SETTLING THE BILL

The Memoirs of Bill Dugdale

SETTLING THE BILL

The Memoirs of Bill Dugdale

endeavour

For Cylla

CONTENTS

FOREWORD

This book has taken nearly five years to write because of inertia and the need, in my eyes at least, to do more important things.

When I came to write about the war I was able to rely on a paper I had written earlier which is now with Leeds University, but on the whole I have relied upon my memory and, on the whole, it has served me well.

Above all it is a personal record – my life, my desires, my likes, my dislikes and my activities. I have obviously omitted a great deal that I found uninteresting in the expectation that the readers, if there are going to be any, would have found them similarly uninteresting.

Being a lawyer and a cautious man I have also omitted stories about the living if I thought they might be upset. Several other stories are also omitted because I disliked the person concerned. Strong dislike colours the judgement in ways that one only realises later.

Chapter 1

CHILDHOOD

I was born on 29th March 1922 and it must have been a Wednesday as Cicely Chamberlayne saw the big flag hoisted at Merevale as she was heading back down the Atterton Lane after hunting in the Wednesday country. I was followed by John in 1923, Susan in 1925 and Judith in 1927.

The Dugdales first came into the realm of knowledge when James Dugdale came from Lancashire to settle in North Warwickshire in the early 16th century. Family legend has it that he was the steward of the Nunnery at Clitheroe and, when the dissolution of the monasteries occurred in 1537/38, he dipped his hand in the Nunnery treasure chest and departed far enough away to be not readily identifiable. He lived a quiet life in Shustoke and his son, John, became tutor to Lord Paulet, son and heir of the Marquis of Winchester. When he had finished as tutor, he married and lived at the Old Parsonage at Shustoke where his wife produced a son, William, in 1605. After education at the Coventry Free School William was married off in 1623 to Marjorie Huntbach, the heiress of the largest landowner at Shustoke who lived at Shustoke Hall (Farm). When his father died in 1625, William purchased the manor of Blyth from Sir John Aston.

Blyth Hall was a typical West Midlands dwelling in red brick with a series of roofs with valley gutters. It had been constructed around 1560, whether by Sir John Aston or an earlier owner is not known. William now began to immerse himself in those antiquarian pursuits which were to occupy him for the rest of his life, compiling materials which were to be the basis of his *Antiquities of Warwickshire*, published in 1656. In 1638 he was introduced to antiquarian circles in London, got access to the medieval records in the Tower of London and to the Domesday Book, and became a junior herald. In 1641, anticipating the destruction and iconoclasm that were to follow during the Civil War, he set out to record monuments, inscriptions and coats of arms in churches round the country. He was at the battle of Edgehill in 1642 as a herald and thereafter at Oxford with the royal court. Meanwhile his wife was at Blyth having a long series of children, most of whom died in infancy.

As a Royalist William had to pay a heavy fine to regain his property in 1646, making ends meet by conducting the funerals of senior Royalists. His great works, the history of English monasticism called *Monasticon Anglicanum* and his history of old St Paul's Cathedral, were published in 1655 and 1658.

At the Restoration in 1660 William became Norroy King of Arms and carried out searching visitations of much of the Midlands, the North East and North West of England, in an attempt to re-establish and purify the rank of gentleman or esquire. His scholarship also continued – into Anglo-Saxon language and history and the history of the law. In 1676 his *Baronage of England* was published and the next year he became Garter King of Arms. If anyone can claim to have laid the foundations for the study of medieval England, then it is he.

John succeeded his father at Blyth in 1686 and in 1692 he re-fronted Blyth and built all the flood protection works. He died in 1700 at the age of 72 and was succeeded by his son William, who had been born in 1664. That William had a son, John, who died without children in 1749 and left Blyth to his sister, who was married to Richard Geast of Handsworth and Bordesley Green, both now parts of Birmingham. Their son Richard took the name of Dugdale and married Penelope Bate, the co-heiress of Francis Stratford of Merevale. He continued to live at Blyth but his son, Dugdale Stratford Dugdale, inherited both Blyth and Merevale and was M.P. for North Warwickshire from 1802 to 1830. He started a long slow business of acquisition of land made possible by the demise of local squires. Baxterley, acquired in the late 1820s, was a major acquisition and the estate gradually grew till it reached its current size. He died in 1836 and was succeeded by his son, William Stratford, who was M.P. for Bramber, near Brighton, and Shaftesbury before representing North Warwickshire from 1832 to 1847. He constructed the present Merevale Hall and built up a large amount of debt as a result, which was not finally cleared until 1927. He died in 1871.

The coal deposits at Merevale had been mined since the Middle Ages, firstly on the surface by the monks, and then at ever-increasing depths as the ability to ventilate and mining skills grew over the years, culminating in William Stratford Dugdale sinking the two Baxterley shafts in the late 1840s to supplement the Speedwell shaft which had been going for some time. Thanks to steam-driven ventilation fans the new shafts were 1000 feet in depth. Their productivity encouraged W.S.D. to overspend in all directions and when he died of cancer in 1871 the estate was heavily encumbered. His son (also W.S.D.) continued the mining and a new boiler, insufficiently protected, provided the spark that led to the Baddesley Colliery explosion on May 2 1882. W.S.D. went down to rescue the entombed miners and a subsequent blast severely burnt him, from which he died nine days later. My father, who now succeeded to the property, aged nine, said he never forgot his screams.

On reaching 21 and gaining control of the estate, Father determined to sink a new shaft and to reopen the mine. This was financed by the sale of a 17th century Dutch landscape picture by Aelbert Cuyp to the Rothschilds for £15,000, now hanging at Waddesdon Manor. Father went to Germany in 1897 and was much impressed by the mining technology there and as a result started his colliery with compressed air as the power source. Not satisfied with this he returned to Germany in the early 1900s and, after a nine month strike because the miners thought that it would cost them jobs, installed electricity in 1911. The future of the pit was assured and it was about the most modern in the business. From then on the profits generated redeemed the estate and family debt and enabled Father to endow his children adequately.

The coal mined from Baddesley Colliery had the highest calorific content for domestic coal in the country and was the nearest decent coal to London, because of the railway line. The colliery worked a six-day week from 1911 to 1947 in an uncompetitive market. It also enjoyed the best labour relations in the industry because whatever the miners asked for, they got. The pit became known in the Depression as the House of Lords because Father insisted that new recruits should be proposed and seconded by people already working at the colliery but who were not relations.

Father was a pious man who continued to read the classics up to his death. While in some ways he was remote from the family he was much loved by all of us. He took a great deal of trouble in getting us interested in all the local activities. A great visitor to museums and art galleries, he similarly got us into the art appreciation world. He had a great sense of humour and was never happier that when playing the fool in the nursery or accompanying my mother, who was on the piano, with a comb and Bronco loopaper. He was an excellent "man manager" and got the best out of everybody without letting them know what he was up to. He was always immaculately turned out and was an early devotee of the motor car. In the 1920s and 1930s he had a series of open Bentleys that we all used to revel in as we hurtled down the roads. He kept many friends from Oxford and Eton who had made their mark in academe. His passions were cars, shooting, Merevale, the family, family history, books and photography. He was Chairman of Warwickshire County Council for 13 years including the years of the Second World War. He and Sir Edgar Stephens were a duo who were much admired in their administration throughout the Midlands.

My mother was Margaret, daughter of Sir Robert Gordon Gilmour of Liberton and Craigmillar (1st Bt). She was born in 1892 and was engaged to an officer in the Scots Guards who was killed in 1916. She became a supervisor in a munitions factory in the Solway area where there was a great explosion and she received the B.E.M. for her work afterwards. Able and intelligent, she was County Commissioner of the Girl Guides and Chairman of the local constituency Ladies' Section for the conservatives.

After the war she worked as a translator at the negotiations leading to the Versailles Treaty in Paris whence she returned regularly to be wooed by my father, who had met her at my Aunt Alice's flat in London in the spring of 1920. He proposed in June and they were married in August 1920. He was well into his forties but had been too preoccupied re-establishing Baddesley Colliery to think of marriage earlier.

We loved her dearly but she was a firm disciplinarian. "Go to Bed and your father will see you on his return" was her dread verdict. She read to us all the Walter Scott books and the Pink and Blue Book Fairy Stories. We prayed together every morning and she or Father would read bits of the Bible to us before they got up. She was very pretty and her picture by de Laszlo at Merevale is just like her, although she did not normally look so startled. She remained a friend and much loved advisor to me, my brother and two sisters till she died.

At Merevale she was crushed by the housekeeper and the cook and so spent much of her time reading in her boudoir. She took on the Merevale Nursing Association which provided care for the aged and for the pregnant women of local parishes. She was a Poor Law Guardian, a Juvenile Magistrate, and involved in the Women's Institute, Mother's Union and many other organisations locally. My father was her first care and looking after him involved much rushing up and down from London. An acute sufferer of train fever, she spent a great deal of time waiting on station platforms.

I had the normal small boy childhood of the period. Nanny was Florence Screech who was born about the same time as my father, and died in 1960. She had been with the Wingfield Digbys at Sherborne in Dorset before she came to Merevale and took me over from Miss Peterkin, the monthly nurse. She was a great believer in "spare the rod and spoil the child" and used to use the back of a big handled hairbrush on us all impartially with devastating effect.

I was about two when my father decided to move to Blyth for two years while Merevale was wired for electric light and central heating was installed, only in the passages and not in the bedrooms! So my earliest recollections are of Blyth. The lawn there was cut with a lawnmower pulled by the house cob, shod in leather boots. I succeeded, at the age of two and a half, in getting my foot run over by the mower and had to be rushed up to Coleshill to have it stitched by Dr. Wall senior, the Coleshill doctor.

Blyth had been the home since 1871 of my Great Grandmother, Harriet Ella (née Portman), when she moved there with her unmarried daughter Mary (Ma). Great Grandmamma died aged 96 in 1903 and Aunt Ma lived there until she died in 1924, when we moved in. Miss Grant, who was a tall, thin and jolly Scotswoman, ran the household. All the rooms had double doors covered in black and speckled Rexene (oilcloth). Great Grandmamma was a very large lady and weighed about 24 stone. Aunt Ma was similarly large so everything was very broad bottomed: the chairs, sofas and even the loos, which were all willow pattern with pull up plugs. Surprisingly, there was only one bathroom and that was for the staff as everyone else used hipbaths in the bedrooms. The cook and parlour maid had bedrooms on the top floor and the three housemaids lived in the barrack room also on the top floor. The butler and hall boy had bedrooms across the courtyard on the first floor. My Great Uncle Sidney, who died unmarried in 1899, had been a very successful Land Agent and his clients included New College, Oxford. He was also the Merevale Agent. His office was in what is now the library and when I moved to Blyth in 1953 his papers were still in cupboards all over the ground floor.

When I was five my mother introduced a governess, Miss Roberts, to the household. She had bright auburn hair which got greyer by the day as term progressed. I hated her but she was without doubt a very good teacher. The schoolroom furniture was from my Great Uncles' schoolroom of 85 years previously and somehow had a look of Struwwelpeter about it.

The great excitement of those years was when I was selected by Great Uncle Will (Earl Beauchamp) to be his page, when he became Chancellor of London University. This entailed carrying his heavy gold-embroidered train around the Albert Hall, where the degree ceremony took place, and attending the formal banquet afterwards. However, one morning when we were hard at work in the schoolroom my mother came in and took down all the photographs of Uncle Will and me. I asked her why she was doing this and she replied, "You'll know when you're older". I had to wait a long time to learn that Uncle Will had had to flee the country because of a homosexual offence, so

Mother thought advertising our relationship was not a good idea. It is now generally accepted that Lord Marchmain in Evelyn Waugh's *Brideshead Revisited* was modelled on Great Uncle Will.

The family returned to Merevale at the end of 1926. Father had a tremendous party at Christmas for everyone who had worked on the house, and everybody else as well. George Ball, the carpenter, played the piano and his nephew, who was famous as the local communist, played the organ and we all sang. *The Daily Express* Community Song Book had just come out and we roared out things like "The Vicar of Bray" and "The Lincolnshire Poacher" together with "Way Down the Swanee River". As always on those occasions I overindulged but I still remember clearly the game of Brandy Snap – with sixpences and florins in a sea of flaming brandy which all the children had to try and fish out. Amusements were much simpler then. Every Sunday night in the winter we had a singsong in the organ hall and everyone in the house came who wanted to. There were tea and crumpets, everyone took it in turn to choose a song and the footmen, who were usually pretty well segregated from the maids, could cuddle up with them on the sofas. I once intruded on my father giving a talking-to to Lawrence, the first footman, who had been caught by Mrs. Tricker, the housekeeper, kissing the still room maid.

The staff was presided over by Mrs. Tricker, the housekeeper, who had come to Merevale in 1873 from Dr. Barnado's at the age of 13, staying until she died in 1950. I have a photograph of her smiling (unusually!) sitting up in bed around 1949. Her acolytes in the housekeeper's room were Tom Hudson, the butler, Mrs. Hawkins, the cook, and Miss Sayer, my mother's lady's maid. The servants' hall (now the kitchen) was overseen by the head housemaid and the kitchen maid. The housekeeper's room and the dining room had the same food. The nursery and the servant's hall equally enjoyed a common menu. Lunch in the servants' hall was at 12.30 p.m. and supper at 6.30 p.m. Lunch was at 1 p.m. in the nursery and was carried up on a tray by Albert, the hall boy, or one of his successors. There was no supper in the nursery. The housekeeper's room lunched at 1.30 p.m. and dined at 7 p.m. The dining room meals were breakfast 8.30 a.m., lunch 1.15

p.m. (later 1.30 p.m.), and dinner at 8 p.m. My parents always changed for dinner whether or not people were staying. Bedtime for them was always 10.30 p.m. unless there was company, and then bedtime was determined by Bridge (auction) or Mah Jong.

The schoolroom came up to the nursery for lunch. The party comprised us four, Miss Roberts and Aggie Brown, the schoolroom maid who was the daughter of the keeper at Shuckburgh, Nanny Screech and Nellie Foster, the nursery maid. Both Nellie and Aggie were very pretty and hotly pursued by the pantry staff: Lawrence, the first footman; James, the second; and Albert, the hall boy. Albert was my particular mate. He was, I suppose, about fifteen, had a bright red quiff and was tall to boot – he was always a very welcome visitor to the nursery kitchen. He taught me how to shoot with a bow and arrow and catapult, in between flirting with Aggie and Nellie.

On summer evenings work in the house stopped at 4 p.m. and, at about 5 p.m., the entire household assembled on the old tennis court. You could play either French cricket and croquet there or tennis on the hard court – at least you could until my cousins, the Blacker twins, dug a large hole in it one morning and it was never the same again. There was also archery, at a target from about 40 yards (Father was a member of The Woodmen of Arden), with lots of bows and arrows available. This went on until the kitchen bell was rung announcing supper in five minutes. In the old days all the water had to be carried from the housemaid's cupboard (really a small room) to the individual bedrooms and put into a hipbath in front of the fire. The fire was then lit and the bath was taken after the dressing gong. After the dinner gong the bath was emptied into the sluice in the housemaid's cupboard, the fire stoked and the bed turned down. There was a gramophone in the servants' hall so there was occasionally dancing; I remember the Tango, Charleston and Black Bottom crazes. Lawrence, the footman, was particularly good at the Charleston and endeavoured to teach us with varying success.

In the stables was Mr. Eyre, the groom (another Albert) – famous for having taught Barbara Cartland to ride. My pony was The Imp; subsequently I was promoted to Teddy, and The Imp was for the others. Brother John got in the way of a rig (a mis-castrated stallion) who attempted to cover The Imp with him on board and understandably rather lost interest. Of my sisters, Susan was a real little goer and would tackle anything on The Imp, Judith was more nervous. Hunting, when we started, was the apotheosis of our childhood world. There were no horseboxes so one hacked to the meets of the Atherstone Hunt and hacked home. The family rule was up to two hours hacking allowed. This got us to Packington (Ashby de la Zouch), Corley Moor, Desford and Seckington, but effectively prevented us from attending meets in the Friday country (Rugby to Leicester). My mother would ring up someone, who she thought would be out hunting, and they would take us in at 2.30 p.m. and give us scrambled eggs and Mr. Eyre a drink, before we hacked home. Most places we would have to lie on a board for 45 minutes after the scrambled eggs to strengthen our spine. Then we were sent on our way, sometimes with a bar of chocolate, and we usually got home at dusk or later. Then a hot bath, toasted cheese and off to bed. Places we used to visit like this were: Thorpe, Mrs. Inge; Twycross, Mrs. Manley; Kirkby Mallory, Old Mr. Russell; Shenton, Mrs. Wollaston (Black Annie); Osbaston, Sir Thomas Cope; Stoke Golding, Mrs. Roberts; Bosworth Park, Mrs. Davies; Whitacre Hall, Mrs. Arthur Lloyd; Grendon, Mrs. Harry Brown; Weston, Mrs. Leyland.

The result of all this was we acquired an encyclopaedic knowledge of the local lanes. Our favourite stops were Thorpe, where Mrs. Inge always made a great fuss of us, and Osbaston where Brigadier Sir Thomas Cope held sway. Sir Thomas had been a hero warrior in the Great War. A regular soldier in the Royal Fusiliers he commanded a Battalion of the Seaforth Highlanders and then a Brigade in the Highland Division. He got a D.S.O. and Bar and retired in 1930. He had a series of fearsome Irish Hunters, all black and, as he had a cut-away black coat and top hat, together with red leather breeches, he was a notable sight. He had been hunting with the Atherstone since childhood and was always worth following, even if he appeared to be going in the opposite direction from the hounds. He was married to a French Baroness in whose Château he had been billeted during the War. She went very odd after the Second World War and, after he had a stroke, she inadvertently starved him to death. She was found near to death herself when people finally wondered what had happened to them. A sad end to a very nice man.

In the War he had an electric vehicle so he was always available to shoot with Father. He would arrive and the battery would be nearly run down; it was then plugged in all day to the electric light so he could drive home again after shooting. There were several sporting parsons who made Father's numbers up. The Reverend Bracebridge Hall of Weddington, a Cambridge rowing blue, had a fearsome tuft of hair at the end of his nose and wore very Edwardian tweed knickerbockers. The other great shooting friend was the Reverend Roland Reed of Clifton Campville. He had four children, two of whom were my contemporaries and great friends: Tony, his second son, who was killed in 1941 at Tobruk in the Tank Corps, and his daughter, Joanna. The Reeds had two nieces, and the younger one, Philippa Robins, was my first serious inamorata. Every year, at Christmas, the Reeds and four other Staffordshire families would give a Junior Ball at The George Hotel in Lichfield. We would go to Clifton Campville Rectory, which was enormous and built onto the 13th-Century church, and then on to Lichfield, where The George Ballroom was filled with about 250 of the local teenagers. Lichfield was the big garrison town of the Midlands – it had two Infantry Battalions, a Cavalry regiment, a Royal Artillery Brigade and the North & South Staffs. Depots. There was no shortage of soldier children to make the numbers up, as well as providing many followers of the Atherstone Foxhounds.

Every Tuesday off we went to Madame Vacani's Dancing Class. It started at Moreton Morrell near Warwick but then relocated to Shugborough Park, the home of the Lichfields, near Stafford. As a result we changed our friends from Warwickshire to Staffordshire. Madame Vacani had trouble with us little boys after the age of six and my dancing skills were limited, until in 1936, I broke my arm playing football at Eton. As the elbow was smashed, I was sent home for three weeks until all the small bones were knitted. My mother, with a flash of inspiration, sent me off to the World Professional Ballroom Champion in Coventry. He, with an equal flash of inspiration, handed me over to his 17-year-old daughter to be initiated in the finer points of ballroom dancing. I fell hopelessly in love and pleaded with my mother to let me continue the lessons in the Christmas holidays. Alas, by then my partner had got herself a regular pair for competition work and my ardour was unrequited, but I had learned to dance – quick, quick, slow and 1, 2, 3 and all that!

When my parents got married my father had a flat in Pall Mall, but shortly afterwards he purchased 18 Berkeley Square, which was situated on the south Bruton Street corner now occupied by the Jack Barclay car showroom. Mr. & Mrs. Hutchins looked after the house. He was a very grand butler of the old school – striped trousers and tailcoat in the morning and white tie and tails after six o'clock. She was a jolly, plump lady who ran the house and did the cooking except in February and March while my parents were having their eight consecutive weeks in London. 18 Berkeley Square was built about 1700 and had panelling in all the entertaining rooms. The large drawing room on the first floor had a log fire on a bed of ash about two and half feet thick, which you only had to stir and throw a fresh log onto for it to burst into flames again. Ma rather enjoyed doing this with us after tea. On the floor above the drawing room was my parents' bedroom and dressing room. The nursery was on the floor above that, with my bedroom and Nellie Foster on the attic floor above.

As a treat on Good Friday 1928, my sixth birthday, we went to the Tower of London. I was standing admiring the Yeoman Warder when I felt an excruciating pain in my leg, and I saw that one of the ravens had buried its beak about two inches into my plump calf. I screamed with pain and was rescued by the Yeoman Warder but I had to have several stitches in the wound. The next day I went down with scarlet fever and was in Berkeley Square for Easter. Old Lady Inverclyde, who lived at number 15, was dying so they strewed straw all the way up the east side of the Square to deaden the noise. However, the next morning the Lifeguards exercised their horses round the Square, making enough noise to awaken the dead (or dying).

Every summer the whole family migrated to The Inch, my mother's home on the outskirts of Edinburgh. My grandfather, Robert Gilmour, was born in 1857 and had had a distinguished career in the army. He started off, after Christ Church Oxford, in the Connaught Rangers and was sent to Africa for the Zulu War. He was the last man to see the Prince Imperial alive, son of the French Emperor Napoleon III and Empress Eugenie. Rather he saw him killed, when a Zulu leapt out of the long grass and skewered him with an assegai. After that he was transferred to the Grenadiers and was in the Guards Camel Regiment sent to rescue Gordon from the Mahdists in the Sudan in 1884-5 – his hall was full of graphic pictures of Tel el Kebir and other battles. He married my grandmother in 1889. She told me that he proposed to her on a bench on which her father and stepmother were also sitting and that her only sex instruction came when she was dressing to go away after the wedding. Her stepmother entered the room and said, "Susie, a word in your ear. Whatever Robert does tonight is right – you understand – is RIGHT!" Anyway, she must have got the message as she produced three daughters: Mary, who married Hughe Knatchbull-Hugesson, the Ambassador in Turkey, who was bamboozled by the German spy known as Cicero – employed as a valet by Uncle Hughe, he sang to him while Uncle Hughe bathed, opened his safe and stole secrets which he then sold to the Nazis; my mother, and Grizel, who married Arthur Hope (Lord Rankeillour) who went bankrupt for £1 million in 1947 and whose only assets were one pair of shotguns and a gold watch; and finally Jock, the only son, who became the top city corporate stockbroker with Joseph Sebag.

There were fourteen grandchildren and, for the first ten years, we were all at The Inch together for the month of August. My mother, as the middle daughter and the last to marry, was the recognised dog's-body who did all Granny's chores and errands. She was always on tenterhooks that we would misbehave and she usually had something awful we had done to apologise for. But it was none the less great fun, swimming at Portobello and North Berwick, golf at Kingston Grange and North Berwick, cricket nets at the Grange Club and, when we were older, grouse shooting at Raeshaw, Caberston and The Glen. My grandfather organised a syndicate with Jock, Arthur Hope, Father,

Roly Cubitt and Jerry Kock de Gooreynd. It coincided with some excellent grouse years in the thirties, and the final years before the war at The Glen were fantastic, with 450 brace being shot on several days. We used to leave at 7.15 a.m. and started walking up the glen to Blackhouse at 8.30 a.m. We got into the butts at 11.45 a.m., had a drive and then walked down and further up the glen for the next drive. Lunch was followed by two more drives further up the glen, and then a race back to Glen House over three hills and two more glens. We had tea and drove home, arriving back at 8.15 p.m. A long day by any measure but to 12-year-olds it was a real stretch.

My grandfather, being a General, was always pleased to be asked to drill us. We did sword drill, arms drill and marched past usually led by someone else staying in the house. Great Uncle Oliver Ampthill really enjoyed marching and drilling with us, so we had no shortage of militaristic exercises. Mr. Blaikie, the professional at Liberton Grange, used to give us all golf lessons and we were very keen on bicycling there and back from an early age. There is too much traffic now but we thought nothing of bicycling all the way to North Berwick (all downhill), playing golf on the children's course, and peddling back (uphill and against the prevailing wind). It took one and a half hours to go but nearer two and a half to come back.

We had a tutor to look after us during the holidays, a prep school master from Cottesmore School, Hove called Jimmy Ford Smith. He was a near-miss cricket blue and a soccer blue from Lincoln College, Oxford. His father was the headmaster of Market Bosworth Grammar School. Jimmy was a great friend and I was the godfather of his child, who was born on the same day that Jimmy was killed at Narvik in Norway in 1940 in the 5th Battalion, The Leicestershire Regiment. The professional at the Grange Club in Edinburgh coached us at cricket. He had played for both Lancashire and Glamorgan and struggled to get us to use a straight bat and to bowl spinners. However, his stories of famous cricketers of the twenties were a great draw and, as Lancashire had been a power in the land, a good many stars had been in the team with him. Cooking lessons from Mrs. O'Gorman, the cook, were another Inch treat. I can still make oatcakes though I suspect my skills with a rolling pin would be rather rusty. And finally there were the trips to Tynecastle to see Hearts play. Mr. Cummings, the chauffeur, was a Hearts fan so we were never taken to see Hibs. He was a boy in the navy in 1916, and used to regale us with stories of having had twelve cuts of the cane from the First Lieutenant for coming late on watch on his destroyer.

Every morning at The Inch the day started with prayers at 8.45 a.m. My grandfather read the lesson, always ending with, "That's all." My grandmother played the piano and the staff took it in turns to choose the hymns. At the end the door was held open by Sandy, the first footman, and he used to give all the pretty housemaids a pinch on the bum as they filed out. Breakfast was in the dining room, which had been the byre in the middle ages. Porridge was eaten with salt and cream, while standing, and then we would sit for bacon and eggs. The walls were implastered stone, with a vaulted ceiling above, so the echo was quite loud. The original staircase was a circular one and went up the house behind the dining room, but there was another staircase straight up to my grandfather's dressing room where he shaved himself three times every morning. The first time with a "cut throat", the second with a Rolls, and the third time with a Gillette. When his health was deteriorating my grandmother tried to get the butler (Mr. Veitch) to do it for him but my grandfather refused to give up the cut throat and came down every day looking as if he had been in a cavalry charge with the Cossacks.

Sunday was a day and a half. Granny and a daughter always went by car to the 8 o'clock Communion and got back for breakfast at 9.15 a.m. At 10 a.m. Grandpa in tailcoat and trousers, a top hat and gold-topped cane preceded the walking party. He led off and was followed by my father and the grandchildren. Mother was whipper-in. The service started at 11 a.m. and was always packed. My grandfather read the first lesson and the sidesmen, about a dozen all in tail coats, formed up in procession to take the offertory bags to the altar. We walked home and got back in time for lunch, which was a very ceremonious occasion. Afterwards everyone was taken around the garden by Grandpa, who enjoyed reeling off the Latin names. The herbaceous borders, like everywhere else in Scotland, were enormous and went all around the kitchen garden and all around the Croquet lawn and shrubbery. Mr. Graham, the head gardener, and the three Mr. Bissetts kept all this in bloom all summer. Mr. Bissett senior drove the Atco motor mower and it was fun to help him empty the grass clippings at the back of the house, into what was presumably the compost heap.

After lunch on Sundays we all went on a walk up to Craigmillar Castle. There used to be enormous games of sardines or kick the can. I was always interested to see how none of the family's dogs would go past the room where Bothwell was put to death by having his veins opened in a hot bath. They would chase behind us, up or down the stairs, until they came to the landing of the room when their hackles would rise and, with tails between their legs, they would retreat in a cowering manner. It was tried on many occasions and with many different dogs ranging from pekes to labradors. Next door to Craigmillar was the Wauchope House where General Sir Alexander Wauchope lived. When he came out of the army he set out to do some repairs and put in a new window. To everyone's surprise, as they took out the bricks, they found a skeleton bricked up in the wall. Murder? or an accident? a priest concealed and the concealer arrested? Anyway it had been there for about 250 years or more. The Scots were a tough race (perhaps still are).

This idyllic August holiday continued every year until 1938 when my grandfather went into a decline and died, aged 81. John and I came up on the Coronation Scot with Bridget and Jean Hope and enjoyed the funeral with the last post and the Grenadier drummer. We were all wearing black and, when we got into the Coronation for the return, the ticket inspector put us all in a reserved 1st class compartment and drew the blinds – as he put it, "There's one of the family not coming back to London." In fact Granny continued to live at The Inch until after the outbreak of war, when she set off for Turkey, where the Knatchbull-Hugessons were ambassador and ambassadress.

Chapter 2

SCHOOLS

I went to Sunningdale School in May 1931, setting off in the Lanchester with my school trunk on the roof. I was pretty sad at my departure so we had lunch at the Randolph Hotel in Oxford and, afterwards, Father took me on a tour of Balliol where he had been from 1891-4. We went up staircase 16 to where Father had had his rooms. We knocked on the door and Father said to the occupant, "Have you seen the ghost?", "Yes," said the occupant, "last November". Father was thrilled with this, as he had seen it several times. In the 1990s Archdeacon Ewbank wrote to the *Balliol Record* to say that he saw it in 1936. I wrote to the editor and told my story, suggesting it was Latimer or Ridley having a perpetual "fry up", which amused Stephen Lukes, the editor. These were the two bishops burnt by Queen Mary outside Balliol in 1555.

Sunningdale was a school of about 120 boys aged eight to fourteen, though most went later and left earlier. It had a good scholarship record and the top class was taken by the redoubtable Mr. G.A. Ling. He was a man of incomparable ugliness and struck terror in small boys. However, he was kind and a brilliant teacher. Sunningdale's record of scholarship to Eton and Winchester was second only to Summer Fields, Oxford which was two and a half times as big. There was no squeamishness about violence to the pupils. The cane was wielded by three of the partner headmasters: Mr. Crabtree, who as an English Amateur Rackets champion, was a dab hand at hitting the target, both backhand and forehand; Mr. Fox, who was a 5 handicap golfer at Sunningdale; and Mr. Burrows, who kept order in the sleeping quarters and therefore inflicted strokes on one's pyjamas. But it was a happy school and we all had fun. The standard at cricket and soccer was good and rugger, which started in my time, rapidly became first class. I failed to make the cricket eleven but was in both the soccer and rugger sides.

The only blot was my mother who, when asked by the matron, a Scottish sister from St. Bartholomew's called Miss Verth, about my medical history, took a deep breath and said that I had syrup of figs every Friday night. The formidable Miss Verth then proceeded to administer a dose which would have cured a hippopotamus of constipation. It took about three years to get this draconian medical treatment abolished.

Like all small boys I took time to realise that school was school and not home and, after two or three disciplinary contretemps, settled down to being a demure and hardworking chap who kept out of trouble. My great friends were Chucks Lyttelton and David Webster, both sadly killed in the war. I learnt the piano from Miss Gertie Ford and drawing from Mrs. Catherine Prescott. The P.T. instructor was Sergeant Buckle, who had been a P.T. instructor in the Royal Artillery. When a small boy's eye was knocked out at boxing he knew instantly how to put it back, thereby evoking our greatest admiration. My brother John had a terrific temper when we were very young once laying me out for dead with a brass-ended cricket stump. When he arrived to join me at Sunningdale he complained that he couldn't read Mother's writing, but when I offered to read her letter to him, he punched me full in the face, again knocking me out. My real friend was Mr. Smithers, the carpentry instructor. He was a scratch golfer for Swinley Artisans and took an infinity of trouble in teaching me how to make things. Merevale had several of my confections on display until recently.

After passing my end of term exams, I finally arrived in Mr. Ling's class. Immediately one was categorised as A – likely to get a scholarship or B – never likely to get one if you tried till 65. I was B but comfortably so. I really enjoyed my Latin and Greek although one was made to look foolish on a daily basis trying to translate Homer and Ovid, or Virgil. When I sat my common entrance in March 1935, I was one of only six boys to take Remove (top grade of the Common Entrance exam to Eton) out of about 120 candidates.

So I arrived at Eton in May 1935. I was in "jackets" as I was under five foot four, the height prescribed for "tails". I was in the house of Mr. Wilfred George Tatham M.C. who was one of the younger housemasters, having only held his house for 15 months. He had been a scholar both at Eton and Kings Cambridge, had been very successful at football and a running blue at Cambridge. He had competed in the 1924 Olympics running in the 440 yards and 440 yards hurdles, but without success. He had a distinguished war in the Coldstream and went back to them in 1939. (In 1942 I was sent in the dark to the Coldstream H.Q. and, on opening the door of a lonely farmhouse in Scotland, I trod on a face, and it emitted a bellow I immediately recognised. So I said, "Oh I am sorry Mr. Tatham sir". He sat up and said, "Why aren't you calling me Gus?" (which was his universal nickname). He was always very good to me but, like all teenagers, I certainly didn't appreciate him at the time. He was recommended for a V.C. at the age of 45, but did not get it – rather unfairly – as they chose to award it to Pat le Patourel who did not achieve nearly so much, but was a regular soldier from the Channel Islands. Gus Tatham had a beautiful snub-nosed wife called Rachel who had a series of affairs with other masters. One Sunday morning at prayers before breakfast her knickers descended to her knees and, as she moved, she kicked up the pink silk (or whatever) and caught them. She sailed out of the dining room to universal applause. As a result the Captain of the House devised a G.T. (General Tanning) and we were all beaten that night for misbehaving. Discipline was kept by the library (the five or six boys who ran the house). It was draconian but, on the whole, fair. I escaped for the first year but then got into regular trouble. I was beaten nine times in all and once three times in a week, with a total of 25 strokes, which was rather more than par for the course and very painful.

If you took Remove you had to score at least 60 per cent in the end of term exams (Trials) or you failed to move up with the rest of your group. I luckily just did it my first half by about an extra five per cent, but thereafter I always got a first class or 75 per cent. It didn't really matter until the last half before you became a specialist in two subjects at the age of sixteen. I got very good marks that half and was therefore right in line for the ten top Oppidans who formed sixth form in the school. I was a long way ahead of any other boys in my house but, to my dismay, Mr. Tatham said he wanted an older boy to be captain before me. I said in that case I am off. My father came to the rescue and as the year before I had just missed a scholarship to Balliol, this was now enough to get me a place there. While at Balliol for the three days of the scholarship exam I was taken out to dinner by Ted Heath on the first night and then Denis Healey on the second, when I got paralytically drunk. My failure to become captain of my house was particularly galling as Bill Gubbins, the chosen one, although a good cricketer and a friend, was as thick as two planks. Poor chap he, like so many of my friends and contemporaries who went into the R.A.F., never came back from a bombing raid in 1943.

The teaching at Eton was very hit-and-miss. The subjects were taught and covered excellently by the Masters but it was up to the pupils themselves whether they benefitted or not. Every fortnight the form order was sent out and one was given a card to be initialled by one's tutors (house and classical). If the results were bad, one was sent to the Head or Lower Master and given a white ticket which meant penal servitude or constant work under supervision of the classical tutor.

After a week one was discharged or the white ticket was renewed. If it was to be renewed a second time one was flogged with a birch. About ten people a term suffered this penalty so it was largely ineffective. However one soon learnt that keeping out of trouble was the best policy. The easy way to amass extra marks was to undertake extra books – for Latin, usually Virgil and for Greek, invariably Homer. I always did both and scored in the high nineties. Only one chap, James Ramsden, scored full marks while I was there but lots of boys scored over 90 per cent. As a result I have kept my knowledge and ability to use Greek and Latin and even to remember bits of it. Once a week one had to learn a Saying lesson, which was five minutes of recitation. I remember struggling with Julian Grenfell's "Into Battle" and John Hills, my history beak, saying that never, in the whole history of English Literature, had a poem been so mangled.

Twice a week one went to "Private Business" in the evenings with one's Classical or Modern tutor. It lasted an hour and, depending on the master concerned, could be a great thrill or a great bore. Cyril Butterwick, Charles Rowlatt, Tom Lyon and John Hills and even Gus Tatham himself all left me amused and excited and keen to read widely. The school library was a haven and, with a wide collection of books not usually found, a good place to dodge going on the river on half holiday afternoon. Francis Warre-Cornish, the Librarian, became a friend, though he had started as a great enemy. My first half he seized my and Tim Cohen's hair and banged our heads together – no doubt for good reason. I discovered a manuscript and typescript by T.E. Lawrence on the crusader castles of Syria and the Lebanon in the library, with the original photographs which Lawrence had taken on his travels between 1911 and 1913.

Clarence Henry Kennett Martin, the Vice Provost, held a book hour once a week in his library in the Vice Provost's Lodge. He had been my father's best friend at Miss Evans's house in the 1880s, had got a double first at Oxford and stayed at Eton ever since. He gave memorable breakfasts on Sunday mornings. He always invited me when my parents were staying with him and, as there was usually an old boy from his house staying too, it was very convivial. He was a bachelor and lived with his sister, who ran his establishment. He had an old spaniel who suffered from eczema and went everywhere with him.

When I was sixteen I was invited to become a member of the Head Master's Essay Society, which met on Monday nights in the Head Master's Study. There were twelve members and each person was asked to do an essay which one had to read out to the assembled company. The Head Master (Claude Elliott) then gave everyone a glass of sherry and the writer was cross-questioned. If the paper was good the questions could last 60 minutes and a second glass of sherry. If papers were bad the Head Master had to do most of the questioning himself. Simon Phipps (later Bishop of Lincoln) gave a paper on the best and worst lines of poetry in English Literature. After spending 50 minutes on Shakespeare, Milton, Shelley, Keats etc. he then considered the worst. I remember his lines to this day:

Ever truthful good at games
Like St Philip and St James
Always helpful never rude
Like St Peter and St Jude.

We got our second sherry and the Head Master grew expansive. He told us he was walking with his uncle on Putney Heath as a small boy when his uncle spied an old gentleman, with an unfurled umbrella, walking towards them. "I'll give you a sovereign, if you go and ask him, 'Excuse me sir have the Hounds of Spring kicked over the traces yet?'" Claude earned his sovereign and the old gentleman, with an oath, started belabouring him. The old gentleman in question being the poet Algernon Swinburne who wrote the well-known poem.

My turn came and, as I was uncertain what to do, I consulted Oliver Van Oss, with whom I did German. We thought up a piece on King Frederick Wilhelm of Prussia and his Grenadiers. I enlisted my father's aid and he got my reading list from the London Library. Several were in German and accompanying them was a letter from the librarian saying that I was the first person to get two of the books out of the library since Thomas Carlyle and would I please not erase or otherwise interfere with the marginal notes in T.C's handwriting. My essay of some 65 pages was duly written and the night before it was to be delivered the Head Master got pneumonia and the meeting was cancelled. So ended my first bid for literary glory. Where the paper is now I do not know, as I have looked for it many times and never found it.

My athletics career at Eton was not distinguished. As I was very small, and was only a Lower Boy on the river my first half, I failed to make my name in any of the Lower Boy races. Although I coxed the second house four, James More-Molyneux in my house was smaller than me so then my chances became nonexistent, and he went on to cox the School Eight. I did better at football and was in the Rugger 15 as Hooker until I was replaced by Billy Straker-Smith. However, as he chipped a vertebra against one of the London Schools, and this was to kill him some forty years later, perhaps I had a lucky escape.

Mr. Tatham's house, being a very good Wet Bob house, had difficulty in raising a cricket XI but what we had was quite useful and we got quite a long way in the House Cricket cup. In the semi-final we played Mr. Sheepshank's house – I went in at number 11 and had to face Ed Garnier and Richard Stanley, the two school fast bowlers. Two nicks through the slips brought eight runs and we went on to get within two runs of winning. Ed Garnier got very cross and bowled me a beamer which went off my hand onto the stumps and that was that. My house colours ended up as my one colour.

The last summer half I was in the chorus of the Musical Society at the school concert and, after thundering out the usual Handel or Haydn oratorio choruses, we came to the Boating Song where the roar of "Swing, Swing together!" caused the chorus rows to swing in opposite directions. I was standing at the end of a bass row next to Mr. Hope Jones, the mathematics master, who was a "character". The middle of the row hatched a plot to send Mr. Hope Jones, or Hojo as he was known, hastily into the wings. As I was next to him I went too and we returned together when we recovered our balance. I thought no more about it but the next morning I was in "The Bill", the malefactor list, to see the Head Master. The conversation went as follows:–

The Head Master (Claude Elliott) "Dugdale you are here for making a dastardly and unwarranted attack on a much-loved senior Master."

W.D. "It certainly was not me Sir."

H.M. "O silence boy, I saw it myself from the front row."

W.D. "I never attacked him, Mr. Hope Jones said so afterwards when I was picking him up."

H.M. "I have a good mind to flog you but you have no record. I will give you a Georgic (500 lines)."

W.D. "As it is the end of the half and I have still got two more exam papers would you please flog me, as it will be much quicker."

H.M. "Two Georgics for gross impertinence and do not argue with me."

I always say that is how I missed the Rosebery Prize for History, won by two marks by John Smith (of the Landmark Trust), and wrecked my beautiful calligraphy.

So ended my Eton career, though in my last summer I was made the secretary of the Dames Golf League and ran the competition. On half and whole holidays we bicycled out to Stoke Poges and played 18 holes as a foursome. Our Dame, Miss Evelyn Strathearn, had played both golf and hockey for Scotland so we usually won – losers bought the winners gin and tonics.

When I returned to Eton after the outbreak of war in September 1939 for my last half, it was clear that my housemaster's thoughts were on rejoining the Coldstream and my own thoughts were on leaving Eton and joining up myself.

Chapter 3

SHORT STAY IN OXFORD

B ut before that, in January 1940 I arrived at Balliol which was not the normal time to start but it was wartime. Oxford had given up large quantities of accommodation for civil service depart- ments and Balliol had a large dose of Chatham House billeted on it. However Oxford bravely continued to behave as if nothing had hap- pened. I shared a room with Ashley Ponsonby on staircase 19, which looked out to the well of a courtyard by the back gate, by the Martyrs Memorial. Our bedroom had two bedsteads which stretched from wall to wall – to get into bed one had to dive over the footboard. Ashley was very studious and usually went to bed before me so, if I had been on the tiles, my dive had to be soundless or I woke him up.

I was reading history and my two tutors were Dick Southern, the Medievalist, and a very good friend though I saw him rarely in later years, and Kenneth Bell. Kenneth was a prolific father and Mrs. Bell looked like Mrs. Sidney Webb – tall, emaciated and her white hair dressed back tightly into a formidable bun. To everyone's surprise Kenneth took off with a nubile lady from one of the Ladies' Colleges whom he had been tutoring (and more) and was away from his home in North Oxford for several months. On his return he was so mortified and no doubt chastened by Mrs. Bell that he took Holy Orders and became the Vicar of Binley to the south of Coventry.

My room was only about 20 yards from the entrance to the bath- house. At Balliol four days a week you had to be in the hall for break- fast by 8.30, or you had to be signed in by Cornell the bath attendant by 8 a.m., or be in chapel for the 9 a.m. service. It was obviously more

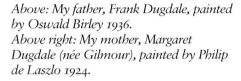

Above: My father, Frank Dugdale, painted by Oswald Birley 1936.
Above right: My mother, Margaret Dugdale (née Gilmour), painted by Philip de Laszlo 1924.

Right: Bill, aged 4.
Below: 4 Dugdales on the step 1928: John, Susan, Judith, Bill.

Left: Bill as page to Great Uncle Will (Beauchamp), Chancellor of London University, before the scandal broke.

Below left: Uncle Hughe (Knatchbull-Hugessen), bathing while Cicero robbed his safe.
Below: Traditional and modern: Grandpa (Brigadier General Sir Robert Gilmour) with H.R.H. The Prince of Wales on Muirfield Links 1927.

Top: *Merevale Hall, garden front – my bedroom is top right with balcony.*
Above: *My first mount,* The Imp *1928.*
Right: *The spirit of Merevale, housekeeper Mrs. Tricker who presided from 1873-1950.*

*Above left: John, tutor Jimmy
Ford Smith and Bill, North
Berwick 1932.
Above: My best friend "Chucks"
Lyttelton, Sunningdale 1932
Left: John, Father and Bill,
Merevale 1933.
Below: Commencing weaving
my spells, John, Judith, Bill and
Susan, Merevale 1937.*

*Above: Bill at Eton in
"jackets", 1935.
Right: My house at Eton
decorated for the coronation
1937.
Below: Annual cricket
match at Eton against
Winchester, June 1939, left to
right: John Dugdale, cousins
John, Elizabeth and Delia
Peyton and Bill.*

Above: Officers and Committee of the Oxford Carlton Club, June 1940, left to right: Father Alfonso de Zulueta, Hon. Edward Douglas-Home, Dr. H.F. Koeppler, Bill, J.R.J. Kerruish. Lord Richard Percy, R. Allsebrook, Colonel Wilkinson, Hugh Astor, R.J. Shrimpton.

Below left: Private Dugdale, Merevale August 1940.

Below right: Flaked at Merevale after two months guard duty at High Wycombe, October 1940.

Above: Bill in front of No. 8 Platoon, 3rd Grenadier Guards winning the 1st Army Forced March competition, Buddon Ness, Carnoustie, October 1942.

Below: No. 3 Company NCOs. Left to right: ?, Sergeant Bruford, C.S.M. Boggis, John Nelson, Sergeant Spiller D.C.M. No. 7 Platoon Sergeant, Bill, Sergeant Nash D.C.M. No. 9 Platoon Sergeant.

Opposite top: Medjez-el-Bab, Tunisia – The River Medjerda and the Roman bridge.
Left: Grenadier Hill, Medjez-el-Bab.
Above: Captain Dugdale, Italy 1943.

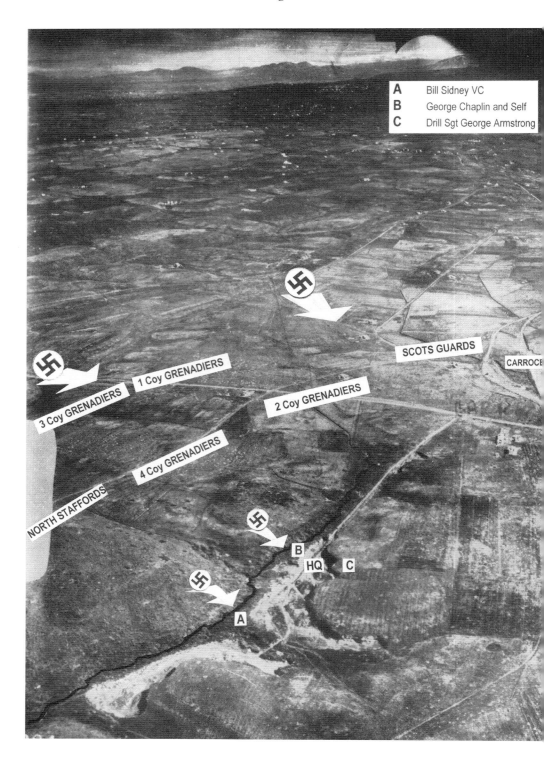

A — Bill Sidney VC
B — George Chaplin and Self
C — Drill Sgt George Armstrong

SCOTS GUARDS

CARROCE

1 Coy GRENADIERS

3 Coy GRENADIERS

2 Coy GRENADIERS

4 Coy GRENADIERS

NORTH STAFFORDS

Above: Detail of the Gully from site of Battalion HQ's tent Anzio. Drill Sergeant Armstrong's shooting position was top left of photograph.
Below: Field Marshal Alexander talking to Francis Legh, Campobasso, Italy, March 1944 having just presented Bill Sidney with his V.C. (Bill Dugdale standing next to the Field Marshal).

Left: Aerial photograph of Anzio beach-head showing Carroceto Station and The Ditch and Gully where the action of 7-8th February 1944 took place

43

Above: The River Po at the point where it was crossed by the 3rd Battalion. This photograph was taken while the Germans were still ferrying over their vehicles, both the ferry itself and some forty lorries can be made out.

Opposite top: Bill (on right) fighting Tommy Reid of 1st Bn. South Wales Borderers on board H.M.T. Champollion, October 1945. Bill lost on points but fractured the winner's jaw.

Opposite middle: Searching the wreck of Jewish ship Hannah Senesh which had landed illegal immigrants at Naharya on Christmas night, Boxing Day, 1945

Opposite bottom: Aunt Baffy (Dugdale) with Dr. Chaim Weizmann, the Zionist leader and Mrs. Weizmann, Rehovot March 1946.

Left: David Rollo and Sergeant of the Trans-Jordan Frontier Force before gralloching our gazelle, 1946.
Below left: My bearers with my 2 Bronneleys duck, Lake Huleh 1946.
Below: David Rollo and Tom Faber with our duck and snipe bag, Lake Huleh 1946.
Bottom: H.M.S. Sirius.

Above: My photos of the Victory Parade in June 1946 which I helped to organise; Senior Heroes in the Victory Parade (General Slim on right).

Below: Field Marshal Alexander.

Above: Photographs I took when escorting German Generals to Nuremberg –
back view of General Blumentritt, Field Marshal von Kleist and Field Marshal von
Rundstedt walking towards the Dakota, Northolt 1946.
Below: Field Marshal von Kleist and General Blumentritt. Note the fur-lined
greatcoat and lack of insignia.

convenient to have a bath so off I went on my first morning – there were about 30 people queuing for the 24 baths. Cornell had a blackboard and, as he had lost an arm at Jutland as a stoker in the Navy, he handed the chalk to you to write your own name. At 8 a.m. he drew a line under the names and he was very quick to spot if you wrote your name above the line subsequently.

You had to wear a gown for hall, for seeing your tutor or the Dean, for attending lectures, and after 7.30 on the way out of college. The commoners' gown was jacket length and the scholars' and exhibitioners' gowns were ankle length. Keeping one's gown from being stolen was a full time occupation – if a gown was lost the easiest thing was to take someone else's. Gowns had also to be worn in the Bodleian. I was taken there by Colin Richardson who had been captain of the school at Eton and was reading Greats. He was a great friend and it was sad when he was killed in Burma. Anyway, one went in and asked for the volumes one wanted and sat at a desk in the Radcliffe Camera scribbling one's card when suddenly the books were delivered. Any urge to study was greatly increased when you saw that the Ladies' Colleges produced a large contingent of fellow readers.

One obtained a list of every lecture and its time and place from the University Office and pored over the list. I was a dilettante lecture taster and went to lots to see if I enjoyed them. Most lecturers were abysmally dull, prolix and usually read from a typescript. However, Canon Jenkins of Christ Church, who lectured on the Holy Roman Empire and the Popes and other aspects of medieval religious events, was a star. He was about eighty and had a shovel hat. He refused to encourage women attending the lectures and, although they comprised 75 per cent of the audience, he ignored questions from them. On my first day I had a note pushed in front of me with a question on it and was asked to stand up and ask it. As the lecture room in the crypt of the cathedral was packed, I was very embarrassed getting on my feet. However reward was at hand, as the questioner was Madeleine Fisher of St. Hilda's College and, after giving her coffee afterwards, I walked her back to St. Hilda's over Magdalen Bridge. Romance dawned until she found Robert Mcsomething of Queens College more attractive.

She was a second-year undergraduate and she took me to lots of parties so I got my feet properly under the Oxford table.

There tended to be a party every night at about 6.30 – sherry etc. – and then there was the monthly dinner drinking parties of mulled wine which went on until everybody passed out. I decided early on that a mulled wine hangover was too mean to be endured in the morning so I cut down on what I consumed, but it was all good fun and it usually meant one avoided Hall in the evening. Balliol gave one a very good breakfast but dinner was awful, although the conversation was fun. I never really got into the J.C.R. way of life, which started with tea and continued with sherry till 7 p.m., and then adjourned to the Buttery under Hall. Seating was in order of appearance and it could either be fun or very chilly according to the person next to one. The Senior Scholar was able to 'sconce' one from a list of offences which now escapes me. If you drank the 'sconce' (a quart of beer) in one go he paid for it; if you failed, it was drinks all round at your table, paid for by you. I got sconced once and managed to drink it up but my beer gut was quite something for 24 hours. I usually dined out, having had lunch in a pub. I joined the two clubs; The Gridiron Club (Grid), that closed down just after I joined it, and The Carlton. Edward Douglas-Home was adept at getting us invited to shoot duck, woodcock and pigeon, and, in the summer, rooks, all over central Oxfordshire. Lectures and tutorials were usually over by lunch so the countryside then beckoned.

As a schoolboy I had joined up at the Honourable Artillery Company on September 4th 1939, and so I had an army number 6464162 and was a member of the Oxford Officers Training Corps. The adjutant was John Chamberlayne of Witherley Hall, near Atherstone who was a Captain in the 16th/5th Lancers so we got on very well. He was always organising military outings although the petrol was tight – often coinciding with a meet of the Bicester or Heythrop who were both hunting on a reduced scale. Anyway it got me into the military life and Oxfordshire society.

Balliol dons were split into four groups. The Reds like the historian Christopher Hill; the "Woolly Uplifters" like the Master (Sandy

Lindsey) and Ashley Ponsonby's tutor, J.S. Fulton; The High Tories like Roger Mynors; and the extreme right of which there was about seven. As a result everything the fellows did was highly political and it prevented Roger Mynors from becoming Master when Lindsey finally went. Dick Southern was a Woolly Uplifter and I never really discovered what Kenneth Bell was; a crypto-High Tory I suspect.

Mrs. Aust was the cook at the Carlton and she had also been Woodrow Wyatt's landlady. Her description of Woodrow's love life used to keep us all in hysterics. Her "digs" were over the river at Folly Bridge, far enough out to be ideal for evading any prowling proctors or bulldogs. Many years later I was sitting in the Gallery over the Government Bench in the House of Commons next to a lady in a light blue coat and skirt. I couldn't see who the current speaker was, as all you could see was a hand gesticulating, shooting out from beneath us. The lady turned to me and said with pride, "Isn't he a wonderful speaker? Although I am a Conservative I never miss him speaking." "Who is he?" I whispered. "My son Woodrow," she said with sparkling eyes.

On a staircase in the Georgian end of Balliol facing the Cornmarket there were suites of large panelled rooms, presumably dating from about 1730. As they were very cold, with no central heating, there were not many takers and I had little competition when I went and asked Sandy Rodger, the Dean, to let me have one which was becoming vacant for the next term. On my new staircase also were Robert Atkinson, Alan Bruce Clark, Graham Leonard (later Bishop of London) and Ronald Griessmann (later Grierson), the renowned banker and industrialist. The bedrooms were small; the sitting room enormous; and there was a large lobby behind one's "oak" (front door). Very cold but very desirable. The only blot was that it was next to the Master's Lodgings and Sandy Lindsey came in once or twice to break up parties when we were making too much noise. Graham Leonard, as one might imagine, was very serious and did not mingle much. Alan Bruce Clark was, on the other hand, a riotous good liver. He was a server at the Roman Catholic Chaplaincy at St. Aldates where Fr. Alfonso de Zulueta had succeeded Ronnie Knox. I went down with him a couple of times to Mass and rather enjoyed it. However my family became alarmed and Aunt Baffy came down from London to discourage me. Still it all added up to several very good free lunches.

One night Fr. de Zulueta came and said he was very worried as he had received an end-it-all note from Alan Bruce Clark. The Blackout lighting was very dim and we searched the staircase with no result. Fr. de Zulueta thought he might be in a bath and there he was, at the bottom of the next staircase – he had taken sleeping pills and opened a vein with a razor blade. We got him out of the bath and called an ambulance via the Porter's Lodge. Alan was removed to the Radcliffe Infirmary with Fr. Alfonso, accompanied by four nuns, to tell the rosary round his bed day and night to pray for his soul and survival. His mother was summoned by the Dean and I took her down to the Radcliffe. When she got to his bed he was lying unconscious and all you could hear was the drone of the Ave Marias from each corner of the bed. His mother was aghast. "What is all this popery for?" she screamed, belabouring the nuns with her umbrella, "Alan is a primitive Methodist." So he was betrayed – no papist from Downside, but a Primitive Methodist from Bristol Grammar School. It was about four hours before the funny side hit me and I collapsed laughing in a dull lecture on Medieval Jewry by Cecil Roth at Merton.

The Trades Unions and the Oxford Labour Club, spurred on by Roy Jenkins and Tony Crosland, produced a mammoth march and demo in favour of the Russian Attack on Finland on May Day 1940. At the Bullingdon Club, led by Richard Percy, we decided to bomb them from above with paper bags filled with soot and water. This caused mayhem and was watched indulgently by the accompanying police until Denis Domvile dropped one too near to a police sergeant who was splattered all over. He immediately came up the Bullingdon Club stairs and arrested us all. As we were taken to New Oxford Police Station in St. Aldates, he more or less apologised although he needed somebody to pay for his replacement uniform. I sat in a cell for three hours until Sandy Rodger came down and bailed me out. I was fined £20 by the Proctors and had to pay £5 towards the new uniform. Two years later, when I joined the 3rd Battalion of my regiment at Perth, I was taken round by the Adjutant to meet people and introduced to the Carrier Platoon Sergeant. "You don't remember me sir?" he said and when I said I didn't, he replied, "I arrested you at Oxford, May Day 1940."

After Madeleine had given me up for a more virile man from Queens, I got friendly with Menara Kumara Mangalam, a communist at Somerville, who came from a very rich family in Madras. Her brother had been captain of Asshetons House at Eton and subsequently became Chief of the Indian General Staff and a Field Marshal. She liked going to the places I liked and I liked being indoctrinated into Marxism. I took her down to Eton and bumped into my Peyton cousins who were taking my brother out with their brother, John Peyton, and we all went off to tea at the Cockpit. All went well until Delia Peyton (Barnett) made some disparaging remark about the Russian invasion of Finland when Menara really cut up rough and we had twenty minutes of virtual mayhem. I extricated her and took her to college chapel where she fumed silently through a long sermon and then was her usual jolly self on the way home. She was an exotic bird and although wearing trousers by day, she would appear with a sari and a bare midriff in the evening. I met her brother at Goodwood many years later, when he was the Indian Military Attaché. When I asked after her he said, "still very busy being a communist".

I had a great friend at Eton called Brian Carritt who was the Eton Rugger 15 Fly Half and keeper of the field. He was a colleger and got a scholarship to Queens where his father was a don. He had an elder brother called Gabriel who was famous as a communist organiser and general troublemaker in the 1930s. Brian, who gave up shaving and was an early proponent of designer stubble, got himself appointed as the Youth Communist Organiser for Cowley and used to spend his evenings spreading the faith. However, about once a month he would come round to my rooms and we would go off to the Carlton Club for dinner washed down by some awful claret. He didn't mind being seen by all his O.E. friends but didn't dare be spotted by a comrade, so in the street he usually had a large muffler wrapped round his face. I never saw him again after I left Oxford as he died of T.B. towards the end of the war.

I had also been appointed the Secretary/Agent of the Oxford Conservatives. The job entailed organising the committee meetings and above all getting out the vote at the Union election. My opposite number on the Labour side was David Ginsburg, also at Balliol. We got on well together and he told me that Roy Jenkins was going to be the Labour candidate for the Presidency of the Union. Jenkins was already the Secretary (the 3rd ranking job) and, as a very good and amusing debater, was an odds-on favourite for the part. David and I had lunch together at an Indian restaurant and I assured him that Roy was a walkover. He was taking his P.P.E. exams and was glad of an excuse not to have to electioneer. I beavered away and got out every Tory voter and some Liberals. As a result Roy was not elected and David came in for a lot of flak. David became M.P. for Keighley and, many years later, I was having lunch in the House of Commons and found myself back to back with him at the next table. I tapped him on the shoulder and said Hello. "Oh," he said, "the man who rigged the Union election". I was too modest to agree but anyway we had a jolly conversation about our time at Balliol. He ended by asking, "How many votes did you stuff into the ballot boxes?" "None," I replied, "but I worked day and night to get the vote out." In fact, the Labour party's support for the Russian campaign and Finland was what turned the vote in the end. So Robert Edmonds, the Tory from Brasenose, was the lucky beneficiary of all the Labour abstentions, while I got elected myself to the Union Library Committee with Tony Crosland as the Librarian in charge.

My academic life continued apace and Dick Southern spurred me on to take my medieval history paper which I duly passed. Kenneth Bell was teaching me the usual 17th century stuff and he was reluctant to let me have a go because he thought I would not pass, but I decided to chance it and scraped through. However, just as I was gearing up to sit the third paper on modern history (post 1832), the war erupted in the Low Countries and the retreat and debacle at Dunkirk stopped all that.

Chapter 4

BECOMING A GRENADIER

When my mother rang and said that she thought I had better sign up and be prepared to fight if an invasion took place, she found a receptive ear. So, after a jolly and boozy lunch at the Carlton Club in George Street, I set off in July 1940 for the recruiting centre on the Iffley Road. I found that I had enlisted in the 8th Battalion Royal Berkshire Regiment and not the Ox and Bucks Light Infantry as I had assumed. I spent two nights sleeping on the floor and was transferred to the 70th Battalion Royal Berkshire Regiment, a new Battalion being formed with college boys from Oxford and, as we were shortly to find out, the sweepings from the prisons and borstals of the Midlands.

The Battalion was commanded by an ex-Regimental Lieutenant Colonel of the Irish Guards, who requested an Irish Guard Regimental Sergeant Major, Sergeant Major Shanahan. The chaps from Oxford in my company were John de Quidt (known as Pluto), a scholar from Queens and Raymond Krailsheimer from Christ Church; John Paul, the actor, from Pembroke College, Cambridge; and one or two public school boys from Rugby, Abingdon and Sherborne. The prisons & borstals intake were much more numerous and I cannot remember their names except for one who was called Robert Foster from Wolverhampton. He had been in approved schools and subsequently borstal for burglary. I took a liking to him and he, in his turn, did his best to wise me up on how to handle and get along with the jailbirds. We were both made up to be Lance Corporals and then Corporals together, but he went AWOL and lost his stripes. He told me that when he arrived as a boy of twelve at his approved school he was given twelve strokes of the cane on his bare behind "to welcome him", as the head said.

My other friend, with whom I shared a double-decker bunk, was Bill Mumford from Arley, near Nuneaton. He had run away from home to avoid going down the pit at Arley and had worked as a boxer in a travelling boxing booth. He had immense shoulders and muscles. He was similarly promoted, but decided he preferred to be a camp cook and asked to be demoted. He told us that if someone looked like winning against the booth-boxer the rounds would be lengthened because, however tough the "punter" was, he would have had a few drinks and was not fit enough. Having seen Bill box, that wouldn't have happened too often.

We were moved from Oxford to Reading for three days to be found some non-commissioned officers. Our Company Sergeant Major was an ex-Marine, who had fought in the Boer War, and was reputed to have been a tramp. He certainly wasn't C.S.M. material but was quite a jolly old villain. He was born around 1884 so must have been just under 60. While in the Marines he had been sentenced to a term in Bodmin Jail, then the naval detention barracks. When he got back to the Marines from Bodmin the Colour Sergeant said to him, "You may want to reform, but I will choose when you are ready to reform, until then you will always be in trouble." He said it was about 18 months before he was sent for and told that he would no longer be considered incorrigible. Our platoon sergeant was a man to whom I took an instant dislike. He had been a regular Royal Berkshire in India, and I doubt he got further than private, but on his return to the colours he was promoted at the Royal Berks depot. He spent his time taking it out of me and Pluto de Quidt.

From Reading we moved to Tythrop House, a stately home of some size near Haddenham in Buckinghamshire. The ablutions were in the garden; likewise the loos, which made for uneasy nights. Our room for 35 or so had been the house's cold larder with the usual slate floor, so it was very chilly in the early morning even on a hot summer's day. The borstal contingent was always very interested in my kitbag and used to go through it on a weekly basis. I lost some things that mattered the first time but subsequently it was merely a bore.

Pluto was very interested in the fair sex and we used to go round the local pubs looking for talent that was in short supply, because most of the girls were already away. However, we found a soul mate in Molly the barmaid at the Wheatley Bridge Hotel. On Sundays the bar closed at 2.30 p.m. and we helped her to do the glasses after which we adjourned to her room in the eaves and had about three hours sleep in a comfy bed. The battalion was used as a guard unit for vulnerable installations and, as we were usually the only N.C.Os in the guard, we went 24 hours with hardly any sleep. It was one guard on and one off, so we got very tired. Molly also had a bathroom so we had a real scrub with hot water.

Guarding the H.Q. of Bomber Command just above High Wycombe I was the only N.C.O. and I had two prisoners in my charge. The Guardroom had no cells and they took advantage of my posting the 2 a.m. reliefs to do a bunk. I reported the matter and, when I came off guard at 4 p.m., Regimental Sergeant Major Shanahan immediately put me under close arrest. After four days in the cells at Abingdon, the Battalion H.Q., they found they couldn't run the guards without me so, after the summary of evidence was taken, I was put on open arrest and returned to duty. Colonel McCalmont then acquitted me, as I obviously couldn't be in two places at once.

On Sunday 9 September I was attempting, for a bet, to drink a pint in each of the 26 pubs in Thame High Street. I had got to number 14 with two sergeants of 1st Battalion Coldstream when a pick-up, with the C.S.M. in the passenger seat, appeared and ordered us all back to barracks. Once there we were given some sandwiches and lots of live ammo and put in buses. We drove off through the night until at dawn we arrived on a beach (subsequently found to be near Ramsgate) and were told to dig in. It was clear the invasion was expected.

Our platoon commander, Lieutenant Rene Lechertier, the esteemed proprietor of Lechertier Barbe, the artists' colourmen in Jermyn Street, sited us just above high water mark and told us to dig in. After 18 inches we struck water and the trench collapsed so we left the beach and started again. We were there for 36 hours with no food, apart from the sandwiches, and no water as the battalion did not have a water cart. Most of us had failed to fill our water bottles in the rush to depart. The Lieutenant took his pick-up and got us some beer from the local pub. However, once the Navy and R.A.F. had sunk the invasion barges we were re-embarked and taken back to Tythrop. If the Germans had landed the 70th Royal Berkshire Regiment were unlikely to have driven them back into the sea.

At the beginning of November 1940 we all went down to the north coast of Cornwall to guard the coastal aerodromes of St. Eval, St. Megan and St. Mawgen. Even though the cliffs were about 250 feet high, if you were on guard you got soaked to the skin from the spray in about ten minutes. One morning in January, after a filthy night of rain and wind, we were just stripping down our Lewis gun when a German bomber flew out of the clouds at about 50 feet. I got two rounds off with my rifle but the Lewis gun did not fire. This was just as well as the red tape to explain why I had fired my gun took all the next day: my one moment of action in the Royal Berks.

I got some leave as I was due to go to Caterham (the Guards depot) in February 1941 to join the Grenadier Guards. On my way home in the dark, near Okehampton, I ran into a police roadblock set up as a prisoner had escaped from Dartmoor. As my Riley 9 had a missing rear door, they thought I had forced it and I was their man. It took an hour and a half and three telephone calls to clear me before I could go on to Churchill in Somerset, where I was entertained to scrumpy cider and dominoes till I passed out and had to be put to bed by the landlord. It is the only time I have drunk myself unconscious though there have been several near misses. Leave was fun at home with the family, but we had an air raid one night with a lost German bomber flying around for about two hours and then dropping his bombs to lighten his load. They mostly fell on Baddesley Common but one was near enough to break all the windows in the laundry block.

For my last month in the Royal Berks I had been acting officers' mess sergeant and I had the stripes to prove it. I learned a great deal from Captain Gordon, the President of the Mess Committee and a former N.C.O. in the Lifeguards, commissioned at the outbreak of war. He had been the sergeants' mess caterer at Knightsbridge and there was nothing he did not know about fiddling the bar takings. He was determined I was not going to do the same and every night he came into my bar to see that the spirit levels in every bottle were marked right way up and upside down. It became, therefore, very interesting to see if he could be outwitted. I finally realised that by the end of the bottle there were so many lines they were self-defeating. I did not like him very much but I thought I would ask him how his system could be wrong-footed. He looked at me for a long time and said, "Finishing the bottle destroys the evidence. But you should be making an unexplained profit of 12½ per cent if you are honest. If you are breaking even you are a rogue!" Information that has been proved right many times over the years.

I turned up at Caterham Barracks Guardroom after a taxi ride with all my kit. The Lance Sergeant in charge of the guard took one look and said, "We had better get those stripes off, before you do anything else," and handed me a Gillette razor blade to nick the stitches. We were to be pay and rations with the Welsh Guards at the far end of the new camp, over half a mile from the guardroom.

The Brigade squads consisted of all the regiments of the Household Brigade; the Scots, Coldstream and Welsh Guards in one squad and the Household Cavalry, Grenadier and Irish Guards in the other. The Grenadier and the Coldstream had coincidentally more candidates. Lots of friends arrived and my bed was between Anthony Courage and Fred Lascelles, both destined for the Grenadiers. There were also three 37-year-olds: Tom Newman, an ex-Oxford rowing blue; Dick Phillips, a Lloyds Broker; and Peter Maclean, a schoolmaster. Tony Bethell, my future brother-in-law and Christopher Petherick, represented the Life Guards; Kenneth Darrell-Rew, Tiny Anderson and Eric Udall, the Irish Guards. In all the Grenadiers had about a dozen out of the 36.

The staff consisted of a Grenadier and a Welsh Guard trained soldier. Our squad instructor was Lance Corporal Stretton, a Metropolitan Police Sergeant from Tottenham Court Road Police Station and the Full Sergeant, who was in charge of both squads, was Sergeant Mason. All the instructors and trained soldiers were reservists and all had been at the depot for a long time and were unlikely to go overseas.

Stretton took everything very seriously and rarely smiled. But he did tell me hardly a week passed without a punter dying on the job in a tart's bedroom in Soho. For £50 the police would dress the corpse, carry it downstairs and duly "find it" in the street. Mason was, I suspect, nearly forty, and was a great joker who enjoyed taking the mickey out of anything that could be laughed at. However, he was a brilliant drill instructor and nothing but the best would pass muster. He could "chase" two squads at the same time, walking backwards and forwards to see what was going on. Our daily drills were enlivened by Tiny Anderson who could only march with the same foot and hand going forward simultaneously. This delighted Mason who used to take him out each evening for special coaching. It took ten days but suddenly Mason came back to the hut with a triumphant bellow and immediately had us all out on the square to prove the problem was no more.

Shining parade every evening meant that everything was up to "duties" standards in a week. My boots were magnificent but they cracked the night before the Adjutant's Parade to pass us off the square and I had to sit up most of the night to get it right. Brigade squads had the first inspection at three and passed out at eight weeks compared to normal units who had it at five and twelve weeks. But the syllabus was the same so it was that much more hard work. The great deal was when Colonel The Earl of Romney, Coldstream Guards, complete with black eye patch – one eye shot out in World War One – passed us out. He addressed us in simple terms about Brigade standards and what would be expected of us, and heigh ho we were off to Sandhurst.

After 72 hours home leave, I reported to the Sandhurst guardroom and went off to join D Company in the new building. The company was commanded by Major Oakeshott of the Welsh Guards who was known as Oakeshott the Big Shott from Bagshott. My platoon commander was Leo Lonsdale, Grenadier Guards, whose wife was a second cousin of my mother; two Scots Guards and one Coldstream officer commanded the other three platoons. The Company Sergeant Major was from the Welsh Guards and the three platoon sergeants were Sergeant Stewart of the Irish Guards (my Platoon), and sergeants from the Grenadier and Scots Guards for the others. I met up with all of these N.C.Os later in the war as Company Sergeant Major or higher.

I parked the car on the square to be greeted by a bellow from R.S.M. "Shagger" Brand, who emerged with his pace stick and said, "What are you doing with that wreck?" I said it had been damaged by a bomb in Cornwall (untrue but it seemed a good thing to say). "What happens if it rains?" he said. "You get wet," I said. "Right," he said, "put it away off the college at once." Luckily Sergeant Stewart knew a garage at Yately, where I took it after unloading. It was to prove a godsend to all of us in the four months we were at Sandhurst as all our recreation and girl-chasing depended on my Riley 9.

Sandhurst was fun although hard work, with tactical and weapon training, assault courses, military engineering (digging), map reading, motor mechanics and lots of drill. One morning with a hangover, at the passing out parade of the company senior to us, on the command "Dismiss!" I failed to turn to my right before saluting. With a bellow "Shagger" said, "Put that man under close arrest." Sergeant Stewart appeared like a lamplighter and I shot across the square into the guard-room. Major Oakeshott was understanding – "a week's punishment drills and don't get a hangover like that again." He made me the Adjutant's Orderly at our passing out parade so I knew I had been forgiven. I was graded A on passing out so I had done OK.

Every month there was a ball on Saturday to celebrate a company's passing out. Michael Christie-Miller was our social secretary, and our usual team of girls consisted of Jane Pleydell-Bouverie, cousin Diana Gilmour, Robbie and Libby Lawrence. We mostly dined at the Pantiles in Bagshot and then went on to the dance in the Mess Hall of the new block. The music was played by the Sandhurst Band and it went on until 1 a.m. when the duty officer closed the bar and the girls went home by whatever means they had devised.

After our passing out parade, where we slow marched up the steps of the Old Building followed by the Adjutant, Captain Clowes of the Scots Guards, we said our goodbyes and had 14 days leave. Ashley Ponsonby and his sister had arranged some stalking in Glen Feshie near Kingussie in Invernesshire, so off we all went. We walked miles on the hill but failed to kill anything other than very small stags. We walked one day after ptarmigan – as it was October they were turning white, ready for the snows to come. You could see them running along in the lichen and then they took off with a whir of wings. On the Sunday we went to the Kirk in Inch and heard a sermon preached at a parishioner with finger pointing in the direction of a nice-looking elderly woman. "Will ye grow old with the silvery graciousness of old age and will ye be a delight to your acquaintances or will ye become a RADDLED AULD HAG hated by all ye know?" The lady in question looked surprised and somewhat mortified but failed to leap up and counter-attack her accuser.

I then went up to London and stayed in our house, 28 St. James's Place (in the 1930s Father had sold 18 Berkeley Square for a very good price and invested in a lease of 28 St. James's Place). It was run by Mr. and Mrs. Clements who had succeeded the Hutchinses when they retired. On the 11th May 1941 I had been having a night out on the town when an air raid started about 11.30. Because of the bombing I had to return to St. James's Place on foot and when I got there, I tumbled into bed oblivious of the continuing explosions. The Clements had long since gone to bed. I awoke about 10 a.m. and was going up to the bathroom on the second floor when I realised there was no back wall. The land mine on Ellesmere House had taken out the rear walls of Nos. 28 & 27. I bathed (with hot water) in full view of the A.R.P. staff, who were clearing up the rubbish in Cleveland Row, and went out to lunch at the Mirabelle regardless. As the house appeared to be structurally sound, apart from the back walls, a tarpaulin was hung down and we continued to use it while father negotiated the surrender of the lease with Jack Spencer, our landlord, who also had had Spencer House damaged by the same explosion. The Clements, having slept through it all too, were now very scared living in the basement using the outside steps, and were trying to get out of London. But I was able to use the housemaid's room and it was very convenient.

Chapter 5

WINDSOR, PIMLICO
AND SCOTLAND

A ll smartened up in our Grenadier uniforms, mine courtesy of Meyer and Mortimer, and after another good lunch at the Mirabelle, we filed into Regimental Headquarters at Wellington Barracks at the end of our leave to be welcomed and exhorted by Colonel Mark Crichton-Magill-Maitland, the Regimental Lieutenant Colonel. The only blot on the landscape was Atty Corbett, who had lost his brown leather uniform gloves and had replaced them with black glacé kid borrowed from his mother, Lady Rowallan, the wife of the Chief Scout. The Colonel's address concluded, we awaited our dismissal – it did not come. Instead he said, "I have noticed with great disquiet that you appear to take a flippant view of your responsibility; for a young officer on the verge of his military career to parade in ladies gloves I find astounding. You are dismissed. Mr. Corbett wait behind." Atty then got a long lecture and was told he would be closely watched in future and might well find himself back in the ranks. The end product was that Atty was the first officer to win the M.C. in the 1st Battalion after D Day.

Arrival at the training Battalion in Windsor was no less hair-raising than one's arrival at Caterham. The only difference was that the Guard Commander saluted before demolishing one and ordering the Drummer to take us to the Officers' Mess. Windsor was very crowded, and again I shared a room with Anthony Courage and Fred Lascelles. The Battalion was commanded by Colonel "Billikin" Cornish, an M.C. from World War I who had a curiously smooth face. We were put on a young officers' squad under Captain Henry Benson and were soon doing all we had done at Sandhurst but this time we were commanding troops, many of whom had been at Caterham with us. It all proceeded very smoothly although Henry Benson could not have been more officious or unpleasant.

In the last week we were bumping across Windsor Great Park with Henry Benson and Fred Lascelles on the tailboard, when someone pushed Atty Corbett and he and the other two shot over the back on to the grass. We were so convulsed with laughter that we didn't tell the driver to stop the truck for about half a mile and, when we got back, H.B. was incoherent and put us all on open arrest. We saw the Adjutant who said it was so grave only the Commanding Officer could deal with it. Billikin said it was a dastardly attack on an impressive Grenadier Officer and sentenced us to 12 punishment route marches of 25 miles, to be done in the evening after normal training in full marching order (i.e. large pack on back and battle pack at one's hip). As we ended training at 4.30 p.m., it meant we started out at 5.15 p.m. and finished around 11.30 p.m. Also, every night after dinner in the mess, H.B. turned up in mess kit and insisted we laid out our packs for a full kit inspection by the side of the road, and he made a great fuss if all was not immaculate. Many years after, H.B., now Lord Benson, was elected to the Jockey Club and came and sat next to me at Ascot. He said, "I don't think we have ever met before", so I enlightened him.

But Windsor was fun. Jackie Philipps of Picton Castle was the Company Commander charged with defending the Royal Family at Windsor Castle. After our training was over he selected the most socially-OK and good-looking officers to join him in the Castle. Of our lot, Fred Lascelles and John Brocklebank were chosen to join Hugh Euston and Joshua Rowley as the four musketeers. John Brocklebank, who was killed at Mareth, was very good-looking, with dark eyes and brown curly hair, and was an immediate hit with the princesses. He was returned to duty, down with me, at the barracks, when Queen Elizabeth thought he might be getting too close to the princesses.

Every Saturday morning Billikin held a Commanding Officers' parade with the whole Battalion in the Barrack Square, with the drums and the band to keep our drill up to scratch. There was a very smart drummer, Boy Mc-something from Liverpool. The R.S.M., Snapper Robinson, was drilling the Battalion when a paper bag was blown across the square. Boy immediately fell out and chased the paper bag and put it in a container. He was punished for this and, after several similar occurrences, he was sent to a psychiatrist who recommended his discharge on mental grounds. As he was walking out of the barracks for the last time a piece of newspaper blew across the guardroom veranda. The Sergeant of the Guard said, "What about the paper?" and the Drummer replied, holding up his discharge, "No need now mate, I've got this."

In December I was drafted to Wellington Barracks in London, where all the dead beats of World War I and the unfits from World War II were based. The Commanding Officer was Lord Eddie Hay, who was the father of a contemporary at Eton. He took an immediate shine to me and I was soon in the orderly room as acting intelligence officer. I was, to begin with, in Douglas Leigh-Pemberton's company and he was a charming and efficient company commander. One did public duties at Buckingham Palace and St. James', with a band but no colours, about once every ten days. The Ensign had to sit up till 2.30 a.m. to do the sentry rounds with the Sergeant and a Drummer. Left alone with the drink, after everyone else had gone to bed, it was easy to over-indulge and from time to time someone got caught out and secured an interview with the Major-General. The Captain of the Guard did his rounds before dinner, and the Lieutenant did his at 11.30 p.m. after the guests had gone, and therefore they were not subject to the same temptation.

There was a mumps epidemic – Eddie Hay and I succumbed on the same day, and were both removed in an ambulance to the North West London Fever Hospital at Hampstead. The nurses were Viennese Jewesses who had escaped in 1939 via the Black Sea. They were very pretty and, for months afterwards, I used to take them out to the Wellington nightclub in Kensington. When my turn came to be discharged and I dressed up in my uniform, the Ward Sister admiringly said, "We had no idea you were an officer," which I took to be a compliment.

On returning I was made an instructor at the newly formed London District School of Street Fighting. We had three bombed streets around

Warwick Way, Pimlico to fight up and down, wickedly running from house to house with long poles with hooks in the end, borrowed from the London Fire Brigade. Of all the pre-warfare training I underwent, this was the most useful because, throughout Italy, nearly every village needed Germans cleared out from cellars, living rooms and bedrooms. As the whole of Pimlico was deserted, we were authorised to use live ammo, and the rattle of Bren and Tommy guns, with the whine of ricocheting bullets, made it very lifelike. And as it was technical rather than tactical, we did not have very long exercises unlike the ones they had at the battle schools.

All this came to an end with the exciting news that I was off to the 3rd Battalion at Castle Douglas. I, luckily, had been judged too stupid to convert to armour, and the 3rd Battalion was where I had wanted to go. It had been the Battalion commanded by my grandfather in South Africa and subsequently at the Tower of London. Known as the "Ribs" after someone said that we were the Ribs of the Regiment, it was commanded by Colonel Algy Heber-Percy and the Adjutant was John Buchanan, later to be headmaster of Oakham School. Just as I was about to join, the Battalion moved up to Perth. So I set sail by sleeper, with Hector my dog, and Guardsman Slater, my soldier/servant. He was a painter and decorator from Blackpool and he remained a firm friend until he died. I reported to the Adjutant and was told I was to go to No. 3 Company commanded by John Nelson. I arrived at Company Headquarters and was told by C.S.M. Boggis, whom I had known slightly at Sandhurst, that I had better be careful as the Company Commander was in a very bad temper. I saluted, the Company Commander grunted and said, "Go down and see Sergeant Bruford" at St. Ninians." St. Ninians was a Church of Scotland church and hall, erected on a new housing estate by the St. Johnstone football ground. I got a lift in the Company 15 cwt driven by Sergeant Hardisty, the company transport sergeant who was a reservist and a traffic policeman in Lincolnshire. He was very pleasant and said, "You'll get along alright with the company, the Major is a good bloke and we're mostly reservists." The 3rd Battalion had had a real party at Dunkirk and had been made up with reservists from the Training Brigade.

Sergeant Bruford, a reservist, was 37 and looked 50. He had been the former boiler engineer at Cardiff gas works, after doing his four years in the colours. I shook his hand and he gave me a grin and said, "Come and meet the boys." They were all cleaning their kit on palliasses on the floor of the church hall, which had the platform for the Minister and elders and a perfunctory sort of pulpit in the corner. I had taken over the platoon from John Henry Lambert, who had gone as a liaison officer to Brigade H.Q., so I said brightly, "I'll come down and make up my platoon roll after lunch." Sergeant Bruford said with a grin, "I've mislaid John Henry's" (sic) and handed over an Eton hardback notebook with most of the relevant details of the platoon. This was to save hours of labour and it somehow typified the way the platoon worked.

Our platoon consisted of Bruford, the gold sergeant, two lance sergeants and one full corporal (the elder brother of Harry Nicholls the V.C.), who had been stripped down to guardsman as a result of a fight in a pub in Louth. The eldest Nicholls brother, Joe (the Tottenham Hotspur goalkeeper) would join us later. All three brothers had been in the Platoon at Dunkirk. There were miners from Lancashire, Yorkshire and Nottingham; a poultry farmer from Ashbourne. My runner was a Co-op milk roundsman from Tamworth and the mortar detachment commander, Corporal Boam, was a brewery worker from Burton-on-Trent. There were policemen from London and Lincolnshire; a bookmaker's runner and two dockers from Liverpool; a professional footballer from Southampton; a rugby league professional from Wigan; some Cockney wide boys; and a bunch of Northampton and Luton factory workers. I was 20 and they were all about 30 or older, except for two or three National Service men from 1939. Sergeant Bruford introduced me round; I shook hands with each one and tried to crack a few jokes, which were received with a hard stare.

I walked back to the company office and John Henry Lambert dropped by on his new motor bike. "They're a tough bunch," he said, "Bruford is very fly but he knows his stuff." With that he roared away. John Nelson came out of the office and said hello to Slater. We got into his pick-up and off we went to Huntingtower, about three miles away, where we had the company officers' billet and mess. David Bonsor was the second Captain, and "Kate" Meyrick and I, the two subalterns. (Tom Faber was to join a couple of months later as the third.) "Kate" was the President of the Messing Committee. He handed me a bottle of whisky (Famous Grouse), wrote my name on the label and said "Guard it with your life." John Nelson had his wife, Jane, and their two small daughters staying in the house. Hunting Tower was the home of Mrs. and Miss Puckle. Colonel Puckle had been commanding a battalion of Green Howards when he had been killed in 1915. The walls were hung with pictures of World War I fighting with the Green Howards and the Leicesters (Puckle's real regiment). I got on a treat with Miss Puckle, who was about 40, and Slater (who was the most adept man at getting his feet under the table) would regularly toast the scones for tea in the private side of the house.

About two days after I arrived, John Nelson laid on a small exercise at Glenalmond, about fifteen miles from Perth. We finished at about 5 p.m. and had our evening meal in the courtyard of Glenalmond House. When it was over, John said to walk home in groups. None of my command wanted to walk home with me, so I set out alone. After about five miles I came to an enormous park wall and went the wrong way. I ended up at 3 a.m. in the signal box at Luncarty, on the Inverness line, and had a whisky and some tea with the signal man. I got back to bed about 6 a.m. After memoranda the next morning, John sent everybody out and gave me a fatherly talking-to about finding my way in the dark. As a result, I took a compass and went out and studied how to get from A to B in the dark, and how to navigate when you had no landmark. This was to make all the difference to my efforts in North Africa. The Dugdale method of foot navigation became standard practice later in the Brigade, after I found my way and others did not. In order to keep your bearing you have to go for a trial walk on the relevant underfoot conditions to accurately get your speed as this can vary from half a mile per hour to two and a half miles per hour and could make all the difference to the logistics of the operation. Having achieved that, you then have to outline some outstanding features on the skyline (if possible in daylight) and use them to get your bearing for controlling your direction in the dark. The Battalion had often practised patrolling but never over the distances required in Tunisia where patrols often had to go 10-15 miles before contacting their objective.

As I knew few people round Perth, I was usually deputed to act as babysitter of the two Miss Nelsons, when John and Jane went out to play bridge. I had been indoctrinated in the arcane art of nappy-changing by Nada Birkbeck at Windsor. A safety pin clamped between my lips became commonplace. When I met Jennifer Arlington at John's memorial service at the Guards Chapel, I rather enjoyed saying "I haven't seen you since I used to change your nappies!" She did not look pleased.

After several marching exercises, there was the 1st Army forced march and shoot at Buddon Ness, Carnoustie. The march was won by my No. 8 platoon and the shoot was won by us as well, primarily because we had 20 minutes to get our breath back before the targets went up. This rather made our name in the Brigade and people began to talk to one.

While waiting to be despatched abroad, we were sent to a large farm at Inchture, near Dundee, to get in the harvest. It was hard and unpleasant work because of the thistles. However, after we had hauled the last load, the farmer gave a big party for the men in the barn and took us out to dinner at a dance hall in Dundee. He drove me home at about 5 a.m. I was later awakened by a phone call from Johnny Bastard to say he had taken one of the ladies back to the North British Hotel and couldn't pay the hotel bill and, therefore, couldn't leave. I borrowed some money from the farmer's cook and set off to find Johnny and the lady still in the double bed, as they didn't dare go downstairs. I handed over the cash and beat a hasty retreat, noting that check-out time was one o'clock.

We were all sent off for a week to do any training we felt our troops needed so, hotfoot, I took a train to Blair Atholl and hightailed up to the estate office. Mr. Pattinson, the factor, let me have the stalking for a week at Forest Lodge up Glen Tilt. So off we went. The Head Gillie, McDonald, and his assistant each took a party and I acted as stalker for the third. Guardsman Macauley, the bookmaker's runner, proved the star rifle with seven stags. It took two blank days for me to get the hang of it but, for the rest of the week, we got as many as the two stalkers. The news of our exploits spread and, one morning, there appeared the Brigadier 1st Guards Brigade (Copland Griffiths), the General Officer Commanding Scottish Command (General Thorne, a Grenadier) and General Officer Commanding London District (Sergison-Brooke). They came upon Guardsman Nicholls, the ex-Tottenham goalkeeper, with a tommy gun. "Are you a good shot?" said General Thorne. "Of course!" said Nicholls and looked up, where a skein of pink feet were winging south overhead, "See those geese!" He let fly with his tommy gun and down came a pink foot. (Thereafter, whenever I saw General Sergison-Brooke he always reminded me of this.) That evening, having been filled in by Bruford, I asked Nicholls about it. "Some people can shoot and some can't," he replied darkly.

After we got back we had 72 hours embarkation leave. Only one Grenadier failed to return – Guardsman Hollis, the assistant company cook. The police picked him up and he appeared before John Nelson. "Hollis, if you do this again I shan't want to take you." Hollis went deep red and said nothing, and was around for the rest of the war.

Chapter 6

OUT TO NORTH AFRICA

When we got back to Perth in November 1942 the Adjutant, John Buchanan, handed out the embarkation orders. He and I, and some others, were the advance party and the remainder of the Brigade followed the following day. We got to Greenock and were told that our ship was the H.M.T. *Leopoldville* – a Belgian tub of about 15,000 tons which did the Antwerp-Congo run before the war. The Quarter Master (Philpott) and I had the job of labelling and allotting the troop decks. The other battalion on board was, I think, the 17th Field Regiment Royal Artillery and Brigade H.Q. We were on the bottom deck, well below the waterline. Anyway the Battalion arrived at about 3 p.m. the following day, having taken from 7.30 a.m. till then to get from Perth to Greenock.

The Battalion was aghast at its quarters; hammocks for some and the rest lay on the decks, on kapok mattresses. The officers were in bunks in cabins but, equally, at very close quarters. I think there were twelve of us in a cabin designed for two. Cooking was on deck, near the loos, in a vast cauldron presided over by a Belgian, with the biggest biceps I've ever seen. There was a tarpaulin rigged over the cauldron, which was heated by steam, which meant the Belgian was permanently sweating, as though in a Turkish Bath, and the sweat dripped off into the cauldron to flavour the grub.

The ship pulled away from the dockside and anchored out in the Clyde, just in from the steel net anti-submarine defences, which were dragged open and shut by two fair-sized trawlers. As soon as the tugs pulled us out into the river they towed another large Nederland Lloyd boat into the quay in our place. We stayed like this for 48 hours, which was useful for getting the routine going and finding our way around. At dusk on the second day we saw the nets being drawn open and, in time, all the tugboats edged us way out into the Lower Clyde. Presumably the plan was to be away from Northern Ireland well before daylight the next morning. As soon as we got out into the Atlantic we were in the midst of a force 9 gale. Seasickness devastated the troops and the officers too.

I am not a seasickness sufferer and was enjoying the icy blast when John Buchanan came up and said I was to do permanent troop officer on the bottom deck, as well as doing my watch on the bridge for keeping station, etc. This was a severe test, as conditions on the troop deck were indescribable. The only plus was that I, and two other officers, breakfasted and dined in state in an otherwise empty dining room. The *Leopoldville* rolled like a tub; we were astern of a Cunarder called, I think, the *Carinthia*, that did not roll much. We were provided with a sextant so that, on watch, one could get the angle of the masts of the ship ahead to prevent our ship from dropping behind or closing up. The convoy proceeded at about 14 knots and I remember very clearly the sight of all these large, ex-passenger ships spread out on a very angry sea. We were guarded by about four Royal Navy vessels and, from time to time, they picked up echoes on their sonars and then departed at speed. On two occasions they dropped depth charges, which sounded terrific when one was below deck.

After two days steaming northwest, we turned south and increased speed. It was completely normal for the troops and junior officers not to know where we were going. The troops were, by now, beginning to get their sea legs. Housey housey became the order of the day, as well as military weapon training and P.T. After about three days going south we turned north east, and then were summoned by Colonel Algy Heber-Percy to a meeting wherein all was revealed; the Battalion was part of the 78th Division that was commanded by General Keightley, and we were going to invade North Africa. We would go through the Straits of Gibraltar that night, and be off Algeria the next evening. After disembarking at Algiers we were to transfer to a fast ex-ferry boat, land

and then capture Bone. However, this was all to be changed overnight, as the French in Algeria did not resist. A rapid deployment group was instead going to try to dash to seize Tunis before the Germans got there. This would include the 2nd Battalion The Hampshire Regiment from our Brigade who were rushed up in a column of all arms, and we would be going up by rail.

We cleaned our weapons and checked our ammo and waited to disembark at Algiers. Hours later we walked down a very steep gangway carrying our full kit which we dumped for the B Echelon to collect. We then fell in and out again about three times until, just as it was getting dusk, we were fallen in and told to march to Maison Blanche, about 20 miles out of Algiers to the east, which was to be our railhead. As we marched off, it started to rain. It penetrated through everything. At the first halt we thought about our gas capes but by then we were all soaked to the skin. Anyway, the march took about six hours and we were billeted in a large agricultural barn which had a roof but no sides, except for a few wires crossing the beams for hanging fodder up to dry. The next morning Chick Plant and Ned Parkes, two of my three Bren Gunners, came to me and said they had thrown away most of the Bren Gun magazines on the march. I thought of courts martial but Sergeant Bruford said why not try 1st Army Headquarters as Fred Turner, the last Quartermaster of the Battalion was camp commandant? I got a lift on the back of a motorbike and marched in very nervously to see Fred. I saluted him (he was by then a Major). He had been right through World War I and got a D.C.M. and M.M., so he knew the form. He roared with laughter and gave me a box of 36 magazines, which I carried back on the pillion to the barracks. I told John Nelson, the company commander and he was furious. He saw both Plant and Parkes, who were regular soldiers and ex-miners. Both of them were excellent shots with a Bren Gun and did their stuff, a fortnight later, to no mean tune.

While we were waiting five days for our train east, Colonel Algy organised a trip to Le Sphinx, the famous Algiers brothel. We had an extremely good dinner at a small French restaurant first. The brothel, presided over by a large woman with an enormous blonde wig, had about 40 girls, all of whom were stark naked apart from a belt round the waist and a pair of high heel shoes. They were encouraged, with lots of occupation francs, to put on a show, which to my callow eyes appeared impossible! Anyway, as some of the boys were eyeing up the girls, Colonel Algy said, "All outside!" and we were driven back to Maison Blanche.

The next day we loaded our transport, and ourselves, on a train and set off eastwards. We were in the famous "Chevaux 8, Hommes 40" type of wagon. My platoon and I took up one wagon and we rumbled on all day, stopping in the evening for a brew-up and the calls of nature, and then rumbling on through the night. After two more days we loaded up our transport and drove to Medjez-el-Bab, where we were based outside the main Tunis-Constantine road where it crossed the Medjerda river.

Every evening at 1650 hrs. we were dive-bombed by Stukas with 250 pound bombs attempting to blow the bridge. At 1700 hrs. R.A.F. fighters strafed us and then, at 1730 hrs., the Americans bombed us. Friendly fire by one's own artillery is all very well as one wants it as close as possible in front, but, every evening, to be dealt with in turn by all three combatants was getting a bit much. After a week we were moved up to what was subsequently called Grenadier Hill. Our trenches and dugouts had been created by the Lancashire Fusiliers, and, as befits miners, they were a very solid and comfortable refuge. The trenches were six to eight foot deep and the dugouts went down about twelve feet and were warm and cosy.

Opposite us, the German lines were about seven miles away and stretched all the way from Longstop Hill to Peter's Corner. One morning I was sent for and told to go to Peter's Corner, and get at least two prisoners. I spent the day watching Peter's Corner (about eleven miles away) and could see nothing. But, as a result of my Scottish disaster, I went out in front with a compass and took Guardsman Quinney, the platoon runner. We both came to the conclusion that two miles per hour would be the maximum speed we could make across the ground. It had been ploughed with a large crawler tractor and a deep digger plough, and had clods about two feet in diameter. We had our supper and set off into the twilight at about 4.30 p.m. We walked on and on in the gathering gloom and I noticed, after 7 p.m. that I was not even

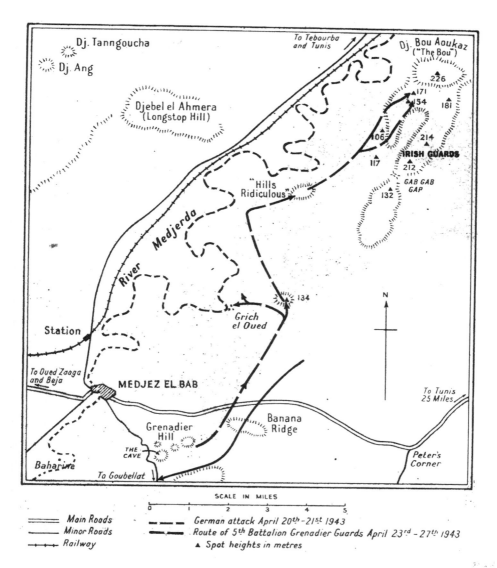

Map 1: Tunisia

half-way. However, the sharp right-angled bend on the concrete road enabled us to keep on track for our objective, which I calculated was about three quarters of a mile to the north of the bend. At about 1 a.m. we blundered into two German sentries, who fired at us and ran away. We lay down because of the flak and the verey lights that the Germans kept putting up. At about 3 a.m. an officer came out, with two men, to see what had caused the trouble. I was in two minds as to what order to give about seizing the party, when the leader trod on Sergeant Bruford who shot him. We all jumped up, grappled his two companions and bore them off into the darkness. As you can imagine, the Germans let off volleys of mortar bombs and lots of flares, but we had got far enough away to be invisible. Having got our two prisoners, the roads appeared less hazardous on the way home. Dawn saw us still about seven miles away and we arrived back at the Battalion well after breakfast, having been walking for about 17 hours. It was my first bit of excitement but it killed a lot of my previous illusions.

A few days later I was asleep in my dugout, when the Company Sergeant Major, Boggis, woke me up. He said that the company was to send out a large fighting patrol to try and rescue Derek Bond, the actor, who had been wounded while out on a similar patrol to our northwest. The patrol had blundered, like we had, into a German patrol. They had not been able to get Bond away because of the machine-gun fire. John Nelson was himself in command and I was to go as second-in-command. There were about 60 of us and we set off walking very fast over the plough as we had about five miles to go. I walked at the rear and was scared stiff all the way. I realised later it was because I had no responsibility and nothing to do, unless John was hors de combat. It was a salutary lesson and, thereafter, I always tried to ensure that everyone had something to concentrate on, as this kept you thinking rather than worrying. Anyway, we tramped right up to the Germans who opened up with everything but, as we were only to rescue Derek Bond, and he was not visible in the almost-daylight of the flares, there was nothing for it but to return empty-handed. Bond had been taken prisoner and re-appeared at the fall of Italy.

At Christmas 1942 the Coldstream mounted a successful attack on

Longstop, lost it, re-took it, handed it over to the Americans, who promptly lost it, and then the poor Coldstream had to go back and try to re-take it. They got half of it but not the crucial feature that overlooked them, so they had to pull back. We had gone forward, up the other bank of the Medjerda, to a village called Grich el Oued (Cricklewood in Tommy talk). We got into the village without casualties and, as we were thinking we were going forward again, we only dug ourselves in as if against shelling and not in defensive positions. That night we were attacked by a stray patrol of Germans. We saw them off, but unfortunately, a hand grenade hit Lance Sergeant Milward, a professional footballer from Southampton. Because of the mud and wet we couldn't evacuate him and he died after 36 hours. It was our first fatality and my first funeral. We had no further incidents and, after the Coldstream withdrew, we were recalled to Grenadier Hill and sent to take over from the exhausted Coldstream. The Germans decided to exploit the recovery of Longstop and sent out a strong patrol, whom we saw coming from a long way away. We lay down in the eucalyptus trees and waited till they had walked past us. No. 2 Company opened up and killed most of them. None of us had yet seen dead Germans so we all took a ghoulish interest in them and their equipment.

We were on the move again. This time up into the mountain range that overlooked Longstop from the north. We marched in pouring rain and, as we got higher, sleet, and then snow, to the mountain fortress of Chaouach. It was situated just below the ridge of the mountain called Djebel Ang, with a pinnacle of rock about 500 feet above the village. We got there well after dark and, as the village appeared to be overpopulated already, had difficulty in finding shelter from the increasingly unpleasant snow and wind. I had carried Harold Slater's rifle for him and had asked him to carry a couple of blankets in a roll over his shoulder. We finally found a storeroom for olive oil where we bedded the platoon down on the floor. Slater made a bed with the blankets and we slept. We were joined by the Gunner Forward Observation Officer, Ian Lawrie, from 17th Field. No. 9 Platoon, under Tom Faber, were out further up the mountain. We had a fairly undisturbed night, although we were frozen solid.

The next morning the officers, led by John Nelson and the French Commanding Officer of the 2nd Tirailleurs Algeriennes, were taken on a reconnaissance to look over the German positions. We climbed gingerly up to the ridge and looked over at about seven miles of corn land in the Bled (plain) along the valley bottom. The French, apart from the officers, were all Algerian Arabs and about five foot tall with World War I weapons and equipment. John Nelson got up to have a look down the rocks on the other side and was greeted with a rattle of fire; so now we knew that the Germans were quite close and were prepared to tough it out. We, therefore, retired back to Chaouach to make our plans for the evening's entertainment.

We were invited to lunch in the French Popotte (Officers Mess) and the Commanding Officer, who was a Viscomte de Saint something or other, was a generous and amusing host. Lunch was surprisingly good and was washed down by copious flagons of Algerian red plonk – a change from the compo rations we lived on. After lunch the brandy was circulated with toast after toast to La Victoire, L'Armée Francaise, Le Roi Britannique, Winston Churchill and Franklin Roosevelt. When lunch concluded, at about 3 p.m., a party, from which I was excluded, went back up the Pinnacle for another look. The Viscomte stood on top of the Pinnacle and looked towards Tunis. A single shot rang out and, pierced through the heart, he plunged down on the German side of the rocks. The French were determined to recover the body that night, which would get in the way of what we were meant to be doing. But, as it grew dark, the Germans, by now thoroughly alarmed, began shooting tracer and hoisting flares all along their lines so we were enabled to see wherever we had to go.

The French were going to do a head-on attack over the pinnacle, but their right flank would be dangerously enfiladed and outflanked by all the Germans to the northeast of the pinnacle. John Nelson was succinct in his orders: Tony Meyrick was to protect the French flank from a possible counter attack, and I was to lead a raid on the German position to the northeast. It was to happen at 2 a.m. Back in my olive store I discussed how to do it with Sergeant Bruford. I was in favour of taking out about six men but Bruford was adamant that more were needed. We also wanted a base established for covering fire. We finally agreed that he would take the platoon, minus my scratch group, and would establish the three Bren guns where they could sweep the ground behind where our raid was to go in. I got my six men and went with them to have a look. The Germans were still letting off flares and regular bursts of tracer from two Spandaus above a deep wadi so we could pinpoint exactly where to go. I also noted that one of the Spandaus was on a fixed line and shooting downhill. The bursts were hitting a cliff then ricocheting up into the sky.

Come 1.30 a.m. and off we went. We had further to go than Tony Meyrick and No. 7 platoon, who were getting shot at from the top of the ridge. When we got to our jumping off point, I said to Corporal Jay, "We must hurdle the fixed line as it is about three foot above the surface, before hitting the ground". We started to run and all got over the fixed line tracer and got into the wadi. I could see two steel-helmeted German heads silhouetted above us, and realised it was now or never. Up we got and raced up the far back of the wadi. By now the Germans had realised their danger and, when Corporal Jay and I reached their position, the two were attempting to take the Spandau off its tripod. I grappled one who was much smaller than me, and the other fell over on top of both of us. I got on top of him and then Corporal Jay and Guardsman Vaughan pulled us apart and we had our prizes. By now the rest of the Germans were sliding down the slope and firing away, so it was time to make our excuses and leave. The whole mountain erupted with tracer and flack. The Germans hailed down a curtain of defensive fire, which luckily fell just behind us as we headed back to Chaouach. C.S.M. Boggis was handing out rum to Tom Faber's platoon so we queued for our share. The French had about five casualties recovering the corpse of the Viscomte and were very angry. The next morning we turned out with a guard of honour as the body of the Commanding Officer was carried on a stretcher through the village, to the sound of "Aux Morts" being played on the Tirailleur trumpets.

It was for this raid that I was given the Military Cross, news of which only came through when I was in Italy. The first time I wore the ribbon was when I went to the General Hospital in Arezzo to visit some guardsmen who had jaundice. The sister was very taken by it and by my youth and so I asked her out to dinner and she asked me home afterwards. So it paid a dividend straightaway.

No. 8 platoon had, by now, established itself as the premier night operator in the Battalion and was being routinely sent out far more than was its fair share. In my turn I had decided that, out of my 33 men, only about eight were safe and reliable in the dark. So it was, I suppose, not surprising that Guardsmen Vaughan and Sergent, my two most invaluable henchmen, should dress up and say that they were being imposed on. We were, by now, back at Grenadier Hill and I sat them down in our deepest dugout and we thrashed it out. They questioned, "Why should we go out every time? With 33 men and only six or eight on the job, surely once every five times or so would be fair?" My point of view was that if I had to go every time, going with the second or third eleven was very dangerous. I could not quite put it that way, but we argued for about three hours and then I heard no more. Guardsman Vaughan was a docker from Liverpool, and Sergent a poultry farmer from north Derbyshire; two better operators would be hard to find. Poor Vaughan was killed on Monte Sole in Italy in 1944, but Sergent survived to send me a periodic diatribe about the horrors of poultry farming.

Back on Grenadier Hill, with the Germans seven miles away and therefore no particular need to be aggressive, filling in the evening after "stand-down" till bedtime was a problem. However, Alfie Moon, a stretcher-bearer and a communist miner, started political discussions; this was strictly against King's Regulations but, to a commie, having a coal owner as your officer was too good an opportunity to miss. So all my miners (about seven in all), my two dockers and my printer used to argue long into the night. This became noticed in and around the Battalion and other miners and activists came along to join in the fun. It never got out of hand and Alfie, who was a regular, became a firm friend. He died from cancer at about 50 when he was the Industrial

Relations Officer for the Kent Coalfield. The other evening sport was bridge; John Nelson organised a four, which had to include me to make up the numbers. The plus was that one got a tea-mug of whisky and I learnt the rudiments of the game, but the stakes were mounting up as I was usually on the losing side.

Chapter 7

FIGHTING FOR TUNISIA

The next excitement was a period of rest in the base area known as Happy Valley, behind the Tebourba plain. We arrived at about four in the morning, having handed over to the Lancashire Fusiliers. We went to sleep in the open and it was a very frosty night. I awakened at about 9 a.m. to hear everyone being ordered out by the C.S.M. and the R.S.M. They sized the company and picked out about forty men to go as guard of honour for General Eisenhower and Admiral Darlan (the Vichy French commander-in-chief) at a ceremony in Algiers.

As might be imagined, this was very unpopular. The chosen men flatly refused to scrub their webbing and then pipe clay it for the flight down to Algiers. Sergeant Bruford came and said to me, "If you are not careful we will have a mutiny on our hands." It appeared to me that we already had one. Bruford and I adjourned to my bivouac where Slater was cooking an omelette. As we ate it Bruford said the only hope was for me to do the cleaning myself. So, after breakfast, I said to the men, "Throw your webbing equipment in to me and I will make a start." Bruford, as a true Welshman, was reluctant to be seen to be strike-breaking so I was on my own. For three hours I laboured at taking each set to pieces, and scrubbing it with my nailbrush until they looked white. Suddenly the strikers came and stood behind me, making sarcastic comments like: "You would never get the Guards Depot to pass that!" or "Didn't your trained soldier ever teach you?" Bruford whispered to me, "Keep going, you've won." And slowly, instead of standing, they all came and sat down in a circle with me and began the boring job of putting on several layers of white & brasso. At 4 p.m., when the R.S.M. re-appeared, all was well. The other platoons did not fare so well and poor Sergeant Nash D.C.M., the hero of Dunkirk, of No. 9 Platoon, was court-martialled and reduced to the ranks, among others.

Whilst at Grich el Oued our first batch of reinforcements had arrived. They were all lousy, having caught it from straw in the cattle trucks of the train on the way up. I thought (DDT only arrived later) that the River Medjerda was the only answer. I made them all strip naked and led them down to the river. All seven of us plunged in. The river was full, icy and running light red from the ironstone soil around. I bullied them all to duck their heads and swim a few strokes. As we clambered out, I noticed that the enormous Grenadier Nicholls (the elder brother of the V.C., and my corporal) had a long scar across his stomach and ribs. "Did you get that at Dunkirk?" I asked. "No Sir, Pongo Waring at Villa Park 1935," he replied. I remembered he had been the Tottenham Hotspur goalkeeper in a cup-tie which I had witnessed, and I also remembered the Villa centre forward had been sent off for kicking a recumbent goalkeeper.

Our few days of rest ended the day the guard of honour returned from Algiers. We were told to be ready to move off at 6 p.m. We found we were to go in Troop Carrying Vehicles (TCVs) to a rendezvous at Djebel Mansour at the head of the Robaa Valley. As soon as we arrived there, John Nelson went off to an order group and I took the opportunity to go through all our weapons, ammunitions and grenades. This proved to be necessary and overdue, as there was a distinct shortage of 303 ammo.

Anyway back came John and called us in to his order group. We were to be the reserve company in the middle, behind 2 & 4 companies, who were to lead the attack on Djebel Alliliga for the Battalion. The left hand was the Para Battalion on Djebel Mansour; and the right flank was a Battalion of the French Foreign Legion. Starting time was midnight and off we went. It was pitch dark and Djebel Mansour was precipitously steep. It was also covered in dense scrub with thorns of about one and a half inches in length. We were making very slow

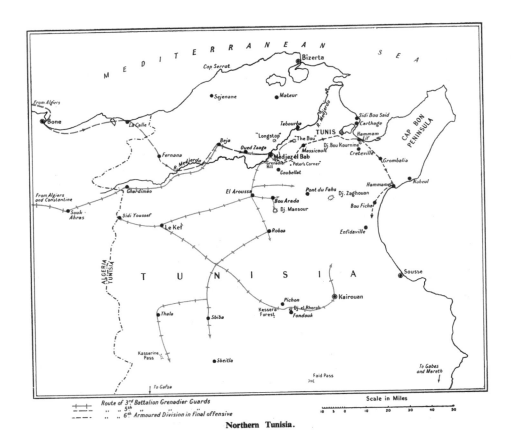

Route of 3rd Battalion Grenadier Guards
"   "   5th
"   "   6th Armoured Division in final offensive

Northern Tunisia.

Map 2: *Northern Tunisia*

progress. It was our first head-on attack, the previous action having all been night patrol work. Suddenly all the German machine guns opened up, and the Paras could be heard shooting with their sten guns. Torn and bleeding from the thorns, we emerged at the final cliff on a pimple in the middle. We kept hearing Caryll Wills' hunting horn as he was the lead platoon of No. 4. Suddenly the horn was silenced; we heard later that Caryll had been killed as he breasted the summit of Djebel Alliliga on the right.

Daylight showed that things were not good. The German counter-attack had come in just after No. 4 arrived on the objective, and they were now about 100 yards below the summit. On our left No. 2 was stuck below their crest and, 600 yards in front of us, the Paras were attempting to ward off a strong counter-attack by a German battalion. John Nelson had established company H.Q. and No. 7 platoon on the absolute summit, and had got there with a rush and scarcely a shot. No. 8 was to the northeast and about fifty feet below the summit. I tried to get my bren gun dug in but it was too stony, so we had to collect small rocks and build a sangar instead. As the rocks were small, an accurate burst of Spandau fire would have knocked the sangar down.

I then went up to company H.Q. and sat and watched and shot at the Germans, who were storming over the far end of the mountaintop, coming in successive waves. No. 4 mounted another attack and got up to their point. So now we had the Paras in front having a hard time, with three Grenadier companies as spectators about 200 feet above them, but unable to help them because of the deep ravine between us. The battle lasted until the afternoon, when it was decided that the Paras would not take the entire mountain as they had finished all their ammunition. The British Army policy of having very fast-firing weapons was a definite handicap. It was almost impossible to prevent soldiers from firing away at full blast in an attack, rather than husbanding their ammunition. The German counter-attack at platoon level came in about ten minutes after the Germans were pushed off their position. I had captured a Contax camera and film during one of our patrols and took several photographs of the battle. But, when the Paras were forced to withdraw, I gave a hand helping carry some of the stretchers with Para wounded and that was the last I saw of my beautiful 35mm camera.

The German officers never led a counter-attack, but remained close behind to take control as soon as the position was retaken. John Nelson had a discussion with the company's N.C.Os and officers to try to improve our performance in this regard. The Germans shoot anyone who wavers in the attack and quite junior N.C.Os do the leading. The British Army places its junior officers in the front of an attack, but the company commander or C.S.M. is needed in the immediate re-organisation after taking the objective. The evacuation of prisoners after a successful attack is another worrying topic. The German P.O.Ws, if not immediately evacuated, had been known to pick up casualties' weapons and resume the fight as their own counter-attack came in. We decided always to have an N.C.O. to deal with prisoners immediately, and get them off site. The only alternative was to take no prisoners, but that was considered too draconian. Later on in Italy the problem again reared its head.

The next morning I walked about two miles up the valley to the French Foreign Legion Battalion which should have taken part in the attack on Djebel Alliliga. Because of bad staff work at Corps H.Q., they had not been included in the Operation Order and had missed the battle. There was the smell of cooking and I updated my French with the C.O. – another of the inevitable Viscomtes. He gave me a glass of wine and said that Mass was about to be celebrated. Shortly afterwards a Legionnaire turned up with a back-pack. He took off his kepi and shirt, opened his back pack and took out and donned a priest's habit of black and white. About a hundred Legionnaires had gathered by the cookhouse. The altar was a door on four jerry cans and the Friar/Legionnaire produced a chalice and candles, which were stuck in wine bottles. Mass then began; no sermon. When it was over the C.O. offered the Friar a glass of wine. He took off his habit, rolled it up and put it back in his backpack. He then put on his shirt and kepi, saluted, drank off the wine at a draught, saluted his C.O. again and went back to duty. I expressed surprise but the C.O. said that he had about six monks – all German – in his ranks and one or the other celebrated the battalion mass every Sunday. By now American stores were reaching the French and their transport and weapons were being brought up to date: contemporary American rather than pre-World War I French.

When I got back to the company after coq au vin with the Legion, I heard we were off again – back to Bou Arada – and Djebel Mansour was to be abandoned to the Germans. We were all depressed as, after the assault and counter-attack, we thought we would remain on our peaks forever. We loaded up the battalion transport and embarked for Bou Arada and the Goubellat Plain. It was long after midnight when we got there and we were immediately told to take off on foot to relieve the Inniskillings, who were on a pimple overlooking the Germans at the far end of the plain.

It was dawn by the time we reached the Inniskillings. I walked into their company H.Q. and failed to salute the company commander, whom I knew, and he gave me a dressing down in front of all my chaps. However, I got my own back by making Bruford check the stores, including the rum which was not there, so I delayed them getting out until he signed a formal take-over note listing the discrepancies. I meet him now from time to time and it has not been forgotten by either side.

The next night I was sent out to cover the Pioneer Platoons who were laying anti-tank mines across the front. We helped carry out the mines, which were the little blue ones with the chemical glass fuse. They were very dangerous and caused lots of self-inflicted casualties. We dug ourselves in and lay and waited. It was very cold and the Germans, who were about half a mile away, kept starting up the engines of their Tiger tanks to keep the batteries and, presumably, the heaters going. Sergeant Bruford and I were gossiping about his youth in South Wales and his days as a regular in the 3rd Battalion, when there was a huge explosion about 600 yards behind us. "That's a mine gone up," said Bruford. "We'd better go and investigate."

I went back with a Canadian officer, who was with us, and found it was the platoon commander who had blown himself up. I got some empty sandbags and put all I could find of him into them. Dicky Braybrooke had been at Sunningdale with me, and had then been a scholar at Eton and Magdalene, Cambridge. His pioneers were very shaken so I had to stay and take over priming and laying the remainder of the mines. Luckily the platoon sergeant, the only man in the battalion with a beard, showed me how it was to be done and everyone rallied round to finish it off before dawn. I took the sacks back to Battalion headquarters and handed them over to the Adjutant. He summoned the padre and Dicky was buried in a temporary grave that evening. I was very upset but the whole thing made me realise how one had to erect one's personal barriers of imperviousness in order to preserve sanity and detachment. I am an emotional man and I found it quite hard.

The Goubellat plain was hell to soldier in. Again, it had been ploughed by enormous French caterpillar tractors with deep digger ploughs and the clods were about eighteen inches in diameter. One progressed across it in a series of sickening slips and slides, ending on our backsides as often as not. In the dark one was lucky to progress further than one mile per hour. The Germans, who had their lines on the north-east edge of the plain, illuminated the night like Piccadilly Circus with parachute mortar flares and star shells so one was continually going to ground. No. 8 platoon seemed to be being sent out every other night and, as we were the front line platoon of No. 3 company, we were getting very tired and short of sleep. The distances were not as great as at Medjez, but the insistent rain made every step a physical nightmare. We twice had encounters with German patrols doing a similar job but, in each case, we heard them coming before they heard us so we had the advantage and incurred no casualties, whilst doing some damage to them.

The war was becoming predictable. The Germans would attack down one of the many valleys, capture some ground, and take prisoners. The 1st Guards Brigade would be engaged and sent round to the south-west of the action. Then they would march up the valley and take to the hills to drive the Germans back off the territory which they had gained. Our counter attacks were usually supported by 17th Field Regiment Royal Artillery, and would come along the ridges. We usually managed to get the ground back with two or three casualties but, from time to time, it developed into a major pitched battle. When the ground was re-captured we stayed on it, until relieved so we could counter the next German raid. As a result of this the Brigade became known as "The Plumbers" – for stopping the leaks.

On one of these expeditions we reached our objective, only to find the enemy had decamped eastwards. It was after dark and, after putting the platoon into their tents, I erected ours. Slater and I settled down under our gas capes for the night. I fell fast asleep and, when I woke up at 2 a.m. to do my rounds, I found that neither of us could move. We were under a blanket of snow about a foot deep. I went round our white outpost and everyone was snowed in, except for the four sentries. They said it had all come down in a blizzard lasting about forty-five minutes. The British Army boot is not designed for snow warfare and we were all glad when it melted in the late morning. Back we went to Happy Valley and we thought a few days of idleness would be a good idea. But, after 36 hours, on February 21st 1943 Bill Pike, the Brigadier Major came along, just as John Nelson and I were discussing possible N.C.O. promotion, and said there had been a disaster down in the south with 2nd American Corps. We were off to stop the rot.

This gave us advance warning and, by the time John was summoned to Battalion H.Q., we were ready to go. In the order of march, No. 3 company was the rear company, and I was the rear platoon. We rumbled off in complete darkness, nose to tail. The Royal Army Service Corps arrived with TCVs to take us south and we piled in. A TCV was designed to take 28 people (small); as my platoon was 36, and guardsmen to boot, it was mayhem behind, as everyone suffered from severe cramp after half an hour on the road. I pulled rank and sat in front beside the driver. On the single track road there were many stops to let transport go by us in the opposite direction. We turned southeast at Khalat Djem and went on into the barren scenery. We halted at a crossroads and, after about an hour with the engine running and the heater turned on, both the driver and I fell asleep.

I awoke to see that, far from being the last platoon in the convoy, I was now alone at the head of my platoon. I said to the driver, "We're going to Kasserine!" and after about five miles, we reached a crossroads in the increasingly desert landscape. A very rickety signpost showed left to Sbiba and right to Kasserine. Well, here was the way and off we trundled. We arrived at the Kasserine Hills at dawn. The road was only a track. I could smell death and we found American bodies lying all over the place: I estimated about 150. They had clearly been caught by the Germans queuing up for a meal, and it did not look as if any fight back had happened. I sent two sections up the hill to get to the top and cover the ground, in case the Germans came back. We put the TCV and the platoon tank under cover, and Sergeant Bruford prepared breakfast.

The Americans did not appear to have any positions dug and were really caught in the open. After breakfast I took the platoon up to the highest point, on the north side of the pass, and considered my situation. There was no sign of the Battalion and no sign of a battle going on, and all was quiet. We dug ourselves in and waited. The road through the pass was a rough track; the road to the north of the high ground in the next valley was better, and beyond there were rolling downs. I had no radio, no communication, and the only thing that happened was that two German ME 190 flew up the pass, saw us, and turned round and headed northwest. I wondered if the Plumbers had been sent elsewhere.

However, at tea time, I saw a cloud of dust and a similar convoy of TCVs drove up to our north, and started taking up positions to the north of the Sbiba Road. After a good deal of peering through my glasses I saw that they were the 2nd Coldstream. About an hour later, a cloud of dust to our west turned out to be the Battalion, bravely headed, I saw, by the Commanding Officer's staff car. It was coming straight down our track. I went down and saluted Colonel Algy Heber-Percy and reported what I had done. "How on earth did you get here first?" he said. "We were sent here by the Military Police Traffic Control," I lied.

Whether he believed me or not, I was sent back up the hill. John Nelson and the rest of the company climbed up and I showed them around. It was now dark and John told me to come and have a whisky and a rubber of bridge if all was quiet at 8 p.m. We played in a sort of shelter on the summit until 10 p.m., when we went back to our position. Stand-to was at 6.30 a.m., but I was woken at about 5 a.m. by a sentry who said that he could hear tanks and traffic to the northeast. I went back to company H.Q. and reported. We were about one mile further towards the east than the Coldstream, and we could make out the column as it came up the road.

It was the perfect battle panorama. We were about 400 feet above the road and could see the great German Tiger tanks, with infantry riding on the engine housings behind the turrets. They didn't seem aware of our presence and went past us, until the Division anti-tank guns shot the three leading Tigers in the flanks. The infantry jumped off the tanks and climbed up the foothills to attack the Coldstream. All day the battle rolled and, once it was clear that our position was not on the agenda, John Nelson, Tony Nation and I sat and watched the contest develop. The Germans were over on the leading Coldstream position but a sharp counter-attack drove them off, and the tanks, both Tiger and Panthers, tried to break through but a combination of six-pounder anti-tank and artillery barrages kept the line intact.

After that I was sent for and told to take a fighting patrol as far as I could, down our pass, to see if there were any Germans in our sector. We set off at about nine o'clock and it was so dark that we kept to the path to avoid falling over a boulder. About three miles down the track I heard a voice and took us off the track into the boulder-strewn hillside. After about five minutes a large German fighting group, of about 70 men, went by on the track. We went on a bit further but found nothing, so we came back expecting to take the Germans in the rear, but saw no one. It had started to rain and the path was becoming sticky and slippery so we made slow progress, as we expected to have to form an ambush at every turn of the road.

The Germans renewed the attack with tanks at dawn but lost two or three to anti-tank guns and, at about 10.30 a.m., called it off and withdrew the way they came. The rain was, by then, making things very unpleasant in our eyrie on top of the hill.

John Nelson was driven over a mine in a Bren gun carrier; the driver was killed and John went to hospital. Tony Nation took over the company and we were now two officers short, as "Kate" Meyrick had become the Transport Officer. Tony was a London solicitor, had been in the Battalion at Dunkirk, and had only come to us when David Bonsor went off to command No. 2 company. A very good bridge player, we got on quite well but I was more gung-ho about things than he liked. He was a competent administrator but had nothing like John Nelson's tactical flair.

The next morning we were off north again, as the Germans had taken advantage of our absence in the south to cause more trouble in the Tebourba Medjez area. This time it was the Medjez-Beja road that the Germans were attempting to cut. However, no sooner had we got there than the Germans withdrew, in order to make a further attack in the Tamera-Sedjenane area. What then followed was one of the most extraordinary incidents of my war.

One morning, when it was not raining and quite spring-like, I was ordered by Tony Nation to have my platoon ready for a patrol. Colonel Algy then appeared in his staff car and led us off in our TCV down to Souk el Khemis and then northeast on tracks for about two hours. I was then invited to get in with Colonel Algy, and we drove up a track to a ridge running north and south. There was a large observation post and a sort of viewing gallery, with telescopes and 88mm gun sights mounted on tripods. Imagine my surprise to be greeted by General Alexander, General Eisenhower and the Army, Corps and Divisional Commanders. I stood behind while probing fingers described arcs moving Tunis-wards on the various maps. After about half an hour I was introduced to them by Colonel Algy. My role was spelt out by the Divisional Commander. I realised that I had to walk all round the bled, within shooting distance of the hills, so the generals could see roughly where the German lines and outposts were. This in broad daylight. The bled led up to the peak of the Tanngoucha of Chaouach Mountain, where I had been before (but on the south side). "How many men shall I take?" I asked. "No more than a platoon," said the Army Commander. This was about 25 men more than I wanted, but I suppose the thought was that fewer people would not get shot at. At the end of the day, the orders meant that I had to walk northeast about 300 yards away from the rising ground for six miles, then turn south for about one and a half miles, and then return the same distance away from the southern side of the bled. Colonel Algy then said that it was a great honour for my platoon to have been specially selected and that he was sure I would make a good fist of the mission.

I went back to the platoon who were now having their lunch of bully beef and tea. When I told them what we were going to do they were incredulous, but orders are orders. We set off at about 1.30 p.m. and headed for the foothills. We had gone about a mile when the first Spandau opened up; the bullets spattered to the ground about ten yards away throwing up divots of mud and corn. We hastily got about another 150 yards further away and continued northeast. The rain running off the mountain had cut deep fissures and gullies into the bled – some of them about fifteen feet deep. We crossed several, leaving a Bren gun team to cover our descent, climbing up the opposite bank and then waiting for them to catch up. When we got to the far end of our first beat, I decided to take about seven men and go in extended order round the north face, as the machine gunning was increasing and they had begun to mortar us as well. I put Sergeant Wright in charge, told him to dig into the banks of the gully and to make his way back to base as the daylight faded. We took advantage of the break to have something to eat and have a brief rest, as we had come about five miles and very fast. This was, as it turned out, a great mistake. Sergeant Wright, a Lincolnshire policeman and a reservist, was a very nice man and a good N.C.O., but recently he had shown signs of becoming jumpy and I should not have asked him to act separately from me. After we had gone, the Germans sent out a fighting patrol and took the fifteen men I had left behind prisoner. I did not hear a fight but Corporal Jay, who was acting as our flank guard, saw them from about two miles away being taken into captivity. We all felt very low about this.

So we set out round the north-east side of the bled and the Generals must have got full value from the flashes and tracers in the darkening afternoon. As we got to the corner to turn for home, the Germans despatched another large fighting patrol – presumably to capture us. They were about 800 yards behind us and lent wings to our cloddy feet. By now it was fully dark and, as I had the usual reliable people with me, we decided to ambush the Germans. But they never appeared, having apparently given up the chase. When we finally got back to the observation post from where we had started, I thought the generals would want to talk to me about it all, but they had gone, leaving Colonel Algy to lead us back to the Battalion area. I was never debriefed on this trip by anyone and could only conclude that the generals and their staff had got all they wanted from noting on their maps the flashes as we progressed along the German front line. This led to the north of Chaouach which was where the 46th division started the Tunis battle some four weeks later, so I suppose it was all of some use. I felt very bad at having lost half of my platoon when I could have got them all to safety if I had kept them with me, but Wright had clearly allowed himself to be surprised.

Chapter 8

NAPLES

In March 1943 I was awaiting the arrival of the re-enforcement draft for my platoon when I was told to go to see the Adjutant, who told me I had been selected to go to the 3rd Division back in England as an assault landing instructor, and I was to fly to Algiers the next day. I asked if I could keep Guardsman Slater and he said I could. We were joined by two from the Coldstream, one or two Gunners and Engineers, and some people from the other Brigade of the 78th Division. We had five days in Algiers until the troopship sailed and were very much at a loose end until we were picked up by some French girls, who worked in the Government offices. This enlivened our stay and improved our French. The troopship was empty except for us, and we had plenty to eat and lots of Algerian wine to drink.

On arrival at Greenock the Welfare officer ordered us to telephone home – in order, he said, to have the lodger's photograph taken down. No one was at home when I phoned so I caught the stopping train from Glasgow to London, and stepped ashore at Atherstone Station at about seven thirty the next morning. I drove home in Mr. Miles' taxi, opened the front door and walked into the pantry to say good morning to Mr. Hudson, the butler, just as he had finished laying up for breakfast. My parents had one big surprise when they saw me tucking into my-egg-and-no-bacon when they came down.

I rang Regimental H.Q. who were equally surprised to hear from me, and they said they would call me back. They rang the next day to say my destination was the 2nd Battalion The Royal Warwickshire Regiment in the north, but I was to give lectures to various units and

particularly the Sandhurst Officers Training Unit. All these I did, halt-
ingly at first but becoming glibber by the minute. The scale of the distances between the opposing front lines seemed to surprise everyone,
and the Dugdale navigation system got several questions as well. Then
off I went to the Royal Warwickshire Regiment with Slater, who was
bored with the London spit and polish. On arrival, the Adjutant of the
R.W.R. said, "Get some proper pips and take your Grenadier flashes
off." Aghast I went out and called Regimental H.Q., who said that, as
the regiment had so many casualties in the Battle for Tunis, I had to
go straight back to North Africa. With some glee I returned and told
the Adjutant who said, "Do have dinner before you go." The 5th Battalion had had very heavy casualties in a long and heavily contested
battle for Djebel Bou Aoukaz. Many officers had been killed, as well as
sergeants and other ranks. The 3rd Battalion had got off more lightly,
but they also had had casualties. So it was a weekend leave and back
to Greenock, with Slater, to catch another boat.

When we got to the infantry base depot on the coast near Cap Bon
in Tunisia it was a case of trying to avoid the tiring and time-consum-
ing route march and battle drills, which took place every morning.
However, John Nelson, by now recovered and second-in-command
to Geordie Gordon-Lennox at the 5th Battalion, arrived and took me
to the 5th Battalion before Colonel Algy had announced whether he
wanted me back (although he said he did after I had gone). Geordie Gordon-Lennox was a tall good-looking man, with fair hair and
moustache, and he walked everywhere with a cromach almost as high
as the one I had made for myself in the borders at Hawick. His adjutant was John Stanley (later Lord Derby), and the Intelligence Officer was a giant, from the Bank of England, called George Chaplin.
John Nelson had also collected Johnny Orme and Johnny Norton (later
Lord Grantly). After Commanding Officer's memoranda, I was sent to
Support Company as second-in-command to Robert Harding of the
Anti-Tank Platoon. The Company consisted of Bill Sidney, the Com-
pany Commander; Johnny Orme, the second-in-command; Michael
Hargreaves, Bren Carrier; Chucks Lyttelton, Mortars; Robert and me.
My platoon was being converted from two-pounder to six-pounder

anti-tank guns and, as I knew nothing of either, I was immediately put down for a course at the Middle East School of Artillery in Tripoli.

Meanwhile, we were searching for equipment left behind by the German and Italian armies. Michael Hargreaves found six BMW motorcycle combinations, and I found about 30 Gilera cross-country motorbikes in a wadi. We all had great fun restoring them by cannibalising them and, after three weeks of intense work, the A/T platoon had six Gileras to ride. I borrowed one of Michael Hargreaves' BMWs, sans sidecar, and set off for Tunis for a night on the town. Driving back at top speed, my bike caught fire and, as my legs became hot, I panicked and slid the bike on its offside cylinder for about a quarter of a mile in a cloud of sparks. The bike was a total write-off but we found another to replace it. The countryside was littered with bikes, Fiats and Volkswagens – we just needed to find out how the armies had immobilised them before leaving.

I thoroughly enjoyed my time at the School of Artillery. There was a large pupillage from both the 8th and 1st armies, and I made many new friends, and gossiped and drank the evenings away. My room-mate was a chap from the King's Shropshire Light Infantry called Murray whom I did not see again until he was head of the T.U.C., and came to watch Leyton Orient v Aston Villa at Clapton. As we had both been through all the Anzio and Italy business we had a very old soldier conversation, helped by two enormous cigars that Harry Zissmann, the Chairman of Leyton Orient, gave us. Lionel Murray or Len, as he liked to be known, had gone from Wolverhampton Royal Grammar School to New College, Oxford on a classical scholarship, and then to the T.U.C. after the war.

Back at Hammamet we lounged on the beach from 11 a.m. till dusk. All training started at dawn because of the heat, and route marches and battle drills were the order of the day. I was made President of the Mess Committee, aided by Johnny Orme, and Guardsman Moran, Chucks Lyttelton's servant. We rescued a couple of Italian P.O.Ws from the cage, who were trained chefs, and we set to work to have a dinner table of incomparable excellence. We had the Commanding Officer to dinner and our fame spread – soon people were clamouring for invitations. Bill Sidney was quick to see the possible advantages and we then entertained all the nobs from Division and Corps, right up to Air Marshal "Mary" Coningham, the Commander of the Desert Air Force. It was all good fun for the boys. We conjured booze up from the cellars of the deserted villas of rich Americans, who had taken advantage of the lax Tunis rules on homosexuality to live at Hammamet and indulge their fancy.

As a reward, Bill Sidney took me to stay with Lord Gort, his father-in-law, at Government House, Malta. There we met Noël Coward, who was entertaining the troops. After dinner Gort's A.D.C. and I were chatting, when Noël Coward, who was clearly intent on making a pass, came and sat on the sofa between us. Lord Gort came up and said to Noel, "What an embarrassing choice you've got to make! Michael (the A.D.C.), Bill or me!" I have never seen anyone, covered in such instant confusion, recover so quickly: "Which one do you recommend?" said Noël.

On the way home we got stuck in Catania, which had just been captured, and it was interesting to see how things were going in Sicily. The 8th Army were stuck on the slopes of Etna and having a very hard time of it, but Catania was quickly recovering. We eventually got a lift back to Bizerta on a B24, and the Captain invited me to go on a raid to Naples, so of course I accepted. As he seemed to be doing this daily, a date was quickly arranged. I climbed on board but as there was no room for passengers I was told to sit on the "potty". Luckily the bomb-aimer had squitters so we changed places, and I went to his place in the nose cone. We were at about 10,000 feet and I could see the flak coming up, fortunately well below us until we got over the targets (the docks). The bomb-aimer came back and, squeezing in with me in the cone, released his load of bombs before returning to the potty. So I had a first-class view of all the proceedings across Sicily and bits of southern Italy. We never saw any German fighters on the flight as they were mostly being used against ground troops in Sicily.

Back home we got down to harder training, with forced marches and hill climbing. Robert Harding, my boss, had a great enthusiasm for manhandling our guns. The Army had produced a vastly underengined tug for moving them, and Robert saw that we would have to learn to handle them, over difficult terrain, at speed. We also had to improve our digging skills, as digging in a six-pounder gun needed a hole of about thirteen feet in diameter.

There was a mammoth party at a villa at Hammam Lif, to which the entire 1st Division was invited. The new Divisional Commander, General Templer, was the guest of honour and it went on till about five, when we were all astonished to see Colonel Andrew Scott of the Irish Guards and Colonel Prince Caraman-Chimay of the Middlesex Regiment having a very aggressive punch up over who should take Laura Twining home. Dicky Twining, the golfer, had been killed fighting in the Welsh Guards at Kairouan and Laura was running a mobile canteen. When the two combatants were at length separated, they were mortified to find that Derek Hague, of the Scots Guards, had already taken her home.

The 78th Division, our former colleagues, had now left the 1st Army and had joined the 8th for Sicily. They had been taken down to Sousse and addressed by General Montgomery. In the course of his address he said, "At last you are joining a fine fighting formation, make the most of it." When, 48 hours later, the Division went to embark, every vehicle had a placard which read, "Any connection with the 8th Army is purely coincidental."

Sicily ended, the 8th Army landed on the sole of Italy and pushed northwards, but were finding the European going tough, so it was no surprise to find ourselves, in October, under orders for the mainland. To celebrate I went down with a high temperature. I had got my sleeping quarters in a mini-mosque, just big enough for a bed and a table and washstand. I had never felt so ill in my life and, as I was still President of the Mess Committee, I had access to the company stores of whisky. I ate nothing for a week but continually imbibed neat whisky. The day we were due to embark I came out all yellow, and immediately felt better. I had Weil's disease. The doctor, "Nelson" Eddy, told me afterwards that whisky was the one thing that should never be taken, and it should have killed me.

On board the American Liberty ship, manned by the American

Coastguard, things were improving because an engaging young man, nicknamed Muscles, had done a deal with the brothel in Bizerta, who had shipped out six young ladies for entertainment. I was in charge of all support companies' vehicles on the Liberty ship with their drivers, so I consulted with the Company Quartermaster Sergeant as to what I should do, "Don't bother Sir," he said with a grin, "it is already done!"

On arrival in Naples, we unloaded in the docks and then moved out to the country around Pompeii, where the various instalments of our transit were re-united. My Gilera motorbike was extremely useful as it enabled me to go anywhere without hindrance, and I was able to explore the Neapolitan hinterland as well as look up friends at Caserta Allied Forces H.Q. This was too good to last and the Battalion was sent across the Apennines to act as coolies for the Royal Engineers, who had to bridge the Sangro. It was quite simple; the October rains had caused the river to flood, so one stood up to one's shoulders in water after carrying the various bits of Bailey bridge down, and then held them up while the Royal Engineers bolted them together. While the rain was lashing down, General Montgomery drove up in his staff car and hurled out a huge bundle of copies of the *News of the World* saying, "There you are my men, news from home!" The bundle fell into the Sangro with a big splash and wetted everything that was not already soaked. Corporal Kettle, who was a Wykehamist failed officer, hurled it back, hitting the General on the back of the head and shouting, "In the Grenadiers sir, we only read the *Sunday Times*!" By the time Monty had turned round, all our hands were aloft supporting the bridge girders.

After four days of this, we were withdrawn and put down on a piece of empty prairie near Barletta, where we lived in two-man bivouacs until just after Christmas. I was given the job of organising the troops' Xmas. I got the Pioneer Sergeant and issued an appeal for bricklayers, which was answered by about ten Guardsmen. My idea was to have an English Inn with fish and chips and Apulia wine, with two roaring fires at either end. Barletta being a fishing port, I thought there would be no difficulty about fish. Cyril Lucas, the Quartermaster, came up trumps and produced a marquee, which would not have been out of place at the Chelsea Flower Show. The bricklayers found some bricks, but had to make do with a lot of granite. In about three days, I had two enormous open fireplaces with chimneys, kept going by hacking down old olive trees from local orchards. The marquee was packed every night; the fish, fried in genuine batter, was washed down with draughts of really black and strong Basilicatan wine. The local Madam entered into the spirit of Christmas, and offered free recourse to her amenities for the most generously endowed guardsman. It was won by Guardsman Skuse, the Carrier Platoon store man, who had been a bearer at George V's funeral - an ex-farmhand from Somerset, with a staggering fourteen inches. He confessed to me afterwards that you could have too much of a good thing. Johnny Orme came back from Egypt with a mammoth supply of Wolfschmidt Kummel, and we arranged our mess festivities around this. Christmas day dawned bright and clear and there were a couple of hundred at church, which pleased the Padre. Our Christmas dinner plus Kummel made certain that we slept anaesthetised against the driving rain and gale.

Two days later, we were told we were off back to the Naples area again, and the convoy set off, without lights, to cross the Apennines once more. I rode up and down the convoy on the Gilera, and generally tried to help the drivers. But, on the descent to Naples, I fell asleep on my bike and woke up to see the Sergeant Major's ammunition truck bearing down on me. I hurled the bike into the ditch and followed it just in time to avoid the wildly overloaded truck from rolling over me and the bike.

We were billeted in Gragnano, a small port at the southern end of the Bay of Naples. Our first task was to go up to Naples and use the newly-discovered DDT to stem the Typhus epidemic raging there. We were handed large flit guns, and were divided between male and female. I got the female set with my platoon, and for four days we did nothing but spray DDT powder into the body hair of thousands of Neapolitan women. In that time the Grenadier and Irish Guards dealt with 441,000 Neapolitans and stopped the epidemic in its tracks, chanting as a sort of litany, "One spray to the left armpit, one to the right, pull open the knickers, one spray to the front, turn round and one to the rear." Once the population realised that DDT really killed the lice they became quite enthusiastic, but the temptation to let the knicker elastic fly back with a ping proved almost irresistible, particularly when it was a granny with about a kilometre of it around the waist.

Naples saved, we learnt we were destined for an amphibious operation, the Anzio landings. The 5th Battalion was a straightforward infantry battalion but, because I had had the combined ops training with the 3rd Battalion in Scotland, I was quite useful in helping with the loading tables, which all had to be written out and duplicated many times over. Every item had to be identified and, as can be imagined, Support Company with carriers, mortars, and anti-tank guns had much more kit than a rifle company. It went on one landing craft, and the Battalion transport went on another. The rifle companies went in much smaller landing craft as they might have to fight their way ashore, and we would come up to the beach twenty minutes later. Getting everyone fit and battle-worthy after a seven-month stand-down was also a problem, but we found time to go to the opera at the San Carlo theatre and also, on January 15th, got an invitation to the annual ceremony of the Liquefaction of the Blood of San Gennaro. The Cardinal Archbishop shook the phial of the saint's blood at half hour intervals and said it had failed to liquefy because of the sins of Naples. "Pray, pray!" he said and, after about four and a half hours, he came up from the crypt and cried triumphantly that the blood was liquefying, whereupon the entire Cathedral went into spiritual overdrive. A large and late lunch of spaghetti completed the proceedings, and we returned to Gragnano in a mood of rampant self-satisfaction.

The weekend before the landing, I was invited to stay at Ravello with the Italian Grenadiers, who were guarding the ex-King and Crown Prince Umberto. I went with Michael Hargreaves and Chucks Lyttelton, and we spent the entire weekend indoors as there was a blizzard and about six inches of snow. The Italian court appeared to be very homosexual and one had to beware of being pounced upon; but the food and comfort was a good deal better than my billet with a Portuguese family in Gragnano. Much warmer too as there were enormous fires in every room. We only saw the King in the distance but we saw quite

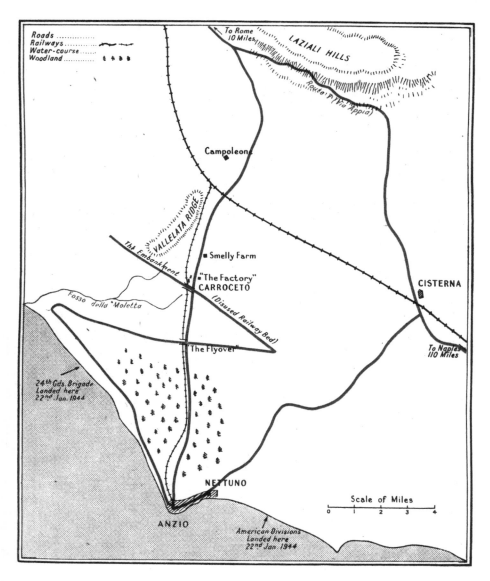

Map 3: The Anzio Beach-Head

a lot of the Crown Prince, who invited us for drinks on the Saturday night and to lunch on the Sunday. The drinks were warm but I asked for grappa and got about a tumbler full, before leaving for spaghetti in a little taverna opposite. Lunch the next day was very formal and went on till about 4.30 p.m. with lots of red wine to wash the osso bucco down. My memories of the weekend remain particularly strong since Michael was killed later that week, and Chucks at the end of our time at Anzio.

The next day was all bustle and preparation as loading of all our transport and heavy equipment commenced on the Landing Ship Tanks (LSTs). Vehicles drove on in a particular order and each one then had to be turned round on the tank deck, and parked. The ship was commanded by a Lieutenant R.N.V.R. (Royal Naval Volunteer Reserve) with two midshipmen, and all three looked about fourteen; one wondered if we would ever arrive, but we finally hauled off into the Bay of Naples and waited till dark, when we set off up the coast.

Chapter 9

ANZIO

The Battalion landed four miles north of Nettuno at dawn on January 22nd 1944. Our LST hit a sandbank about 200 yards off the beach, and we came to a shuddering stop. The Carrier Platoon roared off and disappeared beneath the waves – they survived thanks to their snorkel tubes and, by dint of much revving of the engines, all got ashore. The Anti-Tank Platoon was less lucky, and two of the six tugs sank and stopped in the water with their guns behind. After two hours of hauling and heaving, we finally got a tow-line on them and pulled them through the surf. I emerged from the water, soaking and cross, to be confronted by an immaculate General Alexander in field boots, who said, "You look extremely scruffy," to which the only answer was "Sir" and a salute.

For three days we sat and played bridge, awaiting orders to advance which were not forthcoming from the American Corps Commander. The only excitement was for Michael Hargreaves and his Carrier Platoon who, sent on a recce, drove completely unopposed up the local minor roads to the southwest suburbs of Rome. He finally turned round, as he thought he could be cut off at a street corner. It was the first and only British military visit to Rome until the following June.

The next day the Battalion was ordered to break out at dawn, towards Monte Albano, and capture the "Factory" at Aprilia. I was ordered to be L.O.B. (Left Out of Battle) with about five other officers and the Quartermaster, Harold Lucas. The Battalion moved off and almost immediately the sounds of artillery and small arms fire could be heard. The battle lasted all morning and we heard that the

Commanding Officer, Geordie Gordon-Lennox and John Nelson, the second-in-command, had been wounded, and that John Anthony, No. 2 Company Commander, and Michael Hargreaves had been killed. I went up the next morning with the ammunition and fuel and found Colonel Geordie, lying on a mattress in the Factory compound, directing the repulse of the counter attack. As L.O.B. I was not in battle order or wearing a steel helmet. Geordie beckoned me over and enquired why I was not properly dressed. Whenever we met after the War, he always reminded me of my helmetless state and cheeky retort of, "You're not in a position at the moment, Sir, to do anything about it."

Robert Harding, my boss, was in ebullient mood as our Platoon had accounted for four tanks and two half tracks. The vehicle tugs were refuelled, fresh shells were supplied to the six pounders, and I returned to B Echelon. Thirty-six hours later I was in bed when I was woken and told that Robert, Christopher Ford and Hugh Luttrell had been killed so I was to go and take over the Anti-Tank and Carrier Platoons at once. On arriving at Battalion Headquarters, I found everyone very upset. Christopher and Hugh had been killed, and most of the others wounded when two jeep loads of people on a reconnaissance had been shot up. Eusty Miller, the Senior Company Commander, was now commanding the Battalion, which was to attack through the Scots Guards to the northwest, as the factory had been taken over by the 3rd Brigade. The Germans had now got a very tight grip round the northwest, and north sides of the salient, and every inch of ground gained had to be fought for. To the right (south of Aprilia) was the 56th London Division. I sat on an embankment one morning and watched the extremely gallant efforts of the London Scottish and the London Irish attacking, and attempting to capture Campoleone, across a marsh, where they could not have armoured support. They got to within half a mile of the village, before they were finally pinned down.

The Germans, realising that if the two Naples-Rome main roads were to be cut the whole of their Cassino Line would go, had pulled in every available unit in Italy. Our principal misery was two German 155mm railway guns, which were kept in a tunnel on Monte Albano,

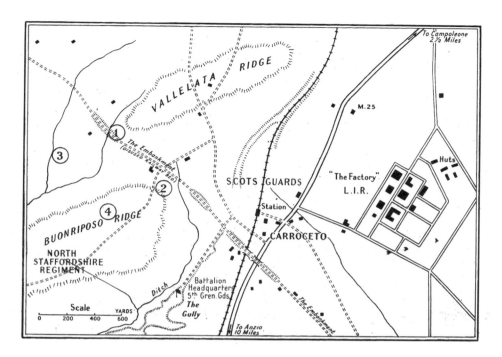

Map 4: The Anzio Beach-Head:- The Embankment and Factory Area

and wheeled in and out for shooting. At breakfast one morning at my Platoon Headquarters, a 155mm shell landed on the breakfast table and killed the six people sitting there – the two of us standing were completely unhurt. It was necessary, in a so-called mobile war with incessant patrol activity on both sides, to move about a lot and, although one had one's hole to bolt to, life under continuous shellfire had to go on.

Day and night, attack was followed by counter-attack. It was the same for both sides: you gained a position one night, and lost it next morning, and took it back again the next night.

After many days of slogging we were told by Brigade to face to the left and take up defensive positions. Brigadier "Glaxo" Murray, our Brigade Commander, had apparently been warned of an all-out effort to flush out the beachhead and drive us back into the sea. So we moved out of positions, and relatively secure trenches, to three open, rolling, cultivated sand dunes that had very little cover on them. They were astride the disused railway line, and had much less to commend them than the positions that we had left.

It had been a bad day, starting with a row with my Company Commander, Bill Sidney, who had complained that my anti-tank six-pounders were sited too far behind the leading companies, and that I was to move them forward to support the front companies much more closely. As they were, all three, on forward slopes, this was not going to get the best out of the anti tank guns. I said that, in my view, they were being put needlessly at risk, as they were liable to be taken out by the earliest wave of an infantry attack. However, the discussion ended with an Imperial Rocket and I was told to comply. So, after walking the ground on foot, I had gone back and collected Sergeant Emery and his gun and crew, and taken them up to No. 1 company. Bob Martin, the acting Company Commander, was very keen to put Emery with the forward platoon but, after a long argument, we compromised, and dug him in behind an old plate-layers' shed on the railway track. The ground was sandy and we made him a good emplacement, with about a 150-degree field of fire towards the east. Neither Emery nor I fancied the position, but we could not find one better. I still had not moved any of the other guns. (Luckily as it turned out).

I was not really concentrating as I was driven back along the disused railway bed to the flyover from No. 1 Company Headquarters at dusk on the 7th February 1944. Suddenly, with a whoosh, a salvo of smoke, shells and mortar bombs fell all around us, and the smoke billowed up in the darkening air. Suddenly a man loomed up out of the smoke, and came up to the gun tug. I told my driver to stop, and leant over to hear what he had to say. He began, "Wo ist" and I realised he was German. My driver, who had joined the Battalion only that morning, realised at the same time and went to accelerate, but only succeeded in stalling the vehicle so I had to draw my revolver and shoot. The vehicle started at the second prolonged use of the starter, and we rumbled off back to Anti-Tank Platoon Headquarters, behind the flyover.

Back at Platoon Headquarters I talked to Sergeant Wilks, who was the Acting Platoon Sergeant, and he said he thought a major attack had started. We had no radio and the nearest field telephone was at the Regimental Aid Post, about 300 yards to the east. I decided to walk to Battalion and Company Headquarters to see what was happening, as the shelling and smoke was intensifying. It had also started to rain heavily. I had not yet been to Battalion Headquarters in its new situation, since it had moved 800 yards north east. It was now sited in a gully, cut out of the terrain by the erosion of countless rainy seasons, and the actual command post was in an American ten-man tent dug into the ground. Support Company Headquarters was about 30 yards away and similarly dug in. Eusty Miller had taken over as Commanding Officer when John Nelson was wounded, and John Stanley, the Adjutant, was busy indoctrinating him in the latest situation.

I ran into Ronnie Taylor, the Signals Officer, who was just about to go out and chase up the telephone lines with Guardsman Fern, who was usually our Company signaller. He told me he thought the attack was on the North Staffs and Scots Guards, but the shelling was on us too, so he thought we would be the next for shaving. Bill Sidney was not at Company H.Q., and C.S.M. Welton, and the Company Clerk were busy priming hand grenades. They told me that Bill had taken three boxes of hand grenades and gone off to survey the gully downstream, with his soldier servant, and had not come back. Small arms fire could now be heard on our front to the north, and I assumed that No. 1 and 2 Companies were being attacked. Chucks Lyttelton, the Mortar Officer, came in and said that he only had one mortar undeployed, and we decided to set it up in the gully about 50 yards away. He had the ranges to No. 4 Company worked out, but we decided that we must also be able to cover the intervening ground between No. 4 and the gully.

In was clear by now that the Germans were launching an all-out attack on the north and west sides of the salient, and the Scots Guards to the north were being heavily attacked. About 9.30 p.m. the firing began at our No. 4 Company, and its position was heavily smoked. The battle lasted for about an hour, or a little longer, and then went quiet. It sounded as if they had been overrun. I climbed up to the top of the gully with George Chaplin, the Intelligence Officer, and Christopher Hodson, the Pioneer Officer, and attempted to see what was happening. The battle still raged to our right, but it was ominously quiet in front, and to our left, where the North Staffs. were. The rain had ceased at about 11 p.m., the moon came out and the temperature dropped like a stone.

In the moonlight we could see a good deal of activity on No. 4 Company's position, but it was too far off to discover exactly what. About 150 yards to the north west of our gully the ground sloped down to a water course, along which there were bushes of various sizes which degenerated into scrub. This gave about 30 per cent ground cover up to where we were sitting. At about 11.30 p.m., large groups of the enemy began to make their way down the slope from No. 4 Company towards us. Almost immediately, I heard Tommy gun firing and hand grenades from about 200 yards to our left. And soon C.S.M. Welton appeared to say that Bill Sidney and his soldier servant were attempting to stop the Germans crossing the water course at an animal crossing lower down.

The stream followed the gully, at a distance of about 50 yards, for about a quarter of a mile, and then meandered off to the northwest. George said that we had better go to the head of the gully and see if there were any other crossings. So, leaving Christopher as the link with Bill Sidney, we walked up to the top and crouched our way back down. We had been joined by a couple of the Pioneer Platoon and my soldier servant, Guardsman Harold Slater, who were all carrying hand grenades and rifles. This went without incident until columns of steam denoted opposition. Grenades from Slater, and shots and a charge from the Pioneers settled the matter, and we got back to the crossing without difficulty. We found a goat or sheep track through the scrub leading to the watercourse. Luckily it appeared to be the only other crossing. Because of the steepness of the bank on our side of the stream, a crossing was only feasible where a track led down to the water.

There were now several hundred people milling about on the German side of the stream, with lots of shouting and Verey lights. George left me to guard the crossing and walked on down, with Christopher, to see if Bill was OK. He came back quite quickly to say that Bill's soldier servant had been killed, that Bill had been wounded, and that Welton had gone to reinforce him with more grenades. The Germans had decided that they were not going to get across at Bill's point, and were now splashing up the water course and walking up the far bank towards us. The frost and the wet meant that, wherever they went, there appeared a cloud of steam above them, which enabled us to see what was going to happen next. Eventually the steam denoted that they had found my sheep track and, after much puffing and swearing, a German emerged a few yards from me, on my side of the stream. I had my Tommy gun on single shots and, taking aim for his midriff, I pulled the trigger. I heard the bullet hit him and he dropped, and all went still.

George, meanwhile, was darting about in the scrubland. His cap comforter had come off and, with his bald head and height of six foot five, it meant that he was an unmistakable target in the moonlight but, as he repeatedly dashed down and fired at the far bank and tossed hand grenades into the stream, the shouts disclosed he was doing damage. This continued for some time. No further attack happened until a German officer came down and rallied his troops. He reconnoitred the stream and decided that our track was the only way. A large group then got into the stream and, I think, pitched the first man up onto the bank and he stood there steaming. I went to repeat the previous scenario, only to find my gun had jammed (it turned out to be a split bullet case). We looked at each other for what must have been a minute, and then a shot rang out and he crumpled. The Germans retaliated with a volley of stick grenades that fell all around.

I had some hand grenades in a sandbag, so I chucked two or three into the stream to more screams. Another German eventually arrived on our side. Again there was a crack, and he dropped. This happened many more times until there was quite a pile of corpses. The Germans seemed to lose their enthusiasm and, again, there was silence. After an interval, they made several more attempts and, each time anyone arrived on our side, he was shot.

Our saviour turned out to be the Senior Drill Sergeant George Armstrong, who had been a member of the King's Hundred at Bisley before the war. He was coming up with the rations and ammo, and had found himself in the middle of the fight. He got up on the south side of the gully with a Lee Enfield and as, from his eyrie, he was only about a hundred yards away from the stream bank, he never missed. Suddenly the Germans could be seen withdrawing up the hill, and Armstrong got a couple more to keep them moving. I went to slither down back into the gully, but it was about a 30 foot drop and I knocked the wind out of myself, not helped when George Chaplin landed on top of me.

I was met by Welton, who had carried Bill Sidney back from the watercourse. Bill was now lying face-down on a stretcher, having lost a lot of blood. With the Company Clerk, we took it in turns to carry him back to the R.A.P., where "Nelson" Eddy, the doctor, gave him a shot; and Welton and me a much-needed whisky. Welton and I then set off back to Battalion Headquarters. When we arrived there, John Stanley emerged to say that he thought we had lost 2 and 4 Companies but 1 and 3, he thought, were still holding out. Eusty Miller was being relieved by Colonel Charlie Huntington, who had been flown out from the 1st Battalion in England. He thought that Colonel Charlie would want to move back to the flyover and he was coming over to make a recce, before deciding. Chucks Lyttelton then appeared – he and Sergeant Hough had fired all their mortar ammo but thought, because of the very short range, they had had very little effect. As I was now the Company Commander, we did a roll call exercise with Welton and tried to revise our order of battle. The Mortar Platoon and the Anti-Tank Platoon had both suffered severely, but the Carriers had escaped comparatively lightly.

It was now getting light and we could see a bit more. No. 4 Company position was apparently deserted, and the intervening ground was bare. But, once the dawn brightened, both sides' automatic weapons ensured that vast amounts of ammunition were expended, with no casualties, though no move could be made by either side. It was now raining again, and George Chaplin and I took it in turns to sit on the top of the gully to see if any signs of a new attack were evident. It continued bitterly cold through that day and, as darkness fell, the shooting stopped and it appeared that preparations were being made for another attack. At 9 p.m. it duly came, with largish numbers of Germans involved and all brought up short by the water course. Hand grenades and volleys of rifle shots were enough to hold the crossing and we looked to be holding our own.

Colonel Charlie Huntington appeared as it was getting light the next morning, and climbed up onto the gully top. He decided that the Battalion had to continue to hold its present position at all costs. He ordered Christopher Hodson, seven Guardsmen, and me to hold the front of Battalion Headquarters and the north west flank; and George Chaplin, the Drill Sergeant and five Guardsmen to go down and hold the area where Bill Sidney had been, before he was wounded. So began the longest, coldest and wettest day of my war.

Any movement provoked a tornado of German spandau machine gun fire. We were ordered not to expose ourselves and not to shoot, unless the Germans attempted to cross the watercourse. Guardsman Slater had an entrenching tool and we passed it, from hand-to-hand, to each dig ourselves a small hole in the sandy soil. This was just as well as at regular intervals we were shelled and mortared and it was comforting to be able to duck below the surface. As we had not had any food or drink for two days, we were glad to be able to jump about a bit after it became dark to restore our circulation. It remained bitterly cold and, as the shooting had ceased at dusk, silence fell until, at about 9 p.m., preparations were made for another attack. When it arrived there was noticeably fewer Germans than the night before. Armstrong was no longer in his eyrie but we all shot away and hurled hand grenades, and the attack petered out. We were left alone in the rain.

We lasted out the night. Charlie Huntington re-appeared and told us to withdraw back to the flyover, and to extract our two 15cwt trucks. They were not four-wheel drive and, after much pushing and cursing, they had to be abandoned. My grandmother, who was in Turkey, had sent me a bright blue pullover and a book called *40 Years Wandering in the Gobi Desert* by two female American missionaries. I extracted both gifts and was glad to put on the pullover as I was shaking with cold and soaked through. I scrambled up the bank with the C.S.M., Guardsman Slater and Guardsman Moran (Christopher's soldier servant) and we made our way back to the flyover, as a volley of smoke shells denoted the launching of another German attack on our gully behind us.

At the flyover I found myself in the middle of yet another German attack. This time they had got on top of the embankment in large numbers, coming from the east, and were shooting up all the people below. Charlie Huntington was attempting to get a General Grant tank, manned by Americans, to machine gun the embankment top, when he was shot and killed instantly. He had commanded the Battalion for twenty-seven and a half hours. The General Grant tank now got the message and shot all the Germans on the skyline. Chucks and the Carrier Platoon climbed up and swept the remaining Germans off the embankment, and then picked off those Germans who had got down on our side of the line and who were cut off between the embankment and the road to Anzio. Meanwhile the code name for every Allied gun to fire had been given, and they pulverised the Germans who were caught in the open, on their way to join the assault.

That night a battalion of the 5th Division relieved us, and we took over their position on another railway embankment, three miles to the south. The Battalion was still facing the enemy but this part of the salient was quiet. The next morning I heard that Chucks Lyttelton had been wounded and, after "stand down", I took a jeep and went back to the Casualty Clearing Station. I asked to see him and a sister said he was not there, but waved towards a line of about 30 blankets. I walked down the line looking at the labels until I saw one that said "Lt. J. A. Lyttelton 5 G.G." I knew the worst – I was the only survivor of the Support Company Officers. I walked back to my jeep and got in to drive back to the Battalion, but there was a touch on my arm. It was the sister with a cup of tea "have this before you go" she said, and I did.

This first major battle for the Anzio beachhead had wiped out the North Staffs and overrun three of our four rifle companies. It had been left to the 55 men of the Battalion H.Q. to stand between the three German Divisions and the Artillery areas of the beachhead. We were down to 29 men at the end but our stand halted the German Divisions and their drive through to the port and embarkation areas. The Germans had received so many casualties that they abandoned their push to the sea, and a three-month war of attrition ensued until the final break out at the end of May. Two days later General Alexander visited the Battalion and thanked us for saving the bridgehead, and said the Battalion and 24th Guards Brigade had performed prodigiously. Bill Sidney got the V.C., George Chaplin the M.C., George Armstrong the D.C.M. and I was mentioned in despatches.

The Battalion was now down to about 80 men as a result of the struggle to retain the beachhead, so it was decided to amalgamate the 5th & 6th Battalions and continue as the 5th. As reinforcements from the 5th Division were brought in to take over from us, we went back to Nettuno and returned to Naples and the infantry base depot. As our two landing craft came alongside we could see Geordie Gordon-Lennox and one or two of the earlier wounded on the quayside. We were all lined up and welcomed formally by Geordie. My personal welcome was actually chilly, as clearly my cheeky reply at Carroceto had not been forgotten or forgiven. I got John Owen, a fellow Balliol alumnus, as my second-in-command of the Anti-Tank Platoon. Chris Oldfield replaced Michael Hargreaves at the Carrier Platoon.

Bill Sidney's V.C. came through almost immediately, as a second

Philip Sidney (the first being the soldier poet Philip Sidney who was mortally wounded at the Battle of Zutphen in 1586) appealed to Winston enormously. General Alexander came down to the Battalion to present him with it at a special parade, and he spoke approvingly of how the Grenadiers had responded to the challenges of Anzio. We all looked to see how Brigadier Archer Clive would react – towards the end of February the ex-commander of the 6th Battalion at Mareth had arrived to replace the Brigade Commander and had immediately infuriated the whole battalion by accusing us of having behaved in a craven way – but he remained impassive throughout. However, the remark of the day went to Sergeant Thomas, a print union organiser at the *Manchester Evening News* who said, "If Sidney was half as beastly to the Germans as he is to us, he thoroughly deserves it."

Chapter 10

A SLOG UP CENTRAL ITALY

The Battalion started to train, harmonising the Middle Eastern approach of the 6th Battalion with the more regimental approach of Colonel Geordie. It was not without friction, and I was glad when I was detailed to go with John Nelson and John Stanley to mentor the 12th Lancers where, at Capracotta and Castel del Giudice, they were having to act as infantrymen up in the mountains. There were about 10 of us in all from the Grenadier and Scots Guards. Capracotta was the highest village in Italy and was above the headwater of the Sangro. The Germans were on the North Bank, but had mostly drawn back to the villages higher up. Each patrol had to walk about seven miles down to the river, and then about a further five miles, before there was any hope of encountering the Germans. We could see occasional enemy movement but, by the time a patrol had been despatched, the enemy had already long disappeared. The 12th Lancers were very conscientious and insisted on going all the way on foot until halted by fire or, more likely, by encountering a minefield of schu mines (the wooden non-detectable anti-personnel jumping mines), as a result of which they lost quite a few people.

However, this idyll did not last long as I and six people were detailed to up and join the Polish Corps at Castrogirardi. To our surprise we found we were to be the carrying party for Brock's fireworks who, on the night of the opening of the final Cassino Battle, were to let off a display to delude the Germans into thinking that the eastern side of the Apennines was the scene of another simultaneous offensive.

The two Brock's people, who had been flown out by Liberator, were still wearing blue suits and bowler hats so we got the Poles to equip them with battledress and boots, as we were in for a long walk and carry. The Poles were fun to be with; they lay naked on their beds in a house, overlooking the river, with a look-out equipped with an 88mm gun sight – if even a solitary German was espied, a fighting patrol was immediately despatched, and told not to return, until they had killed him. They were the Carpathian Lancers and really were a tank and motorised infantry outfit.

The great evening of May 11th arrived. The two Brock's men checked our haversacks to see that we had got all the necessary fireworks, and off we went. The site chosen was meant to be on a line from our gun emplacements to the East and Germany Army headquarters. The fireworks had been chosen to flicker and give a reflection off the clouds as if there were multiple flashes, and to simulate the rumble of far-off artillery. Zero hour was 2145 and for three hours we set up, and the Brock's men lit the fireworks to a pre-arranged pattern. The site was deep in no man's land between the two lines, so we needed our weapons in case we had to extricate the fireworks men. We arrived back about dawn and the Brock's men returned to Caserta. I never heard any feedback as to whether the Germans delayed committing their reserves as a result, but I doubt it.

The Poles had enlarged the jeep track used to supply the infantry on the heights to the north end of the Cassino Monastery to enable their own tanks to get up onto the plateau to the north of the monastery. The Germans evacuated the monastery and it never surrendered. At 9.15 a.m. the morning after, I took my jeep up the tank road and drove to the monastery postern door on the north side. There were about 20-30 long-dead Indians, Ghurkas and Rajputana Rifles, lying outside the postern door. They had been shot by the defenders from the monks' cell windows above, so I presume they had been trying to blow the door in on the first assault in February. The door led into the two vestries of the Great Church. The vestments were hanging untouched but the great chests, where the altar frontals were kept, had been used by the Germans as a latrine, without bothering to remove the embroidery. The sacred vessels store beyond was apparently intact, and had been used as living quarters. The High Altar in the church was more or less intact but damaged, and the rest of the church had been turned into rubble, and was open to the sky.

I went back to the Polish Regiment H.Q. and thanked them for their hospitality. They told me that the Germans, having left the monastery, were making a stand at the next shoulder of the Liri valley and that the 6th Armoured were attempting to clean them out and get up the road towards Rome. I went on round to Cassino town where the 5th Battalion was in the rubble, only to find that John Nelson had gone to take over command of the 3rd Battalion. They had had trouble in their attack with the 6th Armoured, and one of the 3rd Battalion officers had been put out to die on a stretcher, outside the casualty clearing station, as he had had a burst of machine fire through his guts. But, that day, the major-general in charge of surgery arrived from England with the first supplies of penicillin. He operated and sorted things out; he gave him a mammoth dose of penicillin and the chap was alive and kicking in 2004.

When I rejoined the 5th Battalion, it had been in the cellars of the houses in the main square of Cassino for a fortnight. The Germans, until they withdrew on the fall of the monastery, had also been in these cellars. In the square was a shot-up joyriding American jeep containing the bodies of two American Air Force officers and two nurses, who had driven into the square and been shot by the Germans. It was all such close quarters that from 7.30-9.30 p.m. every night the British fired smoke, and replenished their supplies, while the Germans did likewise from 9.45 p.m. till midnight. But we were on the move again and had now joined the 6th South African Division as their motorised infantry.

The route to Rome was slow and tortuous, awaiting the break out of the Anzio troops. Instead of cutting the Germans off at Frosinone, the American 5th Army turned parallel to the German Axis in order to be the first to enter Rome on June 4th. When we got to Rome there was a mammoth traffic jam, but the Roman ladies made us all welcome with garlands, as we sat in endless queues. American jeeps laden with girls flashed by, heading for neighbouring bedrooms. The jeeps, when

Map 5: Northern Italy. Rome to the Austrian Frontier

parked outside, were a sitting target and so, the next day, when we ended up in a field beside the Tiber north of Rome, we had a visit from the Field Security Police who were checking on stolen vehicles. They declared themselves satisfied just as an order arrived for us to ford the river at a cattle crossing.

After about five miles, we ran into the German rearguard, and started getting mortared and having casualties. Colonel Geordie disappeared with a signaller and a wireless set into the scrubby woodland, and, as he crossed the ravine, shouted to me, "Get some vehicles across for me." I walked with two jeeps behind me for about two miles, with the ravine perilously close to the track. I suddenly found a stone bridge, built for oxcarts, over the ravine so I asked Guardsman Gregson, my driver, and Guardsman Mullard, Geordie's orderly, "Can we get across?" Nervously we edged over, with the stream 60 feet below, and no room on either side. Nonetheless, we made it and it then took only five minutes to end up opposite our departure point. As we turned in to go up to Geordie, where the battle was still raging, there was a bellow from across the stream. It was Brigadier Archer, who wanted to hijack our vehicle for himself. I said, in another bellow, that it was for Geordie and I was immediately put in close arrest by the Brigadier. In for a penny, in for a pound, I thought, so I shouted the well known retort with a V sign, and disappeared. I got to Geordie to find him busy listening to the Brigadier, telling of my crimes. Geordie grinned, and the Anzio business was temporarily forgotten.

We struggled up the hill and finally dislodged the Germans, who seemed to be only about a platoon, and so the juggernaut of our advance continued to the next line of vineyards. These were terraced, so launching an assault was very difficult as climbing twelve feet every 30 yards made one an easy target and a very slow moving one as well. Our first officer casualty was Christopher Snell who trod on a schu mine. He was a very old friend from schooldays, and it was eerie to sit by him as his life ebbed slowly away on one of the terraces. Then the Carrier and Mortar platoons were ambushed beneath a cliff and had very heavy casualties, including both platoon commanders. Support Company took this very hard and when, the next day, a despatch rider arrived from the Prime Minister offering Bill Sidney the Chelsea candidature at a by-election, the mood visibly lightened. A regular called David Dixon was coming out to command the company; meanwhile I was the company commander.

We were, by now, well bedded down with the South Africans. They were brave, tactically wise, and good companions. The battle along the shores of Lake Trasimene was much fiercer by the lake than it was for us in the foothills, but the casualties were mounting up for all of us, day by day. My first job was to get the Carrier and Mortar platoons operational again after their severe casualties the week before, and I was lucky when Chris Oldfield and Mark Gilbey arrived as replacements.

The Anti-Tank Platoon was now in the hands of John Owen, a much older chap who had been a scholar at Balliol. He had come to the Grenadiers via being private secretary to Captain Cruikshank M.P. at the Treasury. It was now very difficult because we were in action continuously, with no relief, unless the Battalion got hopelessly stuck. We did most of the fighting by night and the mortars were used for quick support of the attackers, as the artillery found the steep gradient very difficult to fire on accurately. We liked to arrive about 2.30 a.m. to push the Germans out, and the Pretoria regiment would arrive at dawn in case of counter-attack. As the Americans had allowed the German Army to escape through Rome, we were still against our old opponents, 1 & 4 Para Divisions. They mostly departed after we outflanked them, but on three occasions they made a battle of it.

The first one was at Orvieto and we got round the city to the northwest, with the help of the 4th Indian Division. The second was at Castello del Broglio, the vineyard, where the Scots Guards stormed the wine vaults and we attacked the castle. When the doors were blown in the Paras defending the vats produced a hail of fire from on high, and were finally despatched, falling into the vats. So, like the proverbial rats in the Guinness, German Paras were the making of the 1944 Castel del Broglio vintage. Many years later, I told the story to my French Managing Director, who was going on holiday there, and he returned with two 1944 bottles which were consumed with great pleasure, and had a suitable vintage aroma des boches morts.

I went on leave to Rome with Gilbert Lamb and, whilst window shopping in the Via Veneto, we were accosted by an elderly woman. Rome was full of old ladies who were very short of food, and we attempted to give her the brush-off. But, to our surprise, she asked us to lunch the next day. "Who are you?" said Gilbert. "I am Mary Dykes as was," she said mysteriously. She gave an address in the Via and trotted off. The next day, Gilbert and I wandered around the block, and finally came to the conclusion that there was only one unmarked door that fitted the bill. We used the enormous door knocker on the double doors at the end of a sort of arcade. The doors immediately swung open and there stood a Major Domo in a black cloak, holding a large mace and wearing a Wellington type of cocked hat, behind whom were 3 flunkies in red velvet breeches, powdered wigs and blue frock coats. We were just about to turn tail and flee when "Mary Dykes as was", still in her rather dowdy outfit, approached down the stairs, and led us up to the state rooms above. She was the Princess Doria Pamphili, a nurse from Newcastle upon Tyne. She had nursed the prince through the wounds he sustained on the Western Front in World War I and then married him. A further attraction was the daughter, Oriettina, a tall and chilly blonde. I sat at lunch between her and her mother. The Prince, who was Mayor of Rome, was wearing the bluest and opaquest dark glasses, which he had had to adopt as a disguise while on the run from the Germans, and wandering from place to place on his vast estates north of Rome. He was charming, and full of interesting stories of the Great War and the recent German occupation. After lunch we had a tour of the Palazzo and saw all the pictures, including the Velasquez of the family's Pope, Innocent X. I got carried away and asked Oriettina out to dinner, and got smartly snubbed for my pains. Nevertheless, her mother was a great stand-by, and was always good for a meal and a chat whenever I was in Rome.

The next excitement was a private audience with Pope Pius XII (Pacelli). My fellow Grenadier Paul Freyberg had been captured at Anzio and, whilst being marched to captivity, had hurled himself from a bridge over a stream, and hid in the culvert underneath. He was lucky as my old mucker, Anthony Courage, who was ahead of him in the column, looked round and, seeing Paul gone, had made a run for it and was shot by the German escort. Anyway Paul lay low and, walking by night, got into the Vatican City and was hidden by the British Ambassador's butler in a cellar to priests' houses. He turned up, after the fall of Rome, looking like a cross between an opera singer and a gangster. His mother, Lady Freyberg, married to Sir Bernard Freyberg, the general commanding the New Zealand Corps, thought he ought to thank the Pope for his stay, so an audience was arranged.

It was to be a private audience and so, after attending the public one (where we saw the Pope carried in on his sedilia by the Noble Guard of distinguished bearded Romans, in black tail coats and decorations, and snapped by hundreds of G.Is shouting, "Aw, hold it Popey!"), we were escorted down the corridor to one of the private audience chambers, and awaited the arrival of the Pontiff. There were about ten of these private audience chambers, each with a prie-dieu and a small altar and crucifix. After about forty minutes, the door was thrown open and there stood the Pope; tall (over six foot), thin and wearing pancake-white makeup. He spoke to Paul and Lady Freyberg in perfect English but, when they replied, it was clear he was not nearly so good at understanding what was said to him. Anyway, the audience lasted for about ten minutes and then he beckoned us to our knees, blessed us, and proceeded on his way to the next audience. Afterwards, Paul and Lady Freyberg took us off to the Orso restaurant where we celebrated the audience in fine style all afternoon. The Battalion had found itself a flat, where we could stay when in Rome, and it was full of people coming and going all the summer. All good things had to end, and Gilbert and I went back to the Battalion feeling we didn't much fancy the war after all the fleshpots of the Eternal City. But before the slog up central Italy continued, I attended the Missa della Liberazione at Orvieto Cathedral as the Official Allied Representative. It was rather fun sitting in a chair by the High Altar, being covered with incense at regular intervals by the Cardinal and Bishops. The music was much less exceptional than I had been hoping for, but afterwards the Bishops and Town Council and I sat down to an amazing lunch.

It was now that I got myself taken prisoner for ten minutes. After breakfast I had set out with a spade to let nature take its course and was just finishing when someone said, "Hands up Tommy!" I arose and found I had chosen a position about twenty feet below a German artillery observation post. There was an officer and a N.C.O., and a wireless set hidden in the bushes. I put my hands up and they came out to claim me. Luckily Bob Riches, our Pretoria Regimental Squadron leader, was standing on his tank turret, mending his aerial, and saw it happening. So, starting up the tank, he charged out and the biter was bit. We marched them back and then we went and collected their wireless set and glasses, so I had a lucky escape.

I was deputising in Chianti for Ronnie Taylor, our new adjutant who had gone on leave, when a despatch rider from Brigade Headquarters brought the news that Geordie Gordon-Lennox's mother had been killed in the Guards Chapel bombing on 18th June 1944. I went and got a mug of whisky and took it to Geordie, who was working out a fire plan problem with our Battery Commander. I told him and handed him the whisky, "No" said Geordie, "not till I've finished." He completed the task, sent the Battery Commander on his way and then said, "Give me the mug now and leave me alone." From then on Geordie and I got on very well.

The subsequent attack went in and got the Germans out. But, at dawn, they counter-attacked Jimmy Willson's company with at least a battalion, and it was very hard going for a while. But Jimmy and No. 4 Company appeared to be seeing them off so I was sent with a few signallers, and Support Company H.Q., to try to get behind them. As we went down the hill towards Greve, we heard the sound of German voices and discovered that we had found the German Command Post. As we rushed in, they ran away, leaving a state-of-the-art German radio, still spouting the usual battle network. The remnants of the Germans made it back to Greve, where two Tiger tanks were waiting in the square, and they set off for Florence with them riding on the tanks. The Germans blew a couple of culverts, and the Pretoria regiment had to wait while the culverts were bulldozed in by the Royal Engineers.

While waiting, our engineer lorry went up on a mine and I was sent to cover the mine detecting team. I spotted a huge villa with newly painted green shutters and, having nothing much to do, I walked up the drive and saw that the door was secured by an enormous padlock. I shot the hasp off, and went in to see hundreds of pictures stored in racks in every room. I realised that I was the temporary possessor of the evacuated treasures from a gallery. I thought to myself, "This is when the Merevale picture collection is going to be suitably enhanced!" I came out of the front door whereupon two black-leather clad motorcyclists drove up, and held me up with their pistols saying that they were field security police and that they were arresting me for looting. I handed over my tommy gun and then heard a voice say, "Drop those guns!" It was Sergeant Button, who had followed me up the drive; we made them lie down and took away their weapons. They were indeed field security police, but we made them walk all the way back to base and handed them over to our regimental police to be checked on. So ended my brief possession of the treasures of the Uffizi gallery in Florence.

We were now on the final leg into Florence and, on the morning of 4th August, I drove down the hill to the Arno. There was no sign of any Germans. The Ponte Vecchio still stood, but the bridge next to it had been blown, and its rubble was acting as a dam across the river. This didn't matter much because the Arno, by August, had reduced to a trickle. So I thought I would walk across the river on the blown bridge. I got half way across when a Spandau opened up, and then another. There was a hurricane of fire, and I dived into a hole in the bridge. Eventually they became tired of shooting at me and, by dropping down on to the river bed, I got back to the jeep with no further bother. It took a further three days to clear up the scattered German pockets in the city centre – the main force and lines of the Germans had retreated to the rising ground at the northern end of the city, beyond the racecourse and the aerodrome.

Danger always enhances the libido, and the Battalion (and indeed the Army) descended on Florence with a real glint in the eye. The Coldstream took over Mrs. Keppel's villa – she had been Edward VII's last mistress – and the Grenadiers soon found a similar but less exotic one. It was kept by a contessa (all females in Florence are contessas) with a fourteen-year-old daughter. She had a more than spirited approach to life and one evening, when being enjoyed by one of the subalterns, mama appeared and banged on the door and said, "Take me and not my daughter!" "I will," he said, "as soon as I've finished." There was another contessa who had a home up by the racecourse, and she had had a romance with a German graf from the 4th Para. But, as he had had to retire to the north, she was now open to offers, and two officers of our other Battalion used to call upon her, whenever possible. Unfortunately, the graf could see their jeep from his mountain fortress and, one night, he led a patrol which caught the two Grenadiers in flagrante. He spoke good English and, as he beckoned them outside with his luger, he said, "This is a situation which the honour of a German Officer cannot allow to continue." They were led away and driven back to the German lines in their own jeep. That night, as they were being transported up the Futa Pass on the Autobahn, one of the two Grenadiers claimed to have tummy trouble and so sat on the tailboard of the lorry. Seizing his opportunity he rolled back over the tailboard and escaped to tell the tale. His companion finished the war in a P.O.W. camp.

Campbell Holt and I hunted in pairs. We discovered that all the smart Mammas went to Mass on Sundays at 8 a.m. at a church which was the Florentine equivalent of St. Peters, Eaton Square. The mothers all knelt devoutly at the semi-circular altar rail, and their unmarried daughters stood demurely behind them on a stage. By walking behind them on the floor, the girls standing at about shoulder height, we attempted to chat up the prettiest. The girls all got the message and, on the next Sunday, they all were holding out invitations behind them, which Campbell and I collected. In Florentine society most families had a gathering for tea on Sunday afternoon, and it was fun to do the rounds and invite someone out to dinner. The unmarried girls were not allowed out unsupervised, but their elder sisters and sisters-in-law, who seemed mostly to be married to Air Force Officers who had been taken prisoner bombing Malta, were free to do as they pleased.

Chapter 11

In the Mountains, Over the Po

The Fifth Army was re-organised because of the invasion of the South of France and the Battalion was, alas, moved out of Florence, first to Prato and then to Pistoia, so our amusements in Florence were curtailed, but not completely. The assault on the Gothic line, between Genoa and Ravenna, was scheduled for the beginning of September 1944. Before crossing the Arno, north of Pistoia, we spent 36 hours in a vast peach orchard. As the peaches were ripe, just waiting to be picked, and very plentiful, the worst happened and we all had very runny tummies. C.S.M. Welton came to me and said that he didn't think the Company would make the start line. I was aghast as all the orders and fire plans were made. I took a deep breath and ordered all nether garments to be removed, and added that anyone who failed to make it would be court-martialled. So, pantless, Support Company 5th Battalion Grenadier Guards, like the Archers at Agincourt, crossed the river and entered the foothills. We only had a couple of casualties from a stray shell and we took no prisoners so, after a long slog through the night, we were ready for breakfast.

Our axis was the Pistoia-Bologna Road, which went through the woollen mill area of Italy. Perpetually shrouded in mist, we attacked from foothills to hills to small mountains to bigger mountains. Every time we captured a trigonometrical point, there was always another one a bit higher beyond. The weather broke on about the 15th of September, which was about a fortnight early, and we spent a very miserable time in soaking wet khaki drill until someone took mercy on us, and re-equipped us with winter clothing. Parted from our vehicles, the

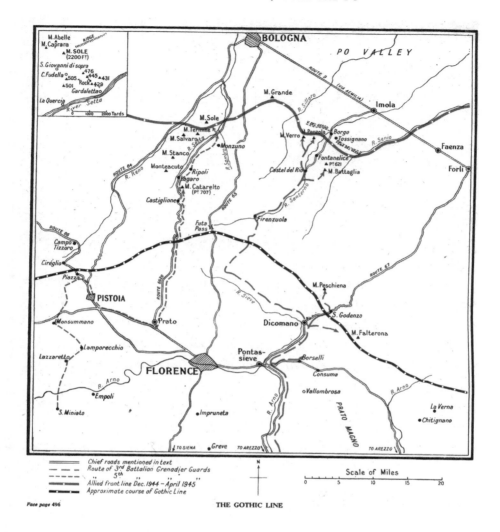

Map 6: The Gothic Line

weapons had to be manhandled. We needed the three-inch mortars and the Vickers machine guns, but had not much use of six-pound anti-tank guns. We were given a supply of explosive shells but, as they had less explosive than a two-inch mortar bomb, it was difficult to make much impression on the Germans. But, from time to time, we found we could bring down a roof or two on German ears. By mid-October we realised we were stuck there for the winter. All the tracks were morasses and one slithered on one's bottom as often as walked.

I took a gamble and decided to go for a hamlet, which appeared on the map as Ca. Cassetta. It proved to consist of two farms, a church and a presbytery, nestling on the north side of a ridge. The church steeple had projected above the ridge and had been duly demolished by the Germans shooting 88mm shells at it. I arrived and was shown round by the priest's housekeeper – a tough looking blonde of about 35 or so. The priest appeared later, unshaven (he only shaved on Saturdays before hearing confessions), and was about 65. I decided to make this my Winter H.Q. We got a tarpaulin to cover the hole made by the demolished steeple. There was a large fireplace and a good supply of firewood (where it came from heaven alone knew as there wasn't a tree for twenty miles). Slater and the housekeeper hit it off; she did the cooking and he scoured the village for eggs. The inhabitants came out of the farm, and we made a defensive position out to the front for nights. Chris Oldfield, his Carrier Platoon and the Anti-tanks were nearly a rifle company so we were an important part of the Battalion formation. We did ten days in the line, and then five days in Prato to recover. By November the first snows came, and the nightly temperature dropped well below zero. We lived in the buildings by day with a lookout, and went onto the forward slope at dusk. The Germans twice sent out patrols to attack us; the first was abandoned when an N.C.O. lost a leg on a mine, and the second was pressed home with a lot of tracer, but eventually came to nothing.

My eyrie bliss was interrupted when Ronnie Taylor went on leave, and I was sent down to Battalion H.Q. to take over as temporary Adjutant. Battalion H.Q. was in a tunnel where the wind blew along the railway like a scythe. There was nothing but drips from the rocks above, and soggy blankets to cower behind. When the Germans came along the railway line through several tunnels, luckily they were spotted and easily repulsed, incurring several casualties before retiring. I was sitting shivering with Colonel Geordie, and imbibing a coffee laced with rum, when he told me that the 5th and 3rd Battalions were going to be amalgamated because of shortages of reinforcements. I was destined to be the next adjutant of the revived 3rd Battalion, succeeding Gerry Micklem. He also said that I was to go to the 3rd Battalion after Christmas and that the amalgamation would take place in late February, prior to the Spring resumption of warfare. Geordie was handing over to Peter Clifton and was going to be G1 Ops (Chief Staff job) of the 5th Division.

But before the take-over took place, we had a bloody battle just prior to Christmas. Two new platoon commanders, when attacked by the usual German patrols, had withdrawn somewhat precipitately and, in the resultant counter-attack to regain our position, Waddie Burke, the No. 4 company commander, was shot and broke his thigh and my old buddie, George Chaplin, the No. 2 company commander, died of wounds. He had been the hero of the battalion defence at the bridgehead, and was one of the few who had been right through it all. So, when Ronnie returned, I went off with Mark Gilbey, the mortar officer, to Florence. Our villa in Florence was run by Rupert Clarke, who was recovering from wounds received earlier in the Autumn; so we had a firm and comfy home with fires and transport to and from Florence. Mark, being a Catholic, had the entrée all round the town so we dined out, almost every night, in some smart apartments. The black market was represented by a Baron Marochetti, who took us out a couple of times, but was eventually rumbled by the Garrison police.

After my leave was up, Slater and I moved down to the 3rd Battalion villa to await joining instructions. The Battalion was up on Monte Sole, a high peak between Firenzuola and Bologna and it took, in the deep snow of winter, about seven hours to get to it. The journey ended in a stiff climb, so one arrived in a muck sweat in very sub-zero temperatures. The Battalion earlier had had a fraught night when a German patrol got behind the forward position and attacked Battalion H.Q. The situation was rescued by Bryce Knox, the Ayrshire Yeomanry Battery Commander, who sorted out the attackers more or less single-handed.

The Brigade was eventually withdrawn from the front line and sent to the seaside at Fano, on the Adriatic, in order to complete the 3rd & 5th Grenadiers' and the 2nd & 3rd Coldstreams' mergers with Peter Clifton and Danny Dixon (Glentoran) as C.O. and second-in-command of the Grenadiers. One day, I received a signal from 8th Army asking me to return the numbers of those of Jewish religion, in order to calculate the supply of unleavened bread required for the Passover celebration. Knowing that unleavened bread was, in effect, Jacobs cream cracker biscuits, I said that we had 73 Jews in the Battalion, hoping that our cheese course would have an adequate supply of biscuits. I thought no more about it until, coming in from football, I saw a grand 8th Army Staff car with a bearded Major-General and Colonel aboard. They turned out to be the Chief Rabbi from England and the Senior Jewish Chaplain in Italy. They said, "We never thought to find so many of our faith in the Guards." I thought that honesty was the only course and told them the truth; that we had only two Jews in the Battalion, both N.C.Os, and that one was in hospital having had a contact with an Italian girl. Luckily they roared with laughter and stayed the weekend, proving most congenial companions at what was also the Easter weekend.

We did a couple of practice Battalion exercises, and then we were off to break through into the Po valley. The initial attack was made by the Coldsteam, who had George Burns as C.O. and Simon Phipps as adjutant. They had a slaying encounter and then, finally, they were through the German lines into the plain. We were launched to leap-frog them and the Welsh Guards and head for the River Po. We had about three skirmishes at bridges, where the Germans tried to hold us up to let the main body get away, but, on the 21st April, we arrived at the banks of the Po at three thirty in the afternoon and hid behind the enormous mud levée. I walked up and peered over.

The Po was in flood with the snow melt from the Alps, and looked about half a mile wide. There was a ramp up the levée to the ferry-man's house, and then diagonally down to the river. When I got down,

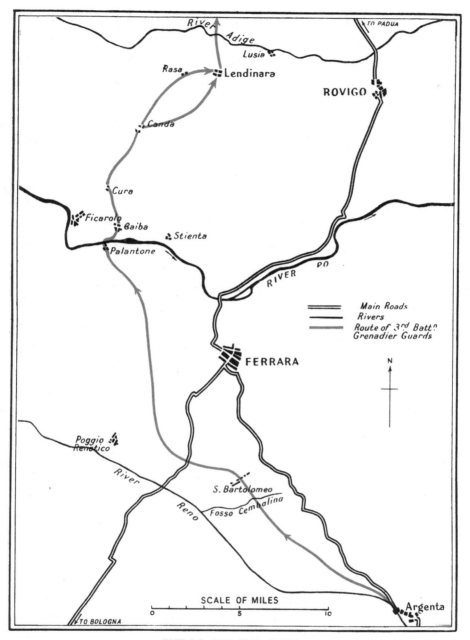

THE PO AND THE ADIGE

Map 7: The Po and the Adige

Colonel Peter was engaged with five generals: the Army commander (Leese), two Corps Commanders, Bernard Freyberg, the New Zealand commander, and the divisional commander. I got into the group with a notebook and heard Colonel Peter saying to them all, " I won't wait, we'll cross at 19.30, no barrage, we'll just go up and launch the tanks and boats and go." He had been allotted a troop of 7th Hussars who had floating Shermans, as used on landings, and we had three large pontoon boats from the Royal Engineers, and one Italian boat from the ferry.

Peter summoned the O group, which met in an outhouse to the ferryman's dwelling, and outlined his plan. "Any questions?" he said and Eric Russell, who was commanding No. 1 company, said, "It's just not on, it can't be done." "Oh Eric," said Colonel Peter very smoothly, "you can go back to B Echelon and send up your 2nd Captain. No. 3 company and Geoffrey (Marriott) can spearhead the operation." There was a perceptible intake of breath from everyone. Eric, a regular soldier, had only just joined the Battalion from a staff job, and Geoffrey was an M.C. holder from the 5th Battalion, who had been all the way as a platoon commander. Eric made a somewhat discomfited exit, and we all got down to planning the follow-up to No. 3 and Geoffrey Marriott.

At 1930 hrs. the tanks rushed up the levée with as many men as could be crammed into the waterproof canvas screens sticking up round their superstructures. The Royal Engineers, aided by No. 2 company, launched the boats. The remainder of No. 3 company jumped aboard, and we were off. The tanks had their tracks on the river bottom, except for about 100 yards in the middle, and the current, because of the bend, forced the boats from one side to the other. My job was to organise the landing point and achieve a quick turn around, so that No. 2 company, and No. 1 following, could be brought over. Geoffrey led his men up the ramp on the far side and shot over the top. The German defenders were all queuing for their evening meal at a field kitchen immediately below. After a couple of bursts of Bren Gun fire, they all surrendered and we were across. They had looted about 50 bicycles, which were stacked on the bank, and Geoffrey mounted a platoon on them and led them off down the road towards the Adige, about seven miles to the north. The Battalion proceeded across and I got Guardsman Gregson and my jeep across at about 2200 hrs., and we were off again. As a footnote, the New Zealand attack at two thirty in the morning was strongly defended and they had about 200 casualties getting across.

At dawn, Geoffrey Marriott radioed that he had reached the Adige and that all was chaos there, so Gregson and I set off. The German pontoon bridge across the Adige had lost one tracking as a result of a R.A.F. Hurricane attack, and no vehicle could get across. There was a huge pile-up of supply vehicles, and the Germans were continuing their flight on foot and by bicycle. Just short of the bridge were two vehicles with trailers and, on inspection, they proved to be the German Army pay office. They were stacked with occupation overstamped Lire.

As the Grenadiers had found the money, I spoke to Colonel Peter who said that the money should be shared between all three Battalions. So Philpott, the Quartermaster, divided the Lire into three. We sent ours straight back to Rome to buy the Battalion Naafi allocation for six months in advance. I then went to Colonel George Burns, the Coldstream C.O., who was standing with Simon Phipps and, after saluting, said that Colonel Peter would like a third share of the money to go to each Battalion. "Very good of him," said Colonel George, and I was on my way. I asked Simon later what they had done with the lolly. "Oh, I told him to burn it as you are always trouble with a capital T."

On I went to Colonel Robin Rose-Price, the Welsh Guards' C.O., and Francis Egerton, my opposite number, to bring them the good news. Colonel Robin put his finger to the side of his nose and said, "Does anyone else know about it?" "Only the three Battalions," I replied. I heard afterwards that they had bought the Welsh Battalion a villa on the Amalfi peninsular. About three years later I was sitting in my office at Lincolns Inn Fields, when I was told that three bowler-hatted gentlemen wished to see me. I went down and found that they were the special investigation branch of the War Office, who were enquiring into the ownership of the Welsh Guards' villa. I couldn't tell them much, and, after questioning me for an hour and a half, they took their leave and I heard no more, but Robin Rose-Price, by then a Brigadier, left the army shortly afterwards.

Chapter 12

PEACE AND PARTISANS

The Italian Partisans, who had been merely a nuisance all the way up from Florence, now became a positive menace. Mostly communists, they were determined to secure an influential position in the Italian state after the eviction of the Germans. Their intervention had been mostly rewarded by the execution by the Germans of innocent Italians in the Apennine villages. I personally came upon two hamlets where the population of aged, women and adolescents had been butchered by the Gestapo, in reprisal for the assassination of a German soldier. Now, every night, the partisans rounded up women who were alleged to have misbehaved with Germans, stripped and shaved them, and tied them to trees and posts for us to find in the morning. As a result our stocks of boiler suits to cover their nakedness soon became exhausted.

The Germans were now surrendering in ever increasing numbers but we just disarmed them and pressed on, leaving them to be collected by following troops. As we approached Mestre there were some explosions and smoke from fires. I left the column of vehicles and drove down the causeway but Venice was further away than I thought and I turned back at the docks, so I cannot say we were the first into Venice. We rushed on eastwards and, as it got dark, billeted for the night in a farmhouse, to be greeted by the usual naked girls in the morning.

We reached Udine and went on to Gorizia. There we came across the worst atrocity where a German S.S. field hospital, in a school, had been captured by Tito's Yugoslav Partisans. The 64 patients had been tied to their beds and a detonator taped in their mouths. A slow fuse had been wound around the back of a chair placed on the table in the centre, so all could see the progress of their end. 63 out of the 64 were dead, missing lower jaws, and the 64th was alive because his detonator had failed to explode. Peter Clifton found he had to go straight into negotiations with the Partisans' Commander. His men were a particularly wild lot and we sat down to negotiate their withdrawal, or at least an end to their retributive activities. The meeting started at 2.30 p.m. and was very hostile. At about 4 p.m. a band of men rushed in from behind us and pointed guns at our backs. I sat with a sten gun pressed to the nape of my neck until, at 6.30 p.m., a tremendous blast of the Battalion drums outside the town hall caused the holder of the sten to rush to the window, and I was able to grab my tommy gun, as did Colonel Peter. Eventually we got the agreement we wanted, and a football match was arranged for the following day.

Colonel Peter said, "We are dumped here till further orders – why don't you take four days off?" So Andy Angus, the signal officer and I, accompanied by Slater and Andy's servant, set off in my four-wheel drive G.M. officer van. We travelled all day and, at 3 p.m., found ourselves in a northern suburb of Milan. We passed an Esso filling station with several dead figures hanging upside down, strung up by their ankles. It was Mussolini and his mistress, Clara Petacci, and their Fascist henchmen, although we didn't discover that till later. Finally we arrived at Bellagio and booked into the enormous Grand Hotel. We asked the Manager, who opened a bottle of champagne for us, if we could dine there, but he said he had no kitchen staff and recommended Silvio's restaurant over the other side of the village. When we arrived there we were told that the war in Europe would end formally on the morrow; more champagne and a surprisingly good dinner followed. Towards the end of dinner a very pretty Italian girl came and asked me to dance. We did the tango and some other paso doble which were beyond me, so she took me into the grove of pines beyond, and stepped out of her skirt.

The next morning we had a long lunch with the girls, and then set out on Lake Como in a rowing boat. It was very hot so we all decided to have a swim. Andy was the first in the water but found, as he dived in, that he went from the warm surface to the arctic six inches below. So instead we decided to row across to the Villa d' Este and look at the azaleas, which were in full bloom. On the way back we were hit by a thunderstorm and the boat took in a lot of water. Andy had rowed at Henley for Shrewsbury so he took over the oars, while the girls attempted to bale out. We just made it back, but the thought of a long swim in the icy water was not appealing.

We motored back through Emilia the next day and arrived at Gorizia to find that we were just in time to move up the Caporetto Pass into Carinthia in Austria. The Battalion stopped at Villach, where the German limbless convalescent depot was situated, and where 16,000 amputees, were recovering and learning to use artificial limbs. There was a grade one brothel for the inmates, both male and female company being provided. The Sergeant-Major put a guard on the front door but failed to do the same at the rear entrance and found, to his dismay, that half the Battalion was struggling to get in.

We went on to the Wörthersee near Klagenfurt where someone had found us the Windisch-Graetz villa as Battalion H.Q., a princely house on the lake, with two speedboats laid up in the boathouse, and a Mercedes and Bentley under wraps in the garage. The Germans had an establishment there working on rocket propellant and the house was lived in by its director, with his wife and two daughters, who were very blonde and very beautiful. The strict non-fraternisation order made social intercourse illegal but, on the first Sunday after our arrival, Peter Clifton had a Battalion church parade to give thanks for victory and arrived at the service without his bible from which to read the lesson. He sent me up to his suite on the top floor to get it and, on crossing the patio, I found the two blondes sunbathing in the altogether. Alas, they had retired to their quarters when I hastened back at the end of church parade. However, our padre, who was a professor of theology in Northern Ireland, was luckier. I went out to dinner with Geoffrey Marriott and No. 3 company and, on coming out, saw the padre's pick-up going up and down in an alarming manner. Believing it was his orderly, I wrenched open the door and out tumbled a blonde and the professor, totally déshabillé, so some people were evading the order.

The first thing we had to do was to disarm the German Army as it returned to Austria from Yugoslavia. For three days, Johnny Norton and I stood on the north end of the bridge over the Drava and, covered by the machine-gun platoon in case of trouble, we got the Germans to pile up their arms and ammo, and then climb into three tonne lorries which, when filled, went off to the cage at Viktring. We had to get the Ayrshire Yeomanry to help with the artillery, of which there was everything from large railway guns, for the coastal defences, to the ubiquitous 88mm. I was instructed to look for an officers' mess chef, and some good riding horses. I found a pastry cook from the Bristol Hotel in Vienna, and two others. I was less clever with the horses, but we got about six officers' chargers.

The Ayrshire Yeomanry were more successful, as the German artillery was still very much horse-drawn. They had a grey horse which, when trained, won at all the local race meetings that were arranged by the 22nd Lancers and the Ayrshire Yeomanry. When John Harding, the Corps Commander, wanted to hold some races at Trieste, the powers that be heard of the prowess of the grey and commandeered it. The horse was dispatched down the Caporetto railroad and, when it was shunted into the marshalling yard at the foot of the pass, it was re-taken by Willie Tulloch of the Yeomanry. He substituted another grey horse, whose previous job had been pulling a medium gun. Brigadier "Perry" Harding, the famous amateur rider and John Harding's Chief of Staff, thought he would ride it and win the opening race. He had been too busy dealing with Tito to have ridden it before. He appeared, immaculate in silk breeches and riding boots, and came into the paddock where his steed was being led round by a horse gunner. He thought it looked a bit common, but, nevertheless, "handsome is as handsome does", so he mounted and set off for the start. By the time he reached the first fence he knew that he was in for a crashing fall, which luckily didn't kill him. All hell was let loose. The Military Police went up the pass and found the champ alive and well, and eating corn chez the Yeomanry. Willy Tulloch and two more were put in close arrest. But in the face of the laughter of the entire army, the charges were dropped and Willy was freed, to resume demobilised life as a Glaswegian stockbroker.

The difficulty of handling the Serbian Chetniks and Russian Cossacks has been well documented. The Welsh Guards had the task of collecting, recording and transporting the thousands of Cossacks wandering around Carinthia and Styria back to Russia. With little affection for the Soviet system, they had been recruited into the German army. The Grenadiers had a lesser but similar task with the Chetniks, who were anathema to Tito's communist partisans since some of them had collaborated with the Germans and Italians. We collected them from the vast camp at Viktring and loaded them onto the first train, made up of the ubiquitous cattle trucks. As the train crossed over the Drava from Austria to Yugoslavia, it halted, and a hoard of Tito partisans poured on to the bridge, climbed onto the roofs of the trucks and, as the train re-started, they commenced firing magazine after magazine into the packed trucks beneath. Our Guardsmen were horrified and, when the next train was loaded, the doors on the other side of the trucks were left ajar so that the Chetniks, driven in from one side at gunpoint, had a means of escape. As a result the local woods became a haven for fugitive Chetniks, and the crime rate increased.

I was ordered by Colonel Peter to organise a 4th of June dinner for all the old Etonians in Carinthia, which was to coincide with the visit of Harold Macmillan and Field Marshal Alexander. The dinner, held in an orchard and washed down with plenty of wine and slivovitz, was attended by about sixty old Etonians including Macmillan and Mc-Creery; Alexander was the only non-Etonian present. When dinner was over, I sidled up to Colonel Peter, who was talking to Alexander and Macmillan, hoping to be congratulated on the dinner, whereupon Robin Rose-Price, the C.O. of the Welsh Guards (who had drink taken), appeared and lambasted the sending of the Cossacks back to certain death. Macmillan, with a cigarette drooping from his upper lip, listened to the tirade and, turning his hands to the front, in the gesture we came to know so well, replied, "How else are we to demonstrate our loyalty to Stalin and the Russians?" He went on to say that an end to the war would not mean the end of hardship, particularly for the losers.

Many years later, when the Sun Alliance took over the Phoenix Assurance, of which I was a director, Toby Aldington, the Sun Alliance Chairman, came to tell us that we were all out of a job. As he shook my hand before lunch I said, "Hello Toby, long time no see," or something similar. He turned to me and said, "Where did we meet last?" When I replied, "At Klagenfurt", he dropped my hand and walked off without another word. It was only months later, when the Tolstoy case hit the papers, that I realised why.

Our idyllic life of water skiing and chasing opera singers (there for the reopening of the Klagenfurt Opera House) soon came to an end with the news that 1st Guards Brigade was to be the British combined operation land force for the invasion of Japan. We were to return to the UK to be re-organised, carry out intensive landing training and then leave for the Far East. We set off for the east coast of Italy, to be flown home from Foggia. Needless to say, when we got there the aeroplanes were not available, and so we spent three weeks at Fano on the beach. As we were to be reorganised there was no point in doing any training, and the most energetic thing I did was to swim out and put a white target on a floating mine, in order to have it sunk by gunfire. When it went off it blew in the windows of all the houses for miles around.

We eventually flew in Liberators to Hyères, near Toulon, whence we boarded the train for Dieppe-Newhaven, and finally home. Everyone who was due to be demobilised before Christmas was out, and we were to be re-manned with recruits from the training battalion. Peter Clifton and I went to Stobs camp at Hawick and tried to make sense of it all. As the Battalion had lost every specialist, it had to replace them with people who had no experience of their tasks. In one instance, a plump lance corporal at Windsor was suddenly promoted to Sergeant, and sent on a cooks' course with a view to becoming the master cook responsible for feeding the Battalion. There was a smattering of regular senior N.C.Os – about 60 per cent of the Gold Sergeants and above. Peter had to get the Battalion operational in about ten weeks, and the quartermaster and I had to deal with the administrative side.

The first complication was that the Colonel, Princess Elizabeth, wanted to come and inspect the Battalion, so I had to get the drill and arms drill up to scratch. This was just up Peter Clifton's street but the necessary drill prevented us from starting the company training. In practice, however, the Guardsmen, fresh from the Guards Depot, were soon up to speed. We were just getting ready for a first landing exercise on the Galloway coast when the atomic bombs were dropped, and Japan was out of the war. As the Battalion was really not going to be up for an official assault landing for months, this came as a very good piece of news. But what next?

Chapter 13

PALESTINE AND
THREE FIELD MARSHALS

The answer when it came was Palestine. The overriding impression when we heard this news was relief that we weren't going to fight the Japanese. We were to go there to shore up the internal security, and keep the Jews and Arabs from attacking each other. Lord Gort, the High Commissioner, had requested urgent reinforcements as the Jews were streaming out of Russia and Europe into the Jewish national state, and the Arabs were getting very nervous and aggressive.

So, after a week's embarkation leave, it was back to Greenock and, this time, onto a purpose-built troopship. The voyage out was uneventful except for a boxing contest with the South Wales Borderers. I got into the final where I met my opposite number, a very nice regular South African with a M.C. He was a really good boxer, and gave me a real thrashing until he knocked me out with an upper cut. As I went down for the count, my knee came up and caught him on the jaw, breaking it in two places. However, he forgave me and subsequently we saw a lot of each other, as we were both in our respective Rugger 15s.

One of the sideline oddities of the war was that Rugby League professionals in the army were allowed to play Rugby Union. As a prime Grenadier-recruiting area was south Lancashire, we had many of Wigan's, Warrington's and St. Helens' finest in our ranks, led by Guardsman Warrior, the Warrington and England fly half. Gilbert Lamb was the Captain, and we were unbeaten all season, adding the Welsh Guards, South Wales Borderers, the Welch Regiment and the

Paras to our conquests. Against the S.W.B., playing wing forward, I was first round the scrum and was laid out for dead by their Medical Officer and scrum half, a Scottish triallist from Glasgow, with an upper cut rather than a hand-off. "Don't worry, we'll fix him," said Warrior and, ten minutes later, the scrum half went off with a broken arm! In the final we beat the Welsh Guards much to their chagrin, as they had four Welsh internationals in their team.

On arrival at Haifa we marched seventeen miles, in full marching order, to our camp on a windy ridge behind Nahariya. The camp had not been occupied for a couple of years, and there was a lot of work to be done to make it comfortable and habitable. Nahariya was a very bourgeois village of Swabian and Bavarian Jews, who used to walk out in leather knickerbockers and Tyrolean hats with shaving brush plumes. I became friends with the village photographer, who was a Leica and Contax enthusiast. There was also a very good restaurant where you could select seafood and, in particular, carp done in several central European ways.

On Boxing night 1945 I had been to a Hanukkah party, and then went out to dinner with two friends at the restaurant, where we dined well and alcoholically. On leaving at 12.30 a.m., we ran into a group of soaking wet people. I enquired whether it had been raining and was told something in Hebrew. We returned to the camp and, at about dawn, I was awoken and told that an immigrant ship had beached at Nahariya. I went down and there was a small motor ship of several hundred tons, rolling from side to side in the surf. I clambered on board, getting soaked, and as I did so, I realised that the wet people in the street were the ship's passengers. There was no sign of them or of the crew. However, someone had left a Leica camera with a couple of lenses, on the saloon table, which were rolling, with the ship, from side to side. I have them still and very good servants they have been all over the world.

The security situation worsened rapidly. The visit of Dick Crossman, the Labour Minister, and the blowing up of the King David Hotel, with so many deaths, resulted in the tension between the Arabs and Jews mounting exponentially. The colonial administration started sentencing Arab and Jewish boys, who were caught rioting and throwing stones, to twelve strokes of the cane as an alternative to locking them up. The British Army Rugby 15, of which I was a member, were due to play the Middle East R.A.F. team and we all went to Petah Tikva, where the Parachute Regiment H.Q. was, to practice and bed down before the game. I was so exhausted after the day's training that I went upstairs for a snooze before dinner. While I was upstairs the Irgun, a Jewish terrorist group, raided the bar and kidnapped four of the Parachute Regiment, who were in it. They were taken to a Tel Aviv cinema, where they were stripped and flogged on the stage before the startled Jewish audience. Nevertheless, they returned to do battle with the R.A.F. with whom we played a nil-nil draw. The subsequent kidnapping and murder of two Intelligence Corps Sergeants reduced our relationship with the Jews to a new low.

I had taken to going to the Jewish frontier settlement of Hanita to help at weekends because there were some pretty milkmaids. I used to help with their dairy herd of very good quality Holstein cattle. One Sunday afternoon I was cleaning out the bull pen, with the enormous Holstein bull safely outside, when two of the settlers rushed up and pushed me outside; as they were all Polish and Russian Jews, the fuss generated was enormous. I was astonished and surprised as I was only doing a routine I had helped with for several weeks already. However, subsequently after I had left Palestine Hanita was raided and searched by the Army, and an enormous armoury was discovered in a cellar under the bull pen, so I suppose I was close to discovering the entrance when the settlers intervened.

David Rollo and I had become friendly with the Mukhtar of Ras al Naqoura, the Arab village on the coast at the Lebanese frontier, and we were invited to lunch. We ate much couscous and Lebanese pastry, washed down by sherbet drinks. His two pretty daughters, who arrived in chadors but reappeared in summer frocks, invited us to go for a swim afterwards. They quickly changed into very revealing swimsuits. We set out and they were much faster swimmers than us. On reaching some rocks about three-quarters of a mile out, they appeared to do a sort of dance. But when they picked up a large package with a cork float and wrapped in oilskin, it became clear what they were up to – collecting the week's hashish supply, which had come down from the Lebanon in the night.

Brigadier Eddie Goulburn decided to give a party for all the village headmen, both Arab and Jews, and we were asked to lay it on in the officers' mess. On the day appointed, we had tables of hard liquor and no pork canapés for the Jews, and tables of soft drink and sherbets for the Arabs. The Arabs arrived first and headed straight for the hard liquor, which they demolished in minutes. The Jews arrived later and looked somewhat askance at the sherbet, so we brought up more supplies of hard liquor. By 10.30 p.m. all inhibitions had vanished and Jews and Arabs were laughing together, as they sought out the last remaining supplies of gin and whisky. The party was considered a great success but it had no influence at all on inter-racial relations, which continued with unabated hostility.

My Aunt Baffy (Blanche) Dugdale was a niece of Arthur Balfour, as well as his biographer. Through him she had come to know the Zionist pioneer Dr. Chaim Weizmann who was largely instrumental in getting Balfour, when Foreign Secretary, to make the Balfour Declaration of 1917, promising British support for a Jewish National Home in Palestine. She became a convinced Zionist, working at the Jewish Agency in London, and through her I was invited to go and stay for a weekend at the home in Rehovot of Dr. Weizmann, soon to be the first President of Israel. I arrived on the Friday evening just in time for the start of the Sabbath routine. Dr. Weizmann was a charming little man with a goatee beard and a bald head. A delightful and very interesting host, I questioned him on the run up to the Declaration and he hinted that if he had invented his explosive material earlier (he was an eminent chemist and physicist and had invented some acetone-based explosive during the first World War), it would not have happened. His wife was an adoring Armenian/Russian lady who referred to him as Master (presumably Raboni in Hebrew) all the time. I stayed till after lunch on Sunday and was invited to propose myself for any weekend. He made a very favourable impression on me, at a time when I was very much inclined to support the Arab cause.

Leave came around and, armed with a copy of T. E. Lawrence's thesis on Crusader Castles and *The Desert and the Sown* by Gertude Bell, David Rollo and I determined to go on a trip round the Lebanon and Syria. We would then head down the Hejaz railway from Damascus to Ma'an and, from there, onwards to Mecca, or so we thought. The first night we spent in Beirut with my cousin and her husband, Elizabeth (née Knatchbull-Hugessen) and Gerry Young. We had been to a nightclub after dinner so it was well on into the following morning when seven of us set off for Baalbek in our little convoy. David and I each had a four-wheel drive vehicle, and there was another with all the fuel for the Mecca trip on board,. The sight of Baalbek in the afternoon sun was amazing, and, after an early night, we went on to Qadisha and Krak des Chevaliers, both of which seemed very well preserved. It was then on to Amman on a very cold and windy day. We refilled our petrol cans from the R.A.F. and set off for Ma'an, about 170 miles to the south. We drove down the rail track (the rails had long since gone) and arrived after dark. We stayed in the Ma'an Hotel, a curious building made of corrugated iron, and when we went into the bar, there was the most amazing collection of whiskies stretching right up to the ceiling; literally thousands of bottles. Who says the Bedouin don't drink Scotch?

The next day we set off for Medina and Mecca, along the Hejaz railway. The rains had come and the desert had become completely green. Some of it was sown corn but most of it was just the dormant weed seeds, germinated by the rain. We startled a gazelle and chased it for about a mile before David shot it, then brought it back to the railway and had gazelle steak for supper, delicious grilled on an open fire of thorn bush. We motored on with mounting enthusiasm for all things desert, but the going got much tougher, and the sand got softer and deeper. We did a calculation every evening when we stopped for the night, and were dismayed to find that our fuel consumption was rising inexorably. On the fourth evening it was clear that we had been much too optimistic and we were not even going to get to Medina. We decided to head due west on a desert track, across the mountains of Moab.

As we came over the plateau of the mountain we could see the ground falling away to the Dead Sea. We found a trout stream, which had cut its way deep into the hill with a series of gorges. We were all fishermen so the wireless aerial was turned into a rod and, with a couple of flies, we caught some very tasty trout up to about one and half pounds. It was fun to strip off and have an evening swim in our pool before grilling the trout for our supper. As we got to the final mountain before the Dead Sea we found an Arab Legion outpost, presumably keeping a watch out for Israeli intruders. They topped up our petrol supplies which were beginning to look parlous. Fuel worries over, we descended and had two days' duck and goose shooting in the Huleh marshes.

Back at work, it was time to act again as escort to Dick Crossman, the Attlee Government commissioner for inquiry into the Palestine problem. He spent his entire time insulting the military, who were attempting to prevent him from being assassinated, including providing a carrier screen to sweep his route. I finally said to him, "Why don't you just concentrate on being rude to the officers and leave the N.C.Os and other ranks out of it?" Whereupon he asked my name and said that he would report me for impudence. However, I heard no more about it and assumed he thought better of it.

One of Aunt Baffy's Jewish contacts was Gershon Agronsky, the Editor of the *Jerusalem Post*, who entertained me to dinner a couple of times. He, it subsequently transpired, was a high-up in the Haganah, the military force of the Jewish Agency, so he was presumably after any information he could get. When the King David Hotel was blown up and we were among the many rescuers picking over the rubble looking for survivors, he appeared on the scene, in his press role, and brought beer for all of us, which was much appreciated.

The British, while I was there, failed to appreciate how brilliantly the whole Zionist refugee problem was being organised, and how the three grades of operations dovetailed: the Haganah was the official Zionist military force whence sprang the whole of Israel's armed forces; the Irgun carried out unofficial operations that the Agency did not want to admit to; finally, there was the Stern Gang for committing terrorist atrocities against the British. After the Holocaust, the Agency was desperate to remove the myriads of displaced Jews from Europe and resettle them in Palestine. The Russians were stepping up anti-Jewish decrees but were not very keen on allowing Jews to leave. On another visit to Rehovot to see Weizmann, he was pretty prescient about the course of events in Palestine for the next few years, but his moderation was becoming increasingly outdated and was outbid by the leaders of the rapidly increasing Jewish population. As the tension rose, the Muslim countries of the Mediterranean and Gulf were causing their Jewish populations, who were mostly Sephardic, to flee to Israel. The Ashkenazi Jews, who had hitherto been in the majority and who had produced all the leaders, began to get anxious, as they felt they would no longer be in the majority in the nation as it evolved.

I had been offered a regular commission but, after discussing it with Father, I decided to leave the Army when my de-mob group came up. The Regiment appointed Alan Breitmeyer to succeed me as Adjutant and I was to go home in April 1946. I had become friendly with the Captain of H.M.S. *Sirius* by providing transport for his crew when they were in dock at Haifa and, as they were going to go home via Athens and Naples, I asked him for a passage back to which he readily agreed. So off I went on leave to stay with my cousin, Elizabeth Young, in Beirut. I had a lovely time and was proposed to by two Lebanese matrons on behalf of their daughters. The Lebanese Christians, being alive to the problems of the Levant and Islam, were anxious to get some European passports flying around their families, and Desmond Cochrane had led the way by marrying Yvonne Sursock in January 1946. The girls were rich, beautiful, clever and very sophisticated, but I thought the quid pro quo would be residence in the Lebanon. Beirut was entrancing in the spring; blossom everywhere, and delicious food and drink in the Aletti and St. George Hotels. Nevertheless, after ten days, it was back to Nahariya to pack up and catch my light cruiser home.

My farewell party in the Mess was proceeding in the usual riotous way when I was summoned by the Officers' Mess Sergeant to speak to the Sergeant of the Guard, who said he had had to put the Picket Officer in close arrest. I went down to the guardroom and, sitting on the bench, was the Picket Officer, Hugh Stanley, clad only in a blanket. Having enjoyed the party too much on a very hot night, he had gone to lie down and had fallen asleep. He had woken, with a start, to see that it was 11.55 p.m., so he had crammed on his forage cap and gone and turned out the guard in his birthday suit and desert boots. I rebuked him and my last act, before leaving, was to give the luckless chap 21 days' extra picket duty.

Captain Smith of the *Sirius* had been in destroyers for most of the war. He welcomed me on board and said that, because they had two officers going home for court martial, I would have to share with him: his state cabin when at sea, and his sea cabin when in port. They were a jolly bunch of officers who had all been in the thick of it for most of the war. I was made welcome and invited to pace the quarter deck each evening, before a pink gin and dinner with all the more senior wardroom officers. We steamed up the Saronic Gulf to the port of Piraeus and had four days in Athens, which enabled me to see most of the sights (and the nightclubs). Then it was on to Naples, where we moored alongside an American battleship, and everyone went back and forth. We gave a party for their officers and, when they reciprocated, we had a jolly time on soft drinks until our hosts said, "Come and see our cabins." On going down, three bottles of bourbon were produced from every bottom drawer. So much for the "Dry" American Navy.

After a brief stop at Toulon, it was the Bay of Biscay and into Portsmouth, with a paying-off pennant at the masthead.

John Nelson was G1 and Brigade Major at London District and he arranged for me to become a learner staff captain in the P.O.W. Department. Andy Angus, likewise awaiting demob, was there too; so that was fun. As a subordinate activity we were both put on to organising aspects of the Victory Parade. Up at dawn, and accompanied by the Garrison Sergeant Major, with a pace stick and a stop watch we marched the entire route, segment by segment, and morning by morning. John Nelson would usually appear at the end in a staff car and, having been greeted by the G.S.M. with a terrifying salute, we all climbed into the car and went through our notes with the boss.

The great day dawned and we were all put in charge of marshalling various bits of the procession. I was given the job of embussing the allied commanders into their scout cars in Park Crescent, Regents Park. The idea was that all the martialled parts would slide effortlessly into the procession, and the march would continue all round central London. Field Marshal Montgomery was the last big shot to appear. I saluted him and indicated his vacant scout car. All the other commanders were sitting with their heads and shoulders showing above their scout cars' combings.

F.M.M. "I am not going to sit like that."

W.D. "It's like all the others including General Eisenhower, Sir."

F.M.M. "Listen, all London and half England have come to see me and I am not going to disappoint them. Get the seat out and put it on the engine cover so I am really visible. I won't get in until I am satisfied."

W.D. "Sir!" (Grenadier for you bolshy bastard)

So off I go to General Eisenhower at the head of the scout car column.

W.D. Salutes and says to Ike – "Sir, Field Marshal Montgomery refuses to get in his car until he can sit on the engine cover."

Gen. E. "That son of a gun would, wouldn't he."

W.D. "Do you want your seat raised Sir?"

Gen. E. "No, certainly not."

I then went and asked all the other commanders if they wanted to sit on top and only General Mark Clark did. So Monty's and General Clark's drivers, both of whom were in the Armoured Corps, had to fix, as best they could, the seats and, as a result, when the Field Marshal consented to get aboard, the start had been delayed by about 35 minutes. As the pace of the procession was controlled by the speed of the W.R.N.S. detachment at the head, it went at about two and a half miles an hour and I was easily able to keep up on foot but I arrived back at Wellington Barracks very tired and footsore at the end of the day.

When the Nuremberg Trials started, London District had to deliver to Nuremberg any P.O.W. who was needed to give evidence or make depositions. They had to be collected from Bridgend in South Wales, brought to London, where they were put in the cage at Kensington

Palace Gardens, and then they were taken by air to Nuremberg from Northolt. The aeroplanes were parachute-dropping Dakotas, and the seats were aluminium benches down each side of the aircraft. On one trip I had to escort Field Marshal von Rundstedt, Field Marshal von Kleist, General Blumentritt, and one other general whose name escapes me. Rundstedt was a nice old man suffering from acute angina and I was handed a box of pills in case of emergency. Our route led over Dunkirk, where Kleist peered out of the window and had a long and excited conversation in German. I asked Rundstedt, who spoke very good English, "What did he say?" "Oh", said Rundstedt, "he said, 'I can see the crossroads where I took the decision that lost Germany the war.'" "What was that decision?" I asked. "Oh," said Rundstedt, "he sent his tanks to St. Valery instead of driving directly into Dunkirk."

We then flew into an electric storm, and the Dakota pitched and tossed. We fastened our seatbelts but Rundstedt, who was wearing a mink-lined field marshal's greatcoat, decided he had to go to the loo. He set off down the polished aluminium floor to the loo at the tail of the aircraft. He lost his balance and shot down the floor and, as the loo door on the left was open, he shot inside. I undid my seatbelt to rescue him and was immediately myself up-ended, and sailed down the plane. As I got to the end, the other door flew open and the Field Marshal shot out, as I shot in by the left-hand door. This pastime continued until the long legs of General Blumentritt caught the skirts of the great coat, and anchored him. I caught hold of Kleist's leg and, between us, we got Rundstedt upright, and chained to his seat. He still hadn't had his pee.

When we got to Nuremberg Airport, we drove in two staff cars to the trial building. The Generals were handed over to the jailers, and I was taken to the mess where all the Allied Staff of the trial slept and ate. Sir Hartley Shawcross and Sir Elwyn Jones were the two leaders of the English prosecution team. Mr. Justice Lawrence (later Lord Oaksey) was the English Judge. I found myself on their table by mistake, but they were very pleasant and continued to talk about the trial all through lunch, which I found very interesting. After lunch, I was taken to the gallery of the court to see the trial.

Goering, much reduced in girth, was seated at the end of the row of the accused. He appeared to have a lot of make-up on. Doenitz was in full admiral's uniform, and looked very smart. The Generals, notably Keitel, were without belts and looked rather scruffy. The cross examination of the witnesses appeared to be carried out by each allied nation in turn and, as a result, the translation into the headphones, with which one was supplied, swayed from the excellent to the impossible to understand. The Judges lolled in their chairs, with only Lawrence and the Russian appearing to be interested in the proceedings.

I was there for three days and found I became bored at the slow pace of the proceedings so went on a tour of Nuremberg, which was surprisingly free of bomb damage. Perhaps that was why it was selected as the venue. Once the deposition from the Generals had been taken, I had to return them to Bridgend via the P.O.W. cage in London. Our journey back was marred by Rundstedt having pains in the chest, but my arsenal of pills seemed to do the trick, and they were safely delivered back the following day.

In early July 1946 I emerged from the demob centre in outer London ready for civilian life, but without the demob suit to which I was entitled because they had none in my size.

Chapter 14

LEARNING THE LAW

Returning soldiers were given the chance to resume their degrees but, after six years as an army officer, I didn't think I would fit in back at Oxford. Whilst I was working at London District, whose offices were in Curzon Street, it was easy to go to lunch at the Guards Club in Charles Street. One morning in 1946 I was sitting at the bar receiving the latest stock market tips from Eddie the barman when Ralph Howard came and sat next to me. He had lost both legs, been recommended for the V.C., and had received a consolation D.S.O. at Monte Camino in Italy. I knew him quite well, and his exploits in the 6th Battalion had been legendary. He wasted no time, ordered us both a gin and tonic and said, "I am looking for a new Articled Clerk in my office, what about you?" I told him that, as I had abandoned my plans to train as a mining engineer because our coal mine had been nationalised by the new Labour government, becoming a lawyer seemed like a good idea.

"Right" he said "start on Monday."

"Not so fast," I replied, "I have just taken a deer forest in Rosshire for the season."

"Well, come in for six weeks and, if you like it, you can sign up."

"Signing up" entailed paying him £3,300 for the first year, £2,500 for the second and the third was a nominal £1,000. In fact, they remitted the third year as, by then, I was earning the firm about £100,000 in fees. So the day after my demob, and with a grade-one hangover, I reported in a black jacket and striped trousers to 28 Lincoln Inn Fields, where Frere Chomeley's offices had been since 1728.

I was taken round by Mrs. Humphreys, who was the chief secretary to Philip Frere, the senior partner, and introduced to everyone in the office. I eyed up the typists, shook hands with the managing clerks and was taken in to see the partners who were not with clients. "I'll put you with Mr. Vale, the probate managing clerk – if you stick with him you'll stick with anything else," said Ralph Howard as he took me out to lunch at Boodles, where he put me up for membership and we returned to the office at about 3.30 p.m. Every morning Ralph had to be dressed by a valet in his room in the Union Club so he didn't arrive in the office till 10.15 a.m. Office hours were 9.45 a.m. till lunch, and then to 7.30 p.m., or later, if one had urgent work to do.

Mr. Vale was in his late seventies, had been a Sergeant in the Royal Fusiliers in World War I, and came to work every day in a frock coat and one of those roll-over starched collars, popular in the 1900s for officials. His department consisted of his deputy, Mr. Fletcher, a south London chap of about 33 who was a keen racing cyclist in his spare time, and about six women ranging from the two senior clerks, who were both about 65, to a couple of pretty north London girls of about 22.

"Here," said Mr. Vale, "the work has to be exact, precise and detailed or the Capital Taxes office will go berserk. The fun is going off and organising funerals away from the office. When you get the hang of it, we'll send you off." My first task, strangely enough, was valuing the stocks and shares of a deceased dowager I knew from Warwickshire. No calculators and the days from the dividend to day of death had to be apportioned, so the Revenue got their fair share. In spite of being taken out to lunch to a pub by Mr. Fletcher, I was very close to chucking after two days. But my father said I'd need to be mad to contemplate that and I should stick it out. So, until August 12th, or 5 weeks later and the start of the grouse-shooting season, I stuck it out, and then decided to pay the Articled Clerk premium. I signed up with the Law Society to take the exams, and with Gibson and Weldon, the crammers, to get the knowledge necessary to pass them.

I had been onto Grants, the Inverness gun dealers, to see if I could get some stalking and mixed shooting in the Highlands. They came up with Corriehallie, an 11,000-acre estate, and while still in the army, I had been up and had a walk over the hill. The lodge was early Victorian and upholstered in Mackenzie tartan, with a large range fuelled by peat in the kitchen, and approached by an eleven-mile track up the Glen. The keeper, called Sandy MacDonald, was 84 years old with a Boer War moustache. He had no gun dog but, instead, a West Highland Terrier called Rache (Heather) who hunted, pointed and retrieved all day. He was a widower and lived with a housekeeper of about 55, who walked down once a week to Muir of Ord to do the shopping.

For three weeks I walked up grouse in waist-high heather in all sorts of weather. Our best bag was fifteen brace; MacDonald was an adequate shot. Apart from three nights, when the weather was so bad that I camped in the lodge, I walked back to the Muir of Ord hotel. Staying in the hotel was a very pretty Wren from Aberdeen, also on demob leave. I took her to the cinema in Inverness a couple of times, and we got along very well, so I thought I would invite her up to the lodge for the weekend. She seemed to like the idea and on the Friday, we each took a back-pack and filled it with groceries and drinks, took the car up to Urray church, and set off up the glen. Halfway up we were met by MacDonald and Rache and, climbing up to the top, we made our way along the side of the glen. We stopped for lunch and had a drink – malt for MacDonald and beer for us – and set off on another sweep. Suddenly, Rache started barking furiously, and I turned round but could not see MacDonald. I went back to the dog and found MacDonald lying face down in the deep heather. I turned him over and he was clearly dead. So my companion and I carried and dropped him down several hundred feet and then, with me giving him a fireman's lift, we got him back to the lodge. When I told the housekeeper she did not seem too surprised, and we laid him out on the bed. It was decided that the girls would stay together and I would go back to Urray church and phone the police from there. The Police Sergeant at Muir of Ord contented himself with a "poor Sandy", and said he would send the constable back with me and phone the undertakers.

On the Tuesday the undertaker came up with the officer and, at 1.45 p.m., from all over the tops, came the locals – keepers, gillies, crofters and lairds. At 2 p.m. we set off down the glen on the track to Urray church, with the housekeeper walking immediately behind the coffin. When the road crossed and re-crossed the River Orrin she merely lifted her skirts, and strode through without a word. The funeral was packed as Sandy was clearly a popular and well-respected man. From then on I was gillie, stalker, and pony man. Right at the end of my stay I shot an outstanding head, with tremendous horns, who weighed 17 stone 13 pounds even at the end of the rut. It was, I am ashamed to say, on the march with Corriehallie and Strathconon and was just over the boundary by about three feet. So I had a long visit to Squeezer Combe, the Laird of Strathconon, to apologise, but the head appeared in the *Field* as one of the heads of the year and is now on the wall at Merevale.

Then it was back to the probate department at Freres. I was becoming more adept at drafting settlements and was allowed to sit in with Ralph when he was interviewing clients. I often took the drafting details for marriage settlements and the like. The work was relentless but, in the late autumn, I was sent down to Torquay to a client, who was sadly on the way out. On arrival, I asked if there was anything I could do. "Yes," she replied, "I have always been a blonde like Jean Harlow and I would like the family to see me like that when they come to say goodbye." The nurse instructed me where to get the peroxide bleach, and we worked away on her hair till Marilyn Monroe wasn't in it. Unfortunately, when the family arrived, they were much more interested in the jewellery and security boxes than in their auntie.

I had now definitely made up my mind to qualify as a solicitor, and hoped to become a partner in Freres. So the first step was the intermediate law and trust accounts exam in the spring of 1947. Being an ex-serviceman, I was excused quite a lot of the syllabus but still had to pass the essentials, including the dreaded trust accounts exam. Gibson and Weldon had a good name for getting "thickies" through so I signed up for an eight-week course. My day was: up at 1.45 a.m., work from 2-7.45 a.m., then breakfast, and on to the office at 9.45 a.m. Gibson & Weldon from 4-6 p.m. and dinner, followed by bed at 9 p.m. I decided not to work on Saturday and Sunday. Anyway my efforts bore fruit and I staggered through at the first attempt. Tommy

Butcher (Philip Frere's articled clerk – an ex-Lieutenant R.N.V.R. and cleverer than me) was a great help as he used to pose questions for us to answer on our way home on the tube.

After six months in probate and trusts, I got myself transferred to litigation and came under the aegis of the redoubtable Mr. Caola, the managing clerk. He passed me on to Mr. Fletcher, the outside clerk, who did the interrogatories with the Master. When you are engaged in litigation intense meetings and negotiations take place between the opposing firms of solicitors and, when you can't agree, it goes before a Master of the Supreme Court for adjudication, who sits in the "Bear Garden" at the Law Courts. If the Master can't agree, it then goes before a judge. Carrying two immense brief cases, together we went first to the Bear Garden, where we stood in a queue to be sworn at by the Duty Master and be told that we had to go back and redo all the documents. We then sat down on one of the stone benches in the corridor to await the arrival of the opposing outside clerks. We then settled what we thought would pass muster the next time, and went off to see one of the agency firms. There were several firms who made it their business to represent provincial firms of lawyers through their processes. The relationship at this level was entirely friendly, as we all wanted to get past the Masters and get our respective litigation partners to proceed to briefing counsel. Our litigation partner was Bernard Sutton (né Sussmann), a Berliner who had fled the Jewish persecution. He was one of the ablest men I have ever come across, and took an infinity of trouble to get me going in his speciality. His early death was a great blow to Freres. They then got Mr. Caola to take the Law Society Finals and become the partner in succession.

One of the first missions in which I was engaged was representing one of the accused in the Sidney Stanley enquiry. Sidney Stanley, another immigrant, ran an import/export agency and, like many others, wanted to be a player in the North London scene. Anyway he got to know many members of the Labour Government and the newspapers ousted him for allegedly bribing government ministers. Unusually, the enquiry, under Mr. Justice Lynskey, was held in Church House Westminster because there was a such a flock of barristers representing just about everybody who had ever spoken to Sidney Stanley. Arnold Goodman sat next to Bernard Sutton, and to my great surprise Lord Goodman's P.A. was Jeremy Tree, who had been a contemporary of mine at Eton and later became a Derby-winning racehorse trainer. The enquiry lasted about 28 days. Hartley Shawcross, the Attorney General, was out for blood, otherwise the Labour Government was in dire trouble. He cross-questioned Sidney Stanley for days. He had a characteristic way of placing his left knee on his chair and, when he went for the jugular, the left foot was then firmly put on the floor with a little thump. I had noticed this little mannerism at Nuremberg and it was even more in evidence at Church House. The result of this enquiry was absolution for the Government. Sidney Stanley was proved a liar, and the fall guy was Mr. Belcher, the Under Secretary for Transport and M.P. for Kettering, who had to resign as a result. While I imbibed the texts around the ceiling of Church House, Freres must have pocketed a great deal of money in fees.

The next excitement on the horizon was a libel case involving Lord Salisbury. There had been a punch-up at his son's, Lord Cranborne's, wedding to Mollie Wyndham-Quin. A *Daily Mirror* photographer, waiting his moment, had got the happy couple cutting the cake or something. Robert Cranborne, who had a noticeably short fuse, had attacked the photographer and jumped on and smashed all his equipment. Lord Salisbury had written a letter to *The Times* criticising the photographer, which was the subject of a subsequent article in the *Mirror*. The case was heard by Mr. Justice Hilbery. My job was to collect the Dowager Lady Salisbury (who was to give evidence) and the bride, escort them to court, and give them lunch somewhere each day. The case collapsed when the photographer, under a savage cross-examination by Val Duncan K.C., was found not to be telling the truth. Old Lady Salisbury tripped when emerging from the witness box and nearly measured her length, but Val Duncan and I shot out of our seats and caught her just before she fell.

We also acted for the public company which owned Chessington Zoo. I was given the job of drafting the bye-laws to control the behaviour of visitors. I wrote to Dr. Gordon, the Superintendent of the

London Zoo, and asked if I could come and consult him. He, a New Zealander, was very kind and I spent about a fortnight with him. We went up on to the Mappin Terrace with field glasses and watched the paedophiles stalking unaccompanied children. When a paedophile was caught by the keepers, he was brought into Dr. Gordon's office and, donning gloves, the doctor gave him a really brutal beating while he was held by the keepers. Six weeks was all it usually took for a paedophile to recover and return to the chase. Dr. Gordon believed that the Zoo bye-laws, which were being re-drafted after the war, did not yet really give quite the control which was needed, so enlisted my help on re-drafting them. When I took my completed document to the partner, Bernard Sutton, he was entranced by one which said "No sacred or secular songs may be sung". When taking my children to London Zoo many years afterwards, I was delighted to see my bye-laws still proudly displayed on the notice-boards.

I got on very well with both Mr. Caola and Bernard Sutton and they cut me in, from the beginning, on many interesting things. By now my Law Society finals loomed. I was beginning to enjoy the solicitor life and, although the routine was often dull, there were sufficient alarms and excursions to make life fun. I got into trouble when I was given the job of advising on the purchase of a property in Buckingham Gate for a well known chancery judge. Although I took income tax into account, I failed to calculate the surtax. The judge rightly took umbrage, and the firm had to stump up. But this was nothing compared to the row when Mr. Underwood, the senior managing clerk, did a deal for Lord Carnarvon, and Mr. Berwick, his sidekick, embezzled £58,750. Mr. Berwick went to prison, and Freres invoked their negligence policy with the Law Fire Insurance. Freres had insured continuously with them without ever having made a claim. As a result, from about 1880, they weren't even required to pay a premium and a Freres' partner sat on the Board. The company paid up without hesitation, but the next year the premium increased, surprise surprise, to £58, 750.

I negotiated time off to go and be crammed at Gibson and Weldon and so was back on the routine of bed at 9 p.m., awake from 2 a.m. till going to work, and then, as before, off to Gibson & Weldon's every day from 4-6.30 p.m. I had moved into 84 Jermyn Street as the third-floor floor tenant. The ground floor was Aykroyd's the estate agent. First-floor was a tart, second-floor a tart. I wanted a pal to share with on the third-floor, and found Mark Gilbey. The fourth-floor was Brigadier A. A. Curry C.B.E., a retired R.A.S.C. supply genius. I had heard of the flat from George Dennistoun-Webster, who was empowered to sell it together with fixtures and fittings, by James Hanbury (then Master of the Quorn) who had just got married. I also inherited the daily lady, a Mrs. Austin. She told me that she came into the flat one morning and saw two heads on the pillow – one definitely James and the other with light red hair. She pulled the bedclothes back and landed a resounding slap on the redhead's bare backside saying, "Time to go home now dearie," only to find that this was the vrai Mrs. Hanbury. Mrs. Austin's daughter was a beauty queen, Miss Hammersmith, and a very pretty blonde of about 20. She deputised for her mother on occasion and caused me once or twice to be very late into the office.

The final law society exam in February 1949 was a physical ordeal; three three-hour papers on three consecutive days. When I returned to Freres, Ralph Howard was drinking more, and working less. I was sent back to work for him on the family side. My first year's salary was fixed at £365 – £1 per day – but I was promised a big lift after a year if I made the grade as an admitted man. I was reluctant to leave Bernard Sutton but he promised to take me back as soon as someone could deputise effectively for Ralph. Ralph had taken to going back to bed at the Union Club as soon as he finished work. It was strange to see him in bed, with his two legs dressed in trousers and shoes sitting in a chair at the foot of his bed. He had a very good mind but, after lunch, he tended to be a bit rambling; it was quite difficult to know at what point to intervene when he was dealing with a client. My partner in crime at trying to help him was Michael Ward, the younger brother of Stephen Ward, the chiropractor who became famous for introducing Christine Keeler to John Profumo. Michael and I shared an office with a legal genius who had won every single prize at the Law Society's exam in 1924. He was a tremendous help whenever legally and intellectually I was out of my depth but, as he had an academic approach of either/or to every problem, he remained a back-room boffin. Less able men became partners because they brought in the business. In 1948 both Mr. Law, the conveyancer, and Mr. Vale, the probate man, each brought in more than £1 million costs and there were others as well; my name remained resolutely low on the list because all the partners for whom I worked collared the costs that were earned by my efforts. Philip Frere had a great deal of work for the Grocer's Company and Oundle School and I was usually called in to help when there were deadlines to be met and the work was running into the evenings. Ralph Howard couldn't sustain the pace and some time later he lapsed into a coma and died.

After the war my father, who was in his late seventies, ran things at home the same way with a much reduced staff and therefore reduced standards of efficiency. Merevale was managed with Hudson the butler, a cook and two daily ladies. The roof leaked. He had a very bad agent who was unqualified but the estate and farms, although subject to wartime regulation, remained much the same as before the war. Father was overwhelmed by the nationalisation of the coal mines. Afterwards he was employed, temporarily, as a business adviser to Sir Benjamin Smith, the ex-taxi-driver who was entrusted by the government with running the West Midlands' collieries. He did the job for 18 months before he was brusquely sacked by Sir Ben, who thought he could go it alone. Father became quite fixated on the loss of the colliery, and his subsequent sacking. As a result, he rather let things slip just as the scramble for compensation for the collieries was hotting up. Also Major Harry Mitcheson, the general manager of Baddesley Colliery, had died in 1947 which meant that Baddesley no longer had a representative on the board of the Mining Association. This put Baddesley at a great disadvantage in the battle for compensation. It was decided by the directors of the Colliery that I would collate and work on the compensation package with Philip Gibbons, the company secretary. Gibbons, an ex-Price Waterhouse manager, had won a M.C. with the Royal Horse Artillery in 1917, and was a little terrier of a man. We got on well and got stuck into Baddesley's problem. It soon became apparent that I needed to devote more time to this than just weekends, so I regretfully handed in my notice at Frere's in the late spring of 1950.

Chapter 15

RACE RIDING

I began to think I ought to learn Estate Management and, after talking to various people, was eventually taken on by Brigadier Ian Watson, the agent to the Garrowby Estate in Yorkshire. Ian, having come down from Oxford in 1938, joined the Ox & Bucks in 1939, and walked out with the 43rd Division at Dunkirk. He turned out to be a supply genius and ended the war as deputy to Gerry Feilden, the Q.M.G. at the War Office. He agreed to let me live with him in the Old Vicarage at Millington, which was about five miles away from Garrowby. I went up to start in June 1950 on the understanding that, if colliery business called, I could defect easily and return home. In the end I worked there for two years, with plenty of interruptions for hunting, shooting and race-riding.

Lord Halifax, the ex-Foreign Secretary and ambassador to Washington, lived in active retirement at Garrowby. He hunted and shot and, in the summer, liked to go riding at seven thirty every morning. It was not long before Charlie, the groom, suggested me as a ride companion. Lord Halifax's talk was fascinating; he appeared on the dot of seven thirty in jodhpurs and hunting jacket and we would ride off in the lovely spring morning in silence for about ten minutes, and then he would begin to talk – about Roosevelt, whom he hated, describing him as the greatest liar he had ever had to deal with. "A promise made by F.D.R. was put on draft first to see your reaction, then to be manipulated when he thought about it more." Early on he had been made a monkey of by F.D.R., when Halifax had communicated what he had thought was a firm commitment to Winston in London, only to have F.D.R. repudiate it when Winston got on the phone. Halifax got on better with Winston but said he could never see himself as one of Winston Churchill's drinking cronies, and therefore there was always going to be something missing in their relationship. He did not want any input from me but just liked to talk about various aspects of his career and life.

One day we arrived at Kirby Underdale just as Mr. Boyes, the village ironmonger and undertaker, was opening up his shop and putting, as ironmongers do, some of the larger items outside. The conversation went like this:-

Lord Halifax "Good morning Mr. Boyes, I hope I see you are well."

Mr. Boyes "Good morning my Lord, what a wonderful morning it is."

Lord Halifax "Are you all ready to bury me Mr. Boyes?" (To me, "Mr. Boyes is going to see me off.")

Mr. Boyes "Whenever your Lordship pleases, I can't wait to polish it up, the coffin is all ready and waiting."

Lord Halifax liked to shoot the partridges early in the season, and the line of guns was always put behind the lowest Wold fence, only about thirty inches high. The guns would kneel behind it and, when the birds appeared, Lord Halifax, who was six foot seven, would rise, like Venus from the foam, and deliver two barrels which usually connected with a bird or two, although he only had one hand. The enormous quantity of rabbits on the Estate were a pest and Lord Halifax arranged for two teams of poachers from Hickleton to come up and run their lurchers and long nets. This was very successful but, alas, they also took a lot of the partridges. Nevertheless, it gave us a breathing space, particularly on the high wold land, where little of the corn survived the rabbits' onslaughts.

Once August 12th arrived the Estate office routine altered; work was dispatched to facilitate everyone's shooting engagements. Ian Watson was a high-class shot and much in demand on grouse moors, where there were still a large preponderance of owner occupiers. The shooting was let wherever possible but the owners were still able to entertain their friends. I did not get many invitations the first year but, during the second year, they began to flow in every so often. The Middleton hounds began cubbing as soon as the corn was cut and, although the early starts were principally for reducing the number of foxes, by mid-October good runs were the order of the day. Neighbouring hunts, the Holderness and the Sinnington, were other alternatives and I got lent horses to go out and school with the hounds. The presence of several pretty girls made a day with the Sinnington a further attraction. Estate work tended to get done in the evenings and keeping up with my correspondence course meant that I was sitting up late quite a lot. I had the room over the kitchen at Millington and one night, after working until about two in the morning with a bottle of wine to help the concentration, I decided to go down and get another book from Ian's bookcase. All the lights were out and I suddenly thought I was being kissed, only to find I was embracing a ham, one of several hanging on hooks to season on the stairs.

In 1947 I had been invited to shoot partridges at Blewbury by my cousin Jean Paul (née Hope) and at lunch I sat next to a very dashing trainer called Major John Goldsmith. I had started point-to-pointing that spring and was absolutely besotted with race-riding. The Major didn't realise that he had a tyro/sucker next to him, but I was thrilled by his stories of the turf and life in France before the war. Anyway, after thinking about it, I rang him up and asked him to find me a horse that I could ride under Rules.

I heard nothing for about three months and then he rang to say he had bought me a horse – "a real little athlete." As I had imagined a great big 17-hand chaser, I wondered how I would fit on board. About three weeks later, he rang again to say that the horse had arrived and would I come and have a look at it. Down I went to Berkshire and was mortified to see a bay entire, of about 15 hands. I was then told I couldn't ride him and, instead, was put on a grey chaser of 18 hands. Up on the downs we went and Johnny Gilbert, the Epsom jockey, was on the bay, Intrepide II; after riding him, he said he was sure to win races.

I went down and rode out with the string as often as I could, until finally, the great day arrived and we were off to Plumpton to race in a novice hurdle. John Goldsmith put Johnny Gilbert in charge of me, and he introduced me to Eddie, the Epsom valet, when we went into the weighing room. On the bench sat Dave Dick and his brother, Ken Mullins, Tim Molony and several others. Johnny introduced me along the line and Dave said to me, "Are you good enough not to cause trouble?" and I replied, "I hope so." Plumpton is a very tight course and there was a big field in the Novice Hurdle. I didn't cause trouble because I missed the jump at the start and was always in the rear. But Intrepide was a tough little number and I moved up at the end of the race, and was only just behind the placed horses. Next it was off to Cheltenham for the October meeting, in a race with only about six or seven runners. Bryan Marshall was on a Walwyn-trained Dorothy Paget hotpot, and Jack Dowdeswell was on a second string. Again I missed the break and rode round with Jack, attempting to copy his technique. Intrepide ran very well up the hill and, although I was last but one, I had the bug in spades.

We decided to enter Intrepide into the seller at Hurst Park, the south-west London racecourse. The hot favourite was an ex-flat horse of Sir Humphrey de Trafford, trained by Willie Stephenson and ridden by Charlie Spares. Johnny Gilbert was on an Epsom-trained horse owned by Stan Wootton and was in the betting. There were about twenty runners. Johnny stood next to me in the line-up for the start – he gave Intrepide a shove as the elastic was released and we got away. I was with the leaders all the way, with Charlie Spares and Johnny Gilbert at it hammer and tongs up the straight, but I was obviously not too hot riding my first finish, and was just out of the money at the end. The next time out was a Novice Hurdle at Manchester on New Year's Day where I met Fred Winter for the first time. He was riding a horse owned by George Archibald. We were neck and neck all the way up the straight but he jumped the last better than me and won by several lengths. But I was second, my first placing and I was walking on air. I had taken my then girlfriend along and we had gone up to stay for both days, with Tiny Goldsmith acting as chaperone. I got to know several of the better jockeys well for the first time – Fred Winter and I hit it off as we both enjoyed much the same things.

Bryan Marshall said to me that owning a hurdler was all very well, but he thought I needed a chaser. He pointed out that nobody was going to "put me up" until I had had a few winners, and that winning hurdle races was much more difficult as all the other jockeys were professionals. He suggested that I ask Fulke Walwyn to look out for a three-mile chaser. When I saw Fulke in the hotel at Manchester, he said he would like to train a horse for me. I was now spending every spare moment in Berkshire. I would go over to George Beeby's to school John Goldsmith's chasers. Martin and Tim Molony would both be there, and I was more than pleased to be asked to ride some of Lord Bicester's young horses with them.

Towards the end of the season, Fulke rang to say he would like to bid for Cloncarrig, the hero of the Grand National finale with Freebooter. Cloncarrig's owner had died and there was an executor's sale at Kempton Racecourse of all his horses. No sooner had I said yes to this, than John Goldsmith rang to say that Percy Thomson, his biggest owner, had had a personal battle with William Hill the boookmaker and been an enormous loser. As a result Thomson had to get rid of all his string including Le Jacobin, his top class two-mile chaser. Both horses had breathing problems and, because Cloncarrig had been hobdayed (an operation on a horse's throat), I got him for just over a thousand pounds. Le Jacobin cost two thousand pounds. I now had a string of three horses to dream about throughout the summer of 1949.

The jumping season in those days started in Devon, occupying all of August and most of September, but only really got going with the Cheltenham October meeting. The whole jumping establishment moved down to the Imperial Hotel in Torquay where the grand (Peter Cazalet and Fulke) had suites and the others had rooms. Lots of owners took the opportunity to come down and enjoy themselves. I got picked up by Mrs. Berker, the beautiful wife of the founder of Berketex, the bridal wear group, and by Mr. Abelson, the owner of National Spirit, the champion hurdler. There was dancing after dinner and the headwaiter, who looked like, and said he was, Billy Nevitt's brother (Nevitt was the northern flat race champion jockey) organised introductions to all the more glamorous diners. If that failed, there was always the Palais de Dance in the town which was much patronised by Yorkshire girls on holiday. One morning, Tony Grantham (Peter Cazalet's stable jockey) appeared with a very exotic blonde with whom he had clearly spent the night. "Where did you pick that one up Tony?" said Peter. The lady advanced on Peter and, putting her head about six inches from Peter's navel, said, "Out of the fucking gutter; where else do you think he would pick me up, you big prick?" We all had hysterics and Peter, who normally adopted a very Olympian attitude, roared with laughter too. The two leading amateurs were Anthony Mildmay and Guy Cunard, who didn't like each other. One day at Lingfield, Anthony had won the race and Guy had had a fall. "Anthony, you put me through the wing," said Guy in the weighing room afterwards. "I meant to," said Anthony and turned on his heel. If crowded out by your fellow jockeys and given no room to jump, you are then forced to have a crashing fall through the wing.

I rode Intrepide in the Novice Hurdle at Newton Abbot and, half way round the second circuit, I found I had a "double handful" and that I was going better than all the others. Having not got off too well, I was in the rear and rather cheekily moved up on the final bend inside "Frenchie" Nicholson, who was on the favourite – a big likely chasing sort. He looked round, saw I was going better than him and made a determined effort to put me and my little horse through the wing. He failed, but I caught my toe in the lattice of the wing and lost a couple of lengths. Frenchie was then weaving about in an effort to stop me going past. He just beat me, and John Goldsmith was incandescent and said "You must object", which I did. However, the stewards were headed by General Sir Richard McCreery, the ex-Commander of the 8th Army, and having heard what I had to say, fined me fifty pounds for making a frivolous objection and overruled my complaint. So I got seventy pounds for being second but lost fifty pounds plus five, net gain fifteen pounds (not to be sneezed at). The race was worth £138 to the winner.

I still had not had my first winner but I was now a member of the Bryan Marshall and Dave Dick set. I was riding out two days a week with John Goldsmith, and two days with Fulke. When staying with Fulke I was allotted the best spare bedroom in Saxon House – down at the end of the passage. This lasted into October; after driving down from Yorkshire late one Sunday night I let myself in and, on entering my bedroom, I found Fulke and Frances Day, his new girlfriend, in the altogether on the bed. Fulke was understandably furious and expelled me there and then. I went down to Bryan Marshall's cottage and slept there. Riding out next morning was a chilly affair; Fulke was not good in the mornings anyway. However, Cloncarrig was getting fit after his hobdaying and was becoming fun to ride. The first time out was the Royal Worcester Porcelain Handicap Chase at Worcester. There were far too many runners – every owner was after the Royal Worcester porcelain dinner service that was to be given to the winner. At the start Dick Francis was riding Possible, the Duchess of Norfolk's good chaser, who was about fifteen and a half hands. I was on one side of him on Cloncarrig (16'3), and Dave Dick was on his other side on a Paget horse, also about 16'3. When we were let go, my horse and Dave's knee were both so close to Dick's thighs that he was catapulted out of the saddle. The subsequent report in Chaseform of "Possible – unseated rider at start" did not amuse Dick.

The second time out was at Kempton in an amateur rider chase. I got unseated when Cloncarrig hit the fence so low that he broke the front frame, which held the birch in place. Fulke, who had been very rude about my falling off, was tackled by the clerk of the course about schooling his horses better, which didn't exactly cheer him up. But things got better almost immediately. I rode Upstanding, a good novice chaser of Colonel Sam Green, in an amateur's race, also at Kempton. Having been last all the way, I found I was going well enough to shoot between the two leaders between the last two fences, and I won going away. My first winner. The celebrations were more expensive that I had hoped (Sam said, "I gave you the ride, you pay for the champagne"), but it still gave me a nice feeling of triumph.

I was brought down to earth the following week in a three-mile chase at Warwick. I found myself alone in the lead because all the other contestants had either fallen or been pulled up, and I was caught on the line, and beaten by a neck, by a horse that had been remounted. Riding Cloncarrig was like playing a salmon and then suddenly losing it. Like a fishing line, Cloncarrig's reins had the disconcerting habit of being very tight as one struggled to hold him, and then suddenly being left with nothing as he chopped the bit. On his day he still took a lot of beating; I made all the running in the Paddington chase at Newbury and he was only caught on the line by Bryan Marshall riding a Peter Cazalet horse.

My exit from Saxon House meant I now lived on the floor in Bryan's scullery with Dave Dick and Fred Winter (when he was there). Bryan would entertain us to dinner but, because his girlfriend, Peggy Miller-Mundy, was very shy about our knowing about her and Bryan, we would all say goodnight and thank you and kiss Peggy goodbye. Then, with much banging of the front door, we would tiptoe round the back and climb in through the larder window. Whether it actually fooled Peggy we never knew.

One day we had all been riding at Leicester during Lester Piggott's sojourn as a jump jockey. Lester had driven us there in the Cadillac given to him by Sir Victor Sassoon for winning his first Derby. It drank petrol like a Tiger Tank and on the way back we stopped to fill up at Market Harborough. Lester was at the wheel with Dave Dick and Bryan Marshall in front; and Fred Winter, me and Bill Rickaby, the flat jockey and Lester's uncle, on the back seat. "Will you pay Uncle Bill – I've no money?" said Lester. "But Lester I saw that man give you a roll of bank notes outside the weighing room," said Uncle Bill. "Oh, they are all in big notes and it would be a shame to break into them," said Lester. Uncle Bill paid, and we went on our way with a full tank.

Intrepide, having run second in several novices at smart tracks, was entered in the seller at Stratford after Christmas. The winner is put up for auction for a specified price – it is a gambling medium and people often got very upset if their horse was claimed. It had two advantages: a drop in class and I could do the weight easily. We got a flyer and I took up the running coming into the straight and won fairly easily by four or five lengths. As it happened, Frenchie Nicholson was second and he told me he wanted some dough out of the race. So he bid me up to a thousand pounds before I got the little horse back. But there it was – my first hurdle winner.

Weight was becoming an ever increasing problem each season. I lived on laxative pills from Dr. Goller in Harley Street, and pills to make me pee from Dr. Gold in Wimpole Street. No jolly bacon and egg breakfasts and only some boiled cabbage for supper. I did 10 stone 3 at Birmingham so I must have got below 10 stone stripped, but I never got as low again. My fleshy bum had disappeared and I had to sit on a sponge in the bath to prevent my ham bones popping through the skin! I lived, and often slept, in the Jermyn Street Turkish Baths. Bryan, Dave and Fred were all regulars, and Charlie Smirke was always there. He would come in on his return from racing, strip off and go into the steam room, crack his fingers, and lose seven pounds in 20 minutes. The next four or five pounds were very difficult to shift. He was fun to listen to and had a fund of stories. When he won the Portland Handicap at Doncaster for Sir Humphrey de Trafford, he started from the favoured position on the far rails when, in fact, he was drawn on the other side. "Were you not had in by the stewards?" asked someone. "What, in Sir Humphrey's colours?" replied Charlie.

I had bought myself a second-hand car from the H.R. Owen Group, which proved to have something wrong with it, so they offered to lend me another one while it was fixed. I collected an old Austin Princess from their Brick Street garage and drove it everywhere for three months. In early November I was due to ride Cloncarrig in the Becher chase at Liverpool, and Fulke was going to drive me to Liverpool in the morning. I spent three hours in the turkish baths and then, wearing my old army greatcoat and a balaclava helmet in order to continue sweating, I set off for Lambourn. When I got to the fountain in Newbury there was a queue of cars and I waited my turn to take the fork up the Lambourn Road. A policeman came down the line and, when he got to my car, he opened the door and said politely, "Excuse me, Sir, do you own this car?" "No," I replied, "it belongs to H.R. Owen," at which he took hold of my right wrist, yanked me out of the car, handcuffed me, took me across the road and pushed me into the back of a police car. The car was driven to the back yard of Newbury Police Station and I was frog-marched into a cell. My companions were two very drunk American airmen from Greenham Common, who spent the next two hours being sick. At one fifteen in the morning I was taken out and sat in front of a table, upon which there was a mug of tea on a tray. "Would you like some tea?" said the nice cop. "Yes," I said, reaching across the table. The nasty cop knocked my hand away and said, "Just as soon as you come clean with a statement".

W.D. "What's it all about?"

P.C. "You have been arrested for stealing or being in possession of a stolen car."

W.D. "I haven't stolen it, they lent it to me."

P.C "That's a good one. Are you off to do a job dressed like that?" pointing to my balaclava.

W.D. "I am riding at Liverpool tomorrow and I have five pounds to lose before."

P.C. "Who for?"

W.D. "Mr. Walwyn."

P.C. "We'll ring him; what's his number?"

W.D. gives it; no reply as it is off the hook to prevent Dorothy Paget calling him after bedtime.

P.C. "Who else?"

W.D. gives Father's number in Berkeley Square. Father is deaf and doesn't pick up the receiver.

P.C. "Where did you get this wallet?"

W.D. "Why?"

P.C. "Well it's got an M.C.C. membership card and a programme of the Atherstone Juvenile Court in it, as well as a lot of money. Where did you steal it?"

W.D. "I didn't, it's mine."

With that I was put back in the cell, empty now, as the Americans had been collected by the Military Police. At 5 a.m. I was released.

P.C. "Sir. Would you please speak to the Detective Inspector at Vine Street."

W.D. is put on the telephone.

Detective Inspector "We are not responsible for your arrest."

W.D. (getting on his high horse) "Well the police arrested me!"

Detective Inspector "On a report from H.R. Owen. Mr. Swain, their managing director, wishes to speak to you."

At any rate he had been got out of bed!

Mr. Swain "Captain Dugdale, I am most upset at what has happened. What can we do to make amends?"

W.D. "Well you can start by letting me have a Bentley and chauffeur for three months."

Mr. Swain "Most certainly sir."

Detective Inspector "I am instructing the Duty Sergeant at Newbury to release you forthwith."

The police, however, had the last laugh as the Berkshire Police refused to release the Princess because it had been reported stolen. So I had to hire a taxi to take me to Lambourn. I arrived at 7 a.m. just in time to ride out the first lot before driving up to Liverpool with Fulke.

Liverpool was a great thrill: Aintree in its glory, the Adelphi Hotel and all the fun of the fair. The entire jumping fraternity at close quarters all combined to make this the event of my jumping career to date. Unlike the National meeting, the one in November had the horses being boxed up just for the day so usually people didn't stay overnight unless they had runners on two consecutive days or they came from far afield.

The Adelphi management organised dancing after dinner. The leading amateur jockey was Peter Chisman, who worked for Fred Rimell's stable. He had succeeded Atty Corbett, after Atty turned professional. And also there was Tilly Joel, the youngest and most beautiful of Stan Joel's three daughters. Peter and Tilly clicked to such an extent that their exit upstairs from the ballroom was noted. Peggy, Bryan, Atty Corbett and Dave Dick then got hold of a pass key and transported all the flowers they could lay their hands on to Tilly's room, where the love birds lay asleep entwined. They did not awake and next morning found their room was like a gangster's funeral. Peter had the last word as he won the Becher Chase the next day.

The following evening I had dinner with John and Tiny Goldsmith, Fulke Walwyn and Ginger Dennistoun. At the next table sat Mrs. J.V. Rank with her boyfriend, who was a professional gambler. Ginger came in tight, and got tighter, when he suddenly took a dislike to the way the professional gambler was treating Mrs. Rank. He picked up an empty champagne bottle and bludgeoned the P.G. over the head, who collapsed on the floor, with blood oozing out of an ear. The Manager appeared and then, almost as if they were waiting in the wings, a sergeant and two Liverpool P.Cs arrived to convey Ginger to the Bridewell (lockup). He later appeared in court charged with GBH, but the P.G. made a generous appeal to the stipendiary and Ginger got off with a large fine.

Anyway, my ride in the Becher Chase was a revelation to the tyro Dugdale. The pace was relatively slow, but the difference between jumping a normal steeplechase fence and one on the National course was that one was in the air for noticeably longer. I went round with Dick Francis, who was riding Irish Lizard for Lord Sefton, and Frenchie Nicholson. Irish Lizard took a run down the near side of every fence and jumped sideways, like a high jumper. I was quite unable to cope as Clonkie, who was going very well, was always watching Irish Lizard out of the corner of his eye. I should, of course, have pulled back and come up on Dick's other side. I lasted until the fence after Valentine's when Clonkie hit it hard and I fell off. I returned to a torrent of abuse from Fulke who thought I should have won it.

I returned from Liverpool determined to sue H.R. Owen for false arrest, defamation and whatever. However, my father said, "Don't do it as everyone will say there is no smoke without fire." So I gave up that idea and continued to work on my riding. Le Jacobin was running at all the smartest courses in non-handicapped two-mile chases. I got several seconds and thirds but did not succeed in raising a flag. Intrepide obliged again in a seller, and I was beginning to kid myself I could ride a bit. Nevertheless, that was dissipated by another moderate performance with Clonkie who looked all over the winner at two and a half miles but, when I asked him to go and win his race, chopped the bit. I felt, once again, I had lost a large fish as the reins went slack in my hands. Fulke was now convinced that I would never pull it off on Clonkie, particularly after the humiliating race at Warwick when I had been pipped to the post by the jockey who had fallen and re-mounted.

After my chase win on Upstanding I was invited to ride a horse by an owner in the bar. I accepted as it was on the second day of the Windsor meeting, and I already had a ride on the first day. I was confident all would be well. But, when I got into the paddock, my horse turned out to be a very weedy brown of about fourteen hands. The favourite was a big brown horse trained by Gerry Wilson, who had been Golden Miller's jockey before the war. I got up and cantered down to the start. Gerry's jockey was a 7lb. claimer – a novice jockey who claimed for seven pounds off his weight – and he had been told to go on the outside for the first circuit. We set off, and my horse ran away with his head so high in the air he wasn't looking at the fences. When we got to the fence he attempted to run out, down the front of the fence, but I kicked and we hopped over. The favourite had no room and refused. I got over two more fences before my horse kindly made a horlicks of the open ditch, and we came down wallop. I got a lift back to the weighing room and, as I came in, I was knocked out cold with an uppercut from Gerry Wilson's jockey, who was anxious to get his own back. I got up, after also having had a good kick in the ribs from him, and was promptly grabbed by Gerry Wilson to prevent a fight developing. I apologised to Gerry, who was most upset, but with the 7lb. claimer rather than me. It was interesting that having done 10st. 7lb. on the first day and, having had only a tonic water and a smoked salmon sandwich between, when I weighed out for the second day I struggled to do 11 stone.

Later that year I "cheated" at Cheltenham by weighing out with a 3lb. saddle with girths, only one iron, and no surcingle. As I sat on the scales "Babe" Mosley, the ex-winner of a champion hurdle and a pillar of the National Hunt Committee and Cheltenham, took the saddle out of my hands, and walked over to the other stewards saying, "Look what that madman Dugdale is trying to ride on." Whether he realised that the saddle was minus an iron etc. I shall never know. I had intended to substitute the saddle for a 5lb. one, and obviously I now could not do so. Nevertheless, Intrepide obliged with a faultless performance and, although I wasn't in the "shake up", I was close on their heels and my bottom never touched the saddle till past the winning post. When I got to the weighing room, there was a cry of "all

Above: Bill mounted on Intrepide *at Cheltenham, 1948.*
Below: Sandown Annual Handicap Chase 1951: Rhetorius *with Tony Grantham up,* Semeur *with Dave Dick up and Bill on* Le Jacobin.

Above: False start in heavy rain at the 1952 Grand National, Aintree.
Left: Bill on Cloncarrig *in paddock before Grand National, Aintree 1952.*

Below: Newscutting from Daily Graphic April 7th 1952 showing melée after first fence, Bill leads away bottom right.

Above: Engagement photo of Belinda, Longford Castle 1952. Left: Blown away on the Normandie *on honeymoon.*

Opposite Top: Jolly times, Morocco.

Right: Blyth Hall 1953.

*Above left:*Top Lodge, Merevale 1961; one of 16 seventeenth-century cottages demolished at the behest of Atherstone Rural District Council because they did not conform to the new rules on ceiling height.
Above right: 3 generations: W.S.D, W.F.S.D. and W.M.S.D., 1959.

Above left: Rufus Beasley, our trainer, imparting wisdom on the gallops at Malton.
Above right: Money to Burn, *favourite for the Cambridgeshire 1956.*
Left: Nanny, Grandnanny and Matthew, 1959
Right: Affiliation Order, *an early success bred at the Merevale Stud.*

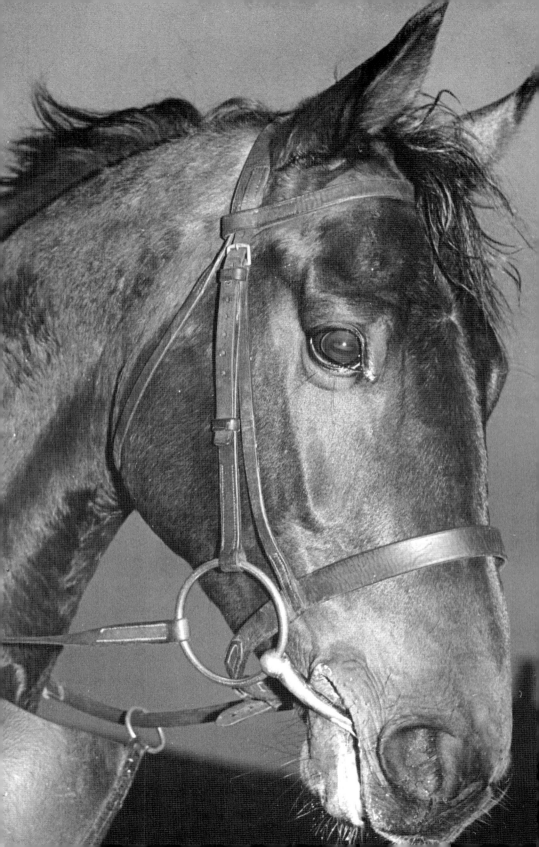

Left: Farm workers: Charlotte, Laura, Tilly and Matthew.

Below: Last photo of Belinda, with Laura July 1961.

*Left: The first brood:
Charlotte with Fuzzy,
Tilly with Ugly,
Laura with Totty
and Matthew 1963.
Below:*The
Ambion *winning at
Newmarket, 1966
Bottom:* Peace and
Concorde *winning
at Maisons-Laffitte.*

Above left: The Trent "can be made potable", 1970.
Above: Bill with Ted Franklin and Rt. Hon. Peter Walker M.P., Secretary of State for the Environment at the opening of Minworth Laboratories, 1972.
Left: Water business with Matt Busby
Below: Mac cartoon during the national water strike 1983.
Right: Cylla having just got her private pilot's licence 1968.

'What d'you say, lads ? Let's call it off, then we can go home and have a nice bath.'

Top left: Bill with Hugh Astor and the Twin Islander lining up at Adelaide for the mass take-off to Sydney, 1970.
Above: En route to Victoria, Canada – up my ladder again on the 3-engined Britten-Norman, 1971.
Left centre: Precious moments on the slopes, Bill and Cyl, 1972.
Left below: Second hatch: Cylla, Bill, Joshua, and Adelaide, 1977.

Above: Cartoon by Jack Bell in Sports Argus October 1977 – more contretemps at Villa Park .
Above Right: Bill with the League Cup, won twice during his reign at Aston Villa.
Below: Ron Saunders, manager of Aston Villa, relaxing in Spain before playing Bilbao 1977

Above: Directors Doug Ellis, Bill and Alan Smith, Villa Park, 1975.
Below: Some of the team warming up in Bilbao, August 1977.

Left: Devoted brothers, John and Bill at Wychnor.

Below: With my grandchildren on my 80th birthday, left to right: Eden May, Amelia Hazlerigg, Belinda Noel, Eliza Hazlerigg, Clemmie Dugdale, Reggie Noel, Viola Hazlerigg, Bill, Lettie Noel, Fernanda Dugdale, Nat Dugdale, William Hazlerigg, and William Dugdale.

Right: Bill and Joshua, 1977.

*Below: The Clan, Blyth,
Christmas 2008.*

weigh", which meant either that the judge hadn't finished the placing or that there was likely to be an objection. I stood at the back of the queue to sit on the scales, and luckily the "all clear" was given. I was still patronizing the two weight wizards in Harley and Wimpole Street and my flesh was falling away. But, even so, my riding weight continued to rise remorselessly and, when I finally gave up in 1952, I had trouble in doing 11st. 7lb.

Life was fun – hard work in Yorkshire in the summer; shooting, hunting and racing from August to Whitsun. Girlfriends were around but nothing very serious emerged as life was too busy. My steady was an ex-wren called Patricia. She worked in a night club in Beak Street and had a flat in Roland Gardens. The night club was shut on Sundays and Mondays so I was usually around by Sunday lunchtime. Uncle Edgar lived at 1 Roland Gardens and Pat lived opposite, so it amused me to lie in bed on Mondays and watch Uncle Edgar shaving. Many years later, I was at Sandown for the Imperial Cup when I was "goosed" from behind and, turning round, saw a small figure dripping in diamonds and sable. It was Pat who had married an old Harrovian Norwegian shipping millionaire; they lived in great style till he died of drink.

Fulke decided that we would open the 1951 season proper with Cloncarrig at Ludlow in October. The ground was very hard, as it had not rained for ages. Cloncarrig jumped out of the tapes and took a real hold for two and three-quarter miles. I was just thinking my first win was on the cards but, as we turned into the straight, his legs went from under him and we slithered off the track and went into a bunker on the golf course. He landed on top of me and, as the bunker was small, he couldn't get up. We lay like this for fifteen minutes until Darkie Deacon, Fulke's travelling head lad, came to look for us. I hadn't been hurt by the fall and the sand was soft but, when Darkie tried to get the old horse up, he did it by rolling him over on top of me, and that really did me in. We hobbled back to the weighing room where I was seen by the doctor and told to get some treatment to my shoulder. Luckily I had a volunteer chauffeur, Jean Walwyn, Peter's sister, to drive me back to London. Off I went to consult Mr Tucker, the orthopaedic surgeon at the London Clinic for sports injuries. He said, "If you were a professional you would be riding again today, but as you are not, it will take ten days."

However disappointing my rides were with Cloncarrig, my rides on Le Jacobin were getting better and better. He was a wonderful two-mile chaser although, as an entire, he did not like Aintree where he found the lack of "rake" on the fences intimidating. After running very well in non-handicapped two-mile chases in the season proper, he became a wow at the smaller courses and I won several races on him. On one occasion when asked, he immediately turned his attention to a hurdle race and won that too.

Then Fulke decided that he would swap a ride on Cloncarrig. He entered Clonkie in a four-mile chase at Hurst Park, and would give Fred Winter or Bryan Marshall the ride. In return, he offered me a ride on his chaser, Silver Drin, in the Past and Present Handicap at the Sandown Military meeting. Silver Drin had 10st. 13 and Le Jacobin, who was also entered, had 13 stone. In the event, the Hurst Park track was flooded and the four-mile chase did not happen. On the morning before Sandown, Fulke said to me that, as Cloncarrig hadn't run, the deal was off. I was furious but clearly Atty Corbett, whom Fulke proposed to put up, was an infinitely better jockey than me and could easily do 10st. 13. I would have had to do some boiling to be sure of doing the weight. So I rang John Goldsmith and arranged to ride Le Jacobin. There were then no overnight declarations so Le Jacobin would be an additional runner as he wouldn't be in the overnight entries. I could easily do 12st. 7 (13st. minus 7lb. claim). As I came into the paddock Darkie Deacon said to me, with a broad grin, "Keep well away from ours as he hates being bumped." When we got down to the start I lined up next to Atty and, as the tapes went up, gave him an old fashioned barge in the girth. Le Jacobin was the class entry and, as he had 12st. 7, I hacked him round in the rear. As we started the long bend into the straight I gave him a push, but he dropped the bit and dawdled. However, as we approached the pond fence at the bottom of the hill, he picked up the bit and started going like a rocket. We jumped up alongside the leader at the last fence, and won going away.

As we returned up the long walk to the unsaddling enclosure, I said to Atty, "What happened to you?" "Oh," he said, "the old dog wouldn't raise a canter all the way." On the Monday, as I was getting Cloncarrig ready to ride out, Fulke came up to me and said, "I suppose you want me to congratulate you?" "Oh no," I said, as sweetly as possible, "I do hope you didn't have a big bet on Atty."

For all our sparring, Fulke was a very good friend to me and took a great deal of trouble to improve my riding, using me to school his jumpers on a regular basis. The final run, before the Grand National, was the Paddington Chase over two and a half miles at Newbury (non-handicapped). All the best stables and jockeys were engaged. I had always thought that, because of his wind infirmity, two and a half miles was now Clonkie's best distance. Anyway, when we set off, he set a tremendous gallop and soon was alone in the lead. I had a double handful all the way and, when Bryan Marshall on a hotpot of Peter Ca-zalet's loomed alongside, Clonkie lengthened his stride and saw Bryan off. Bryan came good as we jumped the last and I have a photograph of me, Bryan and Fred Winter all doing our damnedest at the last. I was finally beaten three-quarters of a length by Bryan. When I came in Fulke said, "Why didn't you put him through the wing when he came up on your inner?" "I didn't think of it," I replied. He said, "You should have closed the gap," and bought me a drink to console me. Neverthe-less I got a good write-up from Quinny Gilbey in the *Racing Chronicle* which massaged my often-bruised racing ego.

April 1952 and it was off to Liverpool for the Grand National, which was the culmination of all my racing efforts so far. We went up for the start of the three-day meeting and stayed at the Adelphi. Cloncarrig had 11st. 7lb. in the National so I had to be a bit careful with my eat-ing and drinking, but not necessarily with my partying. On the first morning Dave Dick and I went down to the Liverpool Municipal Baths at Watton. After stewing ourselves, Dave and I were sitting in deck chairs, sweating away, when a man came up and had a good look at Dave, whose face was concealed behind the *Sporting Life*. "My dear sir," he said, "I do congratulate you." Dave replied, "Poor childhood

– no toys." Dave had a couple of rides that afternoon and won one of them so he was an "in form" jockey for the big event.

Fulke insisted that we walk the course together to plot my route for the following afternoon. At Becher's we bumped into Clive Graham, the Scout of the *Daily Express* and a great friend of Fulke (in fact he married Fulke's girlfriend). After some chat Clive turned to me and said, "You couldn't jump Becher's on foot". "Oh yes," I said and hurtled over; I had a cracking landing on the far side but didn't fall in the brook. Fulke said, "That's one way to avoid taking part tomorrow," and we continued our journey towards the canal turn, where Fulke wanted to demonstrate how not to negotiate it. His advice was, "Do not try and cut the corner and, if you are wise, you will find yourself on the outside for Valentine's and the fences up to the Melling Road. You can come across then, but don't forget this second-time around on the run-in." He further explained that, if I was in the hunt on the second circuit, I should not start riding a finish too early, as it was the longest run-in anywhere. "Even if the horse stays, you won't" was his final admonition.

National day dawned wet and very cold. I decided that I would eat breakfast and forego a sweater to make up for the extra weight. Cloncarrig was given an outing of about two furlongs, ridden by his lad, to clear his pipes and we returned to breakfast at the Adelphi. We went back to Aintree mid-morning as both Bryan Marshall and Dave Dick had rides in the first hurdle race. The weighing room was packed and Eddie, my valet, had a great row of saddles etc. all laid out on part of our bench. At 11st 7 I had the chance of a 7lb. saddle which was a bonus. I usually had to ride on a 4lb. one which, given my height, was very uncomfortable if you had to drop your behind back down to rebalance your mount after a mistake. When I had sorted things out with Eddie, Fulke took me down to the Members' Bar and gave me a large brandy for a "bit of Dutch courage." We were got out early into the paddock for the parade and, by then, it was very cold with snow flurries. I began to regret having breakfast. John Stanley, now Lord Derby, was a Steward and he made a few facetious remarks, from the safety of his thick overcoat, about how cold I looked.

The parade was O.K. and I found Clonkie was enjoying being back at Aintree, and didn't take off cantering down to the start. Fulke's instructions – to go on a wide outside and ride the first circuit as if I was hunting, and to only think about riding a race after Becher's the second time round – enabled me to line up on the outside with my friend Rory O'Connor, who was a fancied outsider. Someone attempted to get a flyer by charging the starter. He refused to give way and, as a result, the whole elastic, frame and all, crashed to the ground. The snow flurries had intensified, and it took over half an hour to get the tapes up and running again. However, off we went at the second attempt and my shivers were initially ended. Rory, who was to be killed tragically at Worcester races later that year, and I were together. The usual lightweight dash for the first fence left us well behind. But, after the second, Rory and I made up ground, and were about five and six lengths behind Tim Molony, who was ahead on the inside. The crack professionals, as a matter of pride, took the inner as the fences were slightly higher there, and the hoi polloi tended to go for the lower middle of the fences.

Pride came before a fall and, at the fence before Becher's, Cloncarrig hit it about half way up and I was deposited. The Marquis de Portago, who was behind me, landed on my left shoulder. The racing plate (shoe) of his horse cut into my shoulder muscles. I walked across to the inside of the course and saw Teal, the ultimate winner ridden by Arthur Thompson, go by on the second circuit. I was asked if I was all right and was put in the ambulance, which took us off to the duty hospital. There the casualty officer – a New Zealander alone in his glory – got very rattled as the Duke of Albuquerque looked increasingly white and traumatized. The Duke of Alba, the Spanish Ambassador, was clucking at the Casualty Officer like a broody hen. The Casualty Officer exploded, "If you don't get that bloody dago out of here right now we'll never save his life." The room emptied, leaving just the wounded sitting there. I got strapped up with acres of sticking plaster, and escaped back to the Adelphi to join in the triumphant Neville Crump-Arthur Thompson celebrations of Teal's win.

Fulke was full of "you fell off" sort of remarks but, when he saw me strapped up, he immediately said, "Could Bryan ride Clonkie at Cheltenham at the April meeting in the Golden Miller Chase over four miles?" I agreed, and Fulke instantly got me a large brandy to deaden the pain. The Adelphi party on National night was always a very jolly do and Jean Walwyn, the sculptress, drove me home the next day. Mr. Tucker said my shoulder would take about six weeks to heal. Nevertheless, I still managed to ride a couple of winners on Le Jacobin at smaller meetings before the end of the season. To everyone's surprise and joy Cloncarrig won the Golden Miller chase at Cheltenham, ridden by Bryan.

My last race was at Worcester in an amateur riders' chase, which I won on Le Jacobin. I only rode nine winners in my career, but they gave me great pleasure and if I had been smaller, I would perhaps have got more rides. Anyway, Cloncarrig had a season ridden by Bob McCreery, a far better rider than me, who got him a very long way in the 1953 National. Le Jacobin injured a leg with a swinging hurdle, and had to be retired. He then became a hunter stallion in Warwickshire. Intrepide, who had been claimed off me at Hereford, emerged to land a gamble at Newcastle in a long distance hurdle and never ran again after that. He was the subject of a police prosecution for neglect against his trainer some time afterwards, which was a very sad end to a lively and opinionated little horse.

Chapter 16

BELINDA, BLOODSTOCK
AND STEWARDING

The evening after my Grand National ride was also notable because Belinda Pleydell-Bouverie, with whom I had quarrelled and was definitely on non-speaking terms, saw me hobbling around with a sling and a crutch and came dashing up to ask if I was OK. I first met her because Ian Watson, a keen and good skier, had arranged a February fortnight in 1950 with Rachel Stuart and her. They came to stay at Millington when I was living there with Ian, and, as I had never skied, I was very out of the conversation. However, Belinda's eagle eye had seen something she liked so, about a month afterwards, I was invited to stay and shoot at Longford Castle. I arrived there in my 1938 Hillman Minx and parked it alongside Belinda's even older Morris. She was just back from staying at Cirencester Park with Lady Apsley, who was very keen on Belinda as a bride for her son Henry. Belinda was full of her trip. She had arrived at Cirencester, had taken the wrong turn and arrived in the middle of the parterre whereupon four footmen came out and bodily picked up ELP 429, with Belinda still sitting inside, and carried it round to the front door.

After dinner Lady Apsley said to her, "Come upstairs, my dear, I have something to show you." She led Belinda up to her bedroom where, laid out on the bed, were the Bathurst family "rocks". "All these, my dear, will be yours if you consent to be Henry's bride." Belinda thought she had, in all decency, to pick up some of the pieces and show some interest and, as she picked up each item, Lady Apsley announced its value. The net effect of all this was the certainty that if the putative mother-in-law had to market Henry like that, he was probably best avoided.

Belinda was working behind the counter at Spinks, the antique dealers in King Street, W.1. She was a very good saleswoman and was soon selling lots of Mr. Spinks' wares, particularly his fine collection of Chinese jade. I went to pick her up one evening and she was busy selling a bracelet to Mrs. Charles Sweeney, who was being wooed by the Duke of Argyll. I stood in the corner by the front door and was amused to see Mr. Spink emerge from his inner sanctum and make frantic gestures to Belinda to cut the sales talk, as he guessed he wasn't going to get the money. However, he was too late and Mrs. Sweeney had the bracelet done up on her wrist like a flash, saying, "Darling, you are sweet." Mr. Spink didn't dare tear it off the elegant wrist – the deed was done, and the bracelet remained unpaid for.

I was working in Yorkshire during the week and going down to London, whenever I could, to see something of Belinda. This carried on through the summer of 1952 until, staying the weekend with Jake, Belinda's eldest brother, I asked her to marry me. She said, "We will discuss it again after breakfast." So I proposed again in the farmyard at Longford Farm and she said yes. But she also said that she was shortly going on the Fastnet Race as a cook and, as she did not want to advertise the fact she was engaged, would I put off seeing her father and telling people about it until the end of August. This suited me just fine as I was off to Newton Abbot and Buckfastleigh for the opening of the jumping season in Devon.

She had a very rough trip in the Fastnet and spent most of the time lashed to the mast, only cutting bully beef sandwiches as it was too rough to use the stove. I had the usual jolly time at the Imperial, again being taken under the wing of Mrs. Berker. There was no shortage of champagne and the problem, as ever, was keeping one's weight down. I had just come in from an early-morning swim when I was called to the telephone. Miss Pugh, my prospective father-in-law's secretary, was on the line and said Lord Radnor wanted to see me immediately, and that "immediately" meant yesterday. I drove up to Longford from Torquay and received an imperial rocket for trifling with a girl by not immediately announcing the engagement. He then said, "Do you want to marry her?" and when I said yes, he pointed out, "Belinda has two great advantages; she cooks really well and I have paid to have her appendix out." On thinking it over, he was undoubtedly right! Anyway, I was immediately sent to Miss Pugh to draft the announcement for the paper and then returned to Torquay, accompanied by Belinda. Belinda's mother had departed from Longford before the war with the amateur huntsman of the Wilton called Selby-Lowndes. December 13th was set for the nuptials at Salisbury Cathedral. On the day before it was icy and, when driving brother John down to Salisbury, I hit a patch of black ice and turned the car round in front of a lorry crawling up the hill – luckily he was able to stop in time. As we waited in the vestry for the bride, I had spilled some brandy on my shirt in an attempt to treat a temperature that I was running. The wrinkling of the nostrils of the Bishop and Dean showed this was easily detectable and established my reputation as a hard drinker. The reception at Longford was quite involved as Belinda's mother Helena had to be kept separate from her stepmother Isabel. However, the champagne mellowed Willie Radnor to such an extent that he patted Helena on the bottom as they gathered at the front door to see us off.

I had chartered a Piper Air Taxi to fly us from Hurn to Le Bourget and, after a bumpy flight, Belinda succumbed to air sickness just as we touched down at Le Bourget. I had organised our trip on the basis that being alone on a honeymoon during the day was a mistake. My French racing friends rallied round, and we were lunched almost every day at a succession of good restaurants. So much so that it was a wrench to take the boat train to Le Havre to catch the *Normandie* to New York, where we were going to stay with Barty and Kay Bouverie on Long Island for Christmas. The weather was vile and the gale was terrific. We dined en prince in the restaurant and retired to our cabin. The boat was due to sail at midnight and, promptly at 12.30 a.m., Belinda became very seasick. So it was quite a surprise to go on deck at breakfast time to find the boat still moored to the quay, as it had been considered too bad for the ship to set sail. It was a very rough trip and, by the time we reached the Newfoundland Banks, there were only two diners – me and Suzy Volterra, the racehorse owner. We dined together and she was highly entertaining. Her husband, the nightclub impresario, had died and she controlled his empire and stable. She had a scar on her face where she said she had been bitten by her poodle, but it was said that it was to remove a large nose during the German occupation.

Long Island for Christmas was terrific. On Boxing Day Barty took us for a walk in the woods and, as we came round the corner, there was a man in a red-and-black hunting coat sitting in a tree holding a rifle with telescopic sights. Barty wished him a happy Christmas and asked him what he was doing. "Waiting for bears," he replied and, not wishing to distract him from his sport, we continued. Shortly afterwards another hunter came along and thought the man in the tree was a bear, and shot him dead. The last bear was killed on Long Island in 1823. On New Year's Eve we left for Acapulco via Mexico City, returning home in mid-January, just as Belinda began to feel ill with No. 1 (Laura). The first morning at Merevale Belinda was tottering along to the bathroom when she ran into Uncle Edgar, who was carrying a full chamber pot to the housemaid's cupboard. "Good morning Uncle Edgar," said Belinda brightly but, to her surprise, got no reply. At breakfast Uncle Edgar came to me and said, "A word in your ear, Bill." And then, "Doesn't your wife know you never greet a man in the morning when he is carrying his pot to empty it? It is an invariable rule." So now we knew.

We moved into Blyth in January 1953 and it has been our principal home ever since. The immediate problems were to make the house watertight and to tackle the Victorian interior. Belinda threw herself into making it a liveable home with a good garden. We worked our way around the house room-by-room and floor-by-floor. Every afternoon and every Sunday we slaved in the rubbish tip at the front of the house. We removed the lone pine and the bushes screening the gents' loos, which were earth closets at the side of the house. My father recalled sitting on one with the door open, facing one of his uncles similarly disposed and smoking a cigar. We settled on a nanny and first set about renovating the nurseries before the arrival of our eldest in September. On taking down Victorian panelling we found some wallpaper dating from around 1700; we also found masses of sawdust piled under the floorboards, presumably to deaden the patter of tiny feet.

However, Blyth was not the only thing requiring renovation. My father had passed on a huge proportion of the estate, and I was busy with plans to upgrade the housing stock. This was not helped by the new rules on ceiling height. As a result, we were made to demolish nearly all the 17th-century cottages. When the heritage movement gained the upper hand twenty years later, we were then ordered by the Council to rebuild the few remaining 17th-century cottages, as they were now listed.

The compensation from the nationalisation of Baddesley Colliery still had to be negotiated. Given the responsibility for nationalisation, Emmanuel Shinwell, the Minister for Mines, had decreed that the global compensation for the coal industry would be decided by a tribunal to be chaired by Lord Cohen, the eminent chancery judge. Thereafter the various mining association areas would fight for their share of the global total. It was then discovered that Scotland, Wales, Durham, Northumberland and the top end of south Yorkshire would get very little because they had been losing so much money and the areas which made money – Nottingham, Doncaster area of south Yorkshire, Warwickshire and Leicestershire – would get a disproportionate share of the money thereby bypassing the big Labour areas that had provided the dynamics for nationalisation. After that the individual collieries would fight for their share.

This system was not ideal from our colliery's point of view as we had had a big fire in 1944 and had made a loss for the first time in 35 years, and the death of our general manager made our hold on the necessary evidence for supporting our claim much more difficult. As a result we were very disappointed with the capitalisation of the colliery but the figures were somewhat mitigated by the good price that we received for the rolling stock of the coal wagons.

I had started farming at home. My system was based on rotation largely copied from Ian Watson's system at Goole – potatoes, wheat, sugar beet, wheat. I soon learnt that it was much too ambitious for the soil type in Warwickshire. With the arrival of oilseed rape I modified my rotation and then we were much more successful, aided by a transfer of livestock from beef to milk. Every year, Coleshill Young Farmers came to see the farm and ask questions. Their leader was Henry Plumb who later (as Lord Plumb) was to be the leader of the Tory MEPs.

When I had got engaged, my father said to me that race riding was not a suitable sport for a married man and, if I gave it up, we might envisage a venture into racing and breeding together. He and I duly went off on a fact-finding tour of bloodstock breeding in France. We stayed at the Royal Monceau and every day sallied forth into Normandy, taken by a Haras Proprietaire (stud owner). We went to see M. Henri Corbière at Nonant-le-Pin. Monsieur Corbière was a very distinguished-looking smallish man with the Legion d'Honneur in his buttonhole, a 1900s stiff collar (which met without wings or rollover) and a cravat. He had had a German military H.Q. in his house continuously from 1940 until June 1944, and had never addressed one word to the conquering Germans. He offered to change some money for us and went to a picture hanging on the wall. This slid aside to reveal a knob, which opened the wall and revealed a safe door. It was stuffed with Franc notes of large denominations. I longed to ask if the Germans had had a look while using the house, but thought better of it.

We were also taken to Normandy by Francois Dupré, the owner of the Hotel George V in Paris, and the owner of the largest stable in France after Boussac and the Aga Khan. We drove down to the Haras D'Ouilly in M. Dupré's Cadillac with a uniformed chauffeur at the wheel. We stopped to allow M. Dupré to pee – the chauffeur took his cap off and placed it on his bosom while the pee continued. We stopped once more at about 11 a.m. for coffee, charcuterie and two Cognacs. The Haras D'Ouilly was enormous. On arrival we immediately sat down to lunch, washed down by pre-war claret and more cognac. First the stallions were paraded, then his personal mares, and finally one or two visiting classic-winning fillies. We then got back in the car and drove back to the George V. Father and I nearly gave up the project after seeing the slick and enormous operations in France. However, a fool and his money…

Back home we pondered the situation. We both knew that we were neither clever enough at bloodstock nor in possession of capital that would enable us to do it in the French style. But we thought that, if we were lucky with successful broodmares, we would be able to grow the operation gradually. We started off with Pretty Girl II, a goodish small filly; two duds bought from Frankie More-O'Ferrall; and Fakhri, a cast-off from the Aga Khan's stud, whose lineage went back to the dam of Mahmoud. We decided to buy a two-year-old filly from Richard Sykes at Sledmere named Persian Queen, and also to buy two or three yearling fillies and that would complete the start-up.

So Belinda and I headed off to the Newmarket October sales. I was sweet on a Borealis filly bred by Bunty Scrope, Lord Derby's stud manager. We had her vetted by Dr. Burkhardt and Mr. Crowhurst, the two most eminent breeding vets. They said fine, but she was a disaster – she was a weaver and a crib biter, which was undiscovered when we bought her. High adrenalin and several drinks with Rufus Beasley (our chosen trainer) saw me emerge from the bar into the sales ring – just as a filly was hanging fire. It was by The Phoenix out of Grandpa's Will, who had bred several very good racers. "Go on Bill, have a bid," said the equally bewhiskied Rufus. One bid at 1050 guineas, and she was mine. On going into the Jockey Club Rooms my adrenalin came down with a bump when I was told by Henry Porchester, "You must be mad, The Phoenix is the kiss of death. Your horse is terribly bosomy and her hocks are in the next county." On inspection – only too true. Nevertheless, she won five races, was favourite for the Cambridgeshire (she came fourth), and we sold her first foals very well.

Our racing and breeding efforts were taking off. Belinda really loved the business. We sent the fillies to Rufus Beasley who was an expert at readying horses for races and a very good judge of a horse. If he was slightly lacking in stable skills, these were provided by his wife, Alexandra. Our first winner was Persian Queen at Thirsk, and thereafter we had a steady flow of them. At first our winners were with bought fillies but soon we had some wins with homebred fillies (we sold all the colts). Belinda wanted to have a trainer in the south whom she could visit from Longford. Fortuitously John Morrison wrote to say that Noel Cannon, who had been J.V. Rank's private trainer at Druids

Lodge until he died, was now very short of owners. John was starting a racing and breeding operation with Noel Cannon and invited us to join. Belinda was delighted and so we sent two fillies. One was looked after by a little billiard ball sort of a man, with pebble lenses, who turned out to have done Minoru, when he had won the Derby for Edward VII. Druids Lodge had the most wonderful gallops on miles of down land. There were also two trial grounds on the far side of the A303 where we would adjourn. The stable jockeys were Scobie Breasley and Jay Purtell, the Australian duo who were enjoying great success.

And Belinda was soon right into the Turfists. With her ready smile and sense of fun we were soon well-known in the flat fraternity. I had been friends of many of the turf journalists such as Bill Curling (*Daily Telegraph*) and Tom Nicholls (*Sporting Life's* "Man on the Spot") and they would come and stay for Midlands' meetings. We would stay with Tom and Tighe Nicholls for Newmarket race meetings – their dinner parties were fantastic, with all the racing correspondents and a good many trainers there. Tighe was a law unto herself, and provided all the sparkle and zest that the slower-tempo Tom lacked. They went to Spain for their holiday one year, and Tighe got herself into the bull-fighting world. She became a groupie for Jean Luis Dominguin, the star matador, and travelled all over Spain in his retinue for months on end.

Rufus Beasley, having been Cecil Boyd-Rochfort's stable jockey for many years, liked nothing more than to get the better of the Captain (B-R). At Nottingham, for our horse Money to Burn's debut, the Captain arrived with one of Lady Zia Wernher's fillies, who was a hot favourite. "Rufus," said the Captain, as we emerged from the lunchroom, "do you fancy yours?" "Oh Captain," said Rufus, eyes wide with Irish honesty, "it's only a moderate maiden. I wouldn't be running her if the owner hadn't wanted to see her before the winter." As Rufus had just told us that it would take a very sharp one to beat her, our eyes were wide open with Warwickshire naiveté. Money to Burn obliged by several lengths and Rufus, eyes wider than ever, went up to the Captain in the unsaddling pen and said, "I'd never believe it, she must be better than I thought." What the Captain thought – he had had a good bet – was not recorded.

Belinda had become quite a backer and had an account with Jack Wolff, the Birmingham bookmaker, with whom she got on very well. One day we had a filly running at Birmingham which opened at 6/4. Jack gallantly said, "It's 6/4 M'Lady, but for you it's 4/1." So Belinda said, "Thank you Mr. Wolff, I'll have £2000 for 500." It was not only her money, but mine and Rufus's and Dai Fetherstonhaugh's as well. Jack stood by it when the filly won, although we didn't tell him it was not all Belinda's dough.

Money to Burn opened her three-year-old career at Thirsk in April 1956 and was about tenth in a field of about 25 (no safety limits then). Rufus was delighted and said that he thought she would be his horse for the Cambridgeshire, which he had already won with Jupiter and Richer. After dinner that night we sat down with "the malt" and plotted and planned her career. The Cambridgeshire entries were made in mid-July for the race in mid-October; the handicap weights were published in late August. We aimed to get the lowest possible handicap weight that a strong jockey could cope with. By timing your horse's races carefully, you should enable it to arrive at the start-line with the best possible chance together with a lot of support from enthusiastic punters. So no race until July after the Cambridgeshire entries and, if all went well, an outing to improve the betting odds. She ran and won a little race over seven furlongs at Haydock in July, and we waited for the weights for the Cambridgeshire to be published. She was given 7st. 9lbs. and we decided to run her in the Dounside Cup over a mile at Ayr. She was quoted in the Cambridgeshire call-over at 66/1 and we then went to William Hill and put £3,000 on (me, Belinda, Rufus and Dai Fetherstonhaugh all contributing). At Ayr she won by twenty lengths, but, as the paper said, it was more like a distance. She immediately became all the rage and, next time out, was 7/2 favourite.

Almost a week before the Cambridgeshire I had a late night call from William Hill who said, "I stand to lose a lot of money on your filly and I will lay it all back to you at 8/1." I was thoroughly out of my depth in these ante-post matters, and wanted to talk to Rufus before agreeing or not. I said I would think it over and call him back. "I'll tell you one thing, Captain," said William Hill, "your filly won't win, so you might as well agree." If a gambler stands to make a lot of money from making a bet at long odds (as we had) and the price radically shortens, it usually makes sense to shorten one's own liability by laying it off with a bookmaker, so we did. As Money to Burn's weight was below what Joe Sime could do, Rufus engaged Paul Tulke, who was that season's star apprentice at Sam Armstrong's. The night before the race the telephone rang in the Tulke home every twenty minutes – they didn't leave the receiver off. We were drawn on the wide outside and, with a westerly gale blowing down the course, the horses drawn on the side of the stands had a big advantage as they were sheltered by them. Money to Burn came from the pack and won the race on the far side, but was beaten two and half lengths by Loppy Lugs on the stand side. As a result of the lay off, the £3,000 was recovered from William Hill plus a little more. We licked our wounds and took Money to Burn to Liverpool, where she won the Liverpool Autumn Cup, under a brilliant ride from Scobie Breasley, in her final race. Not bad for a "bosomy sort with hocks in the next county".

Around 1953 John Willoughby de Broke asked me to start stewarding at the Midlands courses and so I became a steward at Warwick, Birmingham and Wolverhampton. John and Rachel Willoughby ran a very good table at Wolverhampton and it was a much sought-after invitation for trainers and owners to lunch there. Into the stewards' luncheon room came all the big shots of the sport and so we gradually got to know everyone. When John Willoughby became Chairman of Cheltenham, I became his deputy at Wolverhampton and Belinda and I presided in his and his wife's stead.

I was subsequently asked to become a director of Wolverhampton in place of Harry Brown, the only amateur to win the National Hunt jockeys championship, whose many bad injuries were beginning to plague him. John Holloway was the secretary and, in effect, the managing director of the racecourse. He was both energetic and farsighted. We were the second course to stage evening racing and the first to have live groups performing between races. One evening we had a runner in the principal race of the evening. Bernard Norfolk had a peacocky chestnut colt named St. Peter who had, at one time, been favourite for the Derby, but was rather a disappointment. The distant noise of one group from behind the Tattersalls stand caused St. Peter to "draw" and, in spite of all efforts by John Dunlop's travelling head man, he was still erect on going onto the course. Our horse, as a result, won easily. The following week I met Bernard at Newmarket and he said, "What were you doing with that band? It cost me the race." I do not think it did, as St. Peter remained a very reluctant customer.

I was also elected to the Jockey Club Rooms at Newmarket. On my first day there, I was not being spoken to by many people when Lord Sefton noticed me and said, "You Bill Dugdale?" When learning that I was, he carried on, "You and I are going to pay for Harry Brown's hernia operation – he can't manage it himself". We did and Harry continued his sporting career for several more years before he finally pegged it at the end of the fifties.

When I arrived at the first flat meeting at Wolverhampton to start as a steward, there was no period of indoctrination as happens now. New stewards were very small beer and were not allowed to forget it. There was no rotation and the senior steward – Sir Edward, "Johnny", Hanmer who had been the boss for umpteen years and was to remain so until his retirement from stewarding altogether – brooked no nonsense and no interference. No one else was allowed to do much more than nod in agreement.

Woe betide anyone who got him to stay after the last race, whatever happened. As soon as the horses were past the post, Sir Edward would adjourn to the running board of his Bentley and, standing there with his hand shading his eyes from the western sun, he would await the signal that Bill Hawksford would give by waving from the weighing-room door, indicating there was no objection. On the very rare occasions that he had to be summoned back for one, the objector was given very short shrift. On one occasion, when I was in the head-on box, the odds-on favourite – a two-year-old trained by Ted Leader for Jim Joel – got crucified about thirty yards from the line. I rushed over and caught Sir Edward as he emerged from the staircase by the unsaddling enclosure. "Johnny," I said, panting with the effort, "we must object – the favourite got a really bad bump just before the line and the distance was only a short head." Sir Edward eyed me from toe to top and back again – he paused, considered and said, "Is Mr. Joel here?" "No." A further pause and then the K.O. "Well, he would have come, wouldn't he, if he had intended to object." The march to the Bentley running-board was resumed with never a backward glance.

One individual whom Sir Edward had very much in his sights was the trainer Michael Beary. I never discovered what was the reason for this, but Michael had only to set foot in the car park for the Hanmer temperature to begin to climb. Before the race in which a Beary runner was due to compete, Sir Edward would position himself about five yards from the entrance to the old paddock, which was situated immediately in front of the stables, and clutching a huge pocket time-piece, would wait for Beary and horse to emerge. "Beary, you're late," the bark would come and sure enough, Michael would be summoned to be fined the sum of £10. It often seemed to me that Michael had wonderful excuses – like his jockey had ingrowing toenails and could only hobble back to the weigh-in for the previous race. But it was all to no avail and fined he was. This always put the senior steward in a happy frame of mind and he would wonder with a broad smile over his tea-time whisky and soda how Michael ever got his horses to the post at all.

But Sir Edward, who had a very wry and pawky sense of the ridiculous, would keep us amused with his descriptions of contretemps on the turf and his encounters with the civil servants of the Ministry of Agriculture during the war. He had been the Senior Steward of the Jockey Club throughout the war and had achieved miracles in keeping things going, however difficult. He had to go everywhere by train and his descriptions of getting from West Shropshire to Newmarket standing all the way in the corridor and changing at Shrewsbury, Rugby, Peterborough and Cambridge made one marvel at his tenacity and dedication.

The senior member of the Wolverhampton racecourse board was Harry Atherton-Brown. He was the legendary figure who had finished second in the National on The Bore, with the reins held between his teeth. He had left Eton in 1904 and had immediately started to ride winners. He had been at the same house as I was and I had looked him up in the house record book and seen the following entry: "H.A. Brown – an excellent footballer who tackled hard and ran very fast whenever he happened to be unable to go to Sandown." There was nothing that Harry could not do superbly well. He was in every list of the ten best shots, but was never happier than when pottering out after the odd rabbit or partridge with my father. One afternoon on a hot September day, when he did not reappear after a drive, he was discovered flat on his back in considerable distress behind a haystack, having fallen and ruptured himself. He allowed himself to be propped up and proceeded to collect three right-and-lefts running, before departing to have the rupture seen to. Shooting at Laverstoke one day he shot about 30 partridges at one stand and, after the drive was over, he noticed that his young next-door-neighbour had missed everything. Picking up an armful, he deposited them all at his neighbour's place, saying, "I get asked every year, but you won't be asked again if you tell Wyndham (Portal) that you haven't got any."

At Hereford he put Richard Cottrell up in a Hunter Chase and, after Richard had done everything wrong short of throwing himself off, he got beaten a short head. As the defeated odds-on favourite came in, it was greeted with a torrent of booing. All Harry said was, "Bad luck, old boy, if it had been me I would have been beaten a furlong." By the early 1950s many racing injuries had begun to take their toll and Harry, who had had both his collar-bones removed, was rather a light of former days. However, he saw his role as that of the gad-fly and he used to take on the stewards at lunch and pull their legs. He was the only one who dared to pull the Hanmer and Willoughby extremities. Once John Willoughby, who always took the greatest pains to see that all the loos throughout the racecourse were clean and tidy, had despatched Lady W. to see that the ladies' in the Silver Ring were OK. Her Ladyship had sailed through the Tattersalls ones and, heading down into the next enclosure, had gone into the first ones there – only to find they were the men's. This was a constant source of delight to Harry and it was always on the menu when Lady Willoughby came to lunch.

Chapter 17

TORY CANDIDATE

By 1957 I had done several years as a councillor on the Meriden Rural District Council. It was a useful introduction to official life. The one noteworthy moment came after the clerk, Mr. Sidney Woodham, committed suicide one Saturday night. As I couldn't go to the funeral I went to the council offices with a wreath. There I found the whole of the Midlands staff of the National Audit Office going through everything with a fine toothcomb in case the suicide had been as a result of defalcation. However, everything was in perfect order and continued to run like clockwork.

The public service bug had begun to bite and I put my name down as a possible candidate for the Tories. Laura's birth, nine months after our wedding, had been followed by that of the twins, Matilda and Charlotte, in 1955. I was anxious for an heir but we thought we would leave it for a few years before trying for number four. We were confident that we could manage a family and the House of Commons. As the selection committees invariably seemed to be about 70 per cent women, a family was not a hindrance. I went to London and was interviewed by: Robert Grimston in the chair, whom I knew; a Dame – from the west country and dedicated to equal opportunity; and a rather smarmy constituency agent. They questioned me for what seemed like hours but was, in fact, just under an hour. The Dame was very interested in what Belinda would do and I explained that, as we had three girls under three at the moment, she was very busy, but she would always have time to help. About three months later I heard that my name had been put on the panel.

Nothing happened for about eighteen months and then I was ordered to appear at Worcester, where a new candidate was needed after Geordie Ward was ennobled. I was interviewed by the Chairman of the Association (also chairman of Worcester Royal Porcelain) who sported an enormous pair of bugger's grips, and the agent. I got on quite well and I was then (with Belinda) ordered to appear before the selection committee at 7.45 p.m. one evening. What we didn't know was that the whole thing was meant as a lay-down for Peter Walker who was, at that time, the national chairman of the Young Conservatives. I had prepared what I thought was a good speech lasting about thirty minutes. This covered my support for the Tories; my enthusiasm to represent Worcester; and some general thoughts on the way I thought the Tories should proceed. This was received politely with some applause and we were then asked a few perfunctory questions. After we were wheeled out to a gentle handclap, the handsome bachelor Peter Walker was ushered in to loud and prolonged applause. We knew our fate but we continued to sit in the cold room for about an hour until the chairman came out and sent us on our way. I was downhearted at what I thought was an exposure of my limitations, but cheered up when I received a letter from Jack Galloway, the West Midlands' Central Office agent. He apologised for "using me as a stalking horse" – explaining that they had needed someone quiet in order to show off Peter's obvious advantages.

Belinda and I had a long discussion and decided my address should be shorter, punchier and more about my advantages rather than about current politics; her skirt should be shorter; she should not sit behind the Union-Jack-draped table but out where her legs could be seen to best advantage; questions to me should quite often be answered by us jointly; and I should avoid a one-to-one situation and try to be one of four or five at the selection meeting. "Favoured son" anointing should be avoided.

About nine months later I was invited to be interviewed by Ludlow, where Christopher Holland-Martin had died, and got on the short list along with Robin Maxwell-Hyslop, a Rolls Royce salesman and later M.P. for a Devon constituency, and Jasper More the favoured son.

Order of batting was Maxwell-Hyslop, me and then Jasper. Maxwell-Hyslop was in and out in three-quarters of an hour, and then Belinda and I went in. She had to sit in a chair at the side of the table, so legs were much in evidence. My speech went very well and the questions to us both were helpful and encouraging. I was asked whether I would live in the constituency. I said I didn't think you could run Ludlow without a base there, but that I would continue to bring up my family where we were. We left to extended applause, and Jasper and Mrs. More followed last. They reappeared after an hour, at 10.45 p.m. Belinda and I expected the worst, and thought we would be told about twenty minutes later. But, instead, we sat there until 2.15 a.m. accompanied by the noise of prolonged arguing and shouting. Then the vice chairman came out and said, "Congratulations Jasper, come in and make your acceptance speech." Mrs. More had had too long worrying, within reach of the bottle of Gordon's gin, and was unable to get up. Maxwell-Hyslop and I, ever the gentlemen, lifted her up and handed her her handbag. We shook Jasper's hand. Afterwards I got several angry letters saying the vote was rigged; I had apparently won by two votes but then they counted again and I had lost by one. So they counted again – this time it was a tie and the chairman's casting vote saved the day. The altercation had been about the recounts and the chairman's role. I didn't hear from Jack Galloway this time but I remained good friends with the Mores all the time Jasper was M.P. for Ludlow.

We were next summoned to Cambridgeshire, which was going to be a lay-down for Francis Pym. I had known him slightly at Eton and didn't fancy the idea of once again being the stalking horse for a local hot favourite. Pym, the descendant of the most important Parliamentarian figure in the run up to the Civil War in the 17th century, carried too much local ballast compared to a chap from the Midlands. The result was as expected.

Every May we went to stay with Dick and Heather Bearsted at La Serena, their marvellous villa in Cap Ferrat. Nightly, after dinner, we went to the Casino at Monte Carlo. Belinda was soon hooked on roulette and, as we were very short of foreign currency, we agreed that we would start off with £20 and play rouge et noir and pair et impair until she had enough to go to the wheel proper. On the third night, at about 2 a.m., Belinda had made enough to go to the table and take a seat. She put a stash on o and it came up. She left it on and o came up again. She let out a squeal and one of the old biddies at the table said loudly, "Elle est encore jeune." Unfortunately, our luck didn't last and we gave it all back over the rest of the week. En route to Cap Ferrat we called on any of our mares who were visiting French stallions in Normandy, before making our way south on local roads. We visited most of the three-star restaurants en route but, as we became more sophisticated, we looked out for very small restaurants and usually did very well.

At home we continued slogging away at the garden. Mr. Price, the gardener was a very old man. He had been a tool-room man at Rolls Royce in Derby but, disliking all the strikes in the 1920s, had changed career and taken the job at Blyth. He was brilliant in the kitchen garden but, beyond a few roses, he refused to come around the front, so the first herbaceous border all had to be done by us. We also began to reclaim the peninsular garden behind the stable yard. Mr. Price used to come round and watch as we worked and then, sadly shaking his head, would walk silently away. As he was nearer 80 than 75 I thought it was time to get someone younger. I went to see him and said I thought he ought to retire. He burst into tears and I was completely unable to control the situation. Later his son came to see me – he owned a chain of carpet shops – and said he was sure I was right and that he would take his father (now widowed) away where he and his wife could look after him. I replaced the outmoded staff accommodation in the stable yard, which had just been condemned by the Council, with two modern cottages behind the garden, and then looked for a new gardener. I advertised and only had one reply, from the gardener in charge of six at Alderman Byng Kenrick's at Handsworth Wood in Birmingham. This was Mr. Woodedd, who stayed for about 25 years before semi-retiring and going to work in the greenhouses at Arbury. The lawns soon looked greener, the kitchen garden was fully cultivated and the greenhouses re-activated.

Matthew was born in 1959 and so we now had four in the nursery and considered our family complete. When I was finally given the possibility of standing as the Prospective Parliamentary Candidate for the safe seat of Oswestry in 1961, Belinda's surgeon said that he thought I would be most unwise to let my name go forward as Belinda had become very ill as a result of an ovarian cyst. This ended, for the time being, any ambitions I had of becoming a Tory M.P.

At the December Newmarket sales in 1960 Belinda woke one morning in great pain; so much so that she wanted to be driven home at once. The next day she went to see Sam Davidson, the surgeon, and he put her straight into Birmingham General Hospital. Her ward was run by the redoubtable Sister Underwood like the Guards' Depot, with all the nurses parading in line to be inspected, before coming on duty. One day a particularly pretty staff nurse said, "I am going out with Dr. – (one of the registrars)." She replied, "Nurse, your sex life is of no interest to me". But, later that evening, when sitting on Belinda's bed, she told us the story adding that, "Of course, the nurse's sex life is of great interest to me – that girl is determined to catch a doctor, but that particular doctor is No Bloody Good." Many years later I was at Windsor races and was shouted at by a couple having a glass of champagne. It was Sister – now retired and married to a Birmingham tycoon – who had a string of horses in training.

After two operations and no improvement I thought it was time for a second opinion so asked Sam. He bridled rather before saying, "Who do you want?" Belinda had heard of a Professor Stallworthy at the Radcliffe Hospital in Oxford and said his name. Sam said, "That is the one I am prepared to have a second opinion from." Off we went to the Radcliffe and I waited outside until Belinda was being helped into the car. The professor called me back and said, "I will write to Sam. Sam has done everything he can, but now we must just hope." Belinda came out of hospital at the beginning of June and, for three weeks, we had a very happy time at Blyth with the children. But one morning her tummy blew up like a balloon and, on ringing Sam, he said, "Bring her in at once." After seeing her she was admitted to the Queen Elizabeth Hospital in Birmingham.

A week or so later I got chicken pox and had a very high temperature. I was just recovering when I had a recurrent bout of malaria, which I had first contracted during the war. I felt very seedy. However, late one night my telephone rang and it was Sam: "I have to tell you now that Belinda is a dying woman." I dressed and went into the hospital where Belinda was propped up, with a nurse in attendance. Sam was there and said it would be about 24 hours. I went down and rang Jane Bethell, her sister, and asked her to prepare the family. She nobly said she would come down early next day, and appeared at the hospital by lunch. We saw the next night out but Belinda was visibly sinking. I sat on one side of the bed holding her hand, and the nurse held her wrist and her pulse on the other. She died at 3.30 p.m. I didn't realise she had gone until the nurse lifted the sheet over her face and said, "that's over."

When I got back to Blyth I was met by our G.P., Dr. Wall, with sleeping pills for a week. I had to tell Nanny and the children, and ring both sets of parents. I found arranging the funeral very cathartic; my sister-in-law Kath was just about to deliver Mary but brother John was a great help arranging the service, until he was called to the delivery ward. I sent the children down to Longford to avoid the funeral and I was told later by Isabel Radnor that on arrival, Charlotte, who was just six, skipped into the house and said to Grandad, "Have you heard Mummy's dead?" and skipped out. So the worst of the situation for them was avoided until later. I went away immediately after the funeral for five days to sister-in-law Jane Bethell and was kept busy with Rise Estate matters and helping to arrange the Holderness puppy show. But it was grim when I returned home to our empty house. I dived into the whisky bottle every night.

My catharsis came about six weeks later. I had been up at Farrers, our solicitor, sorting out Belinda's probate and all the consequent problems of trustees for the children etc. I left Farrers about 5.30 p.m. on Friday and drove towards the A5, filling the car at the Shell station on Bayswater Road. As I was leaving the attendant said, "I am just off – will you give me a lift?" I took her northwards towards Lancaster Gate and, on arrival she said, "Do you want to come up?" I said, "Yes." She took off her Mrs. Mop headgear to display black curls. Going up in the lift she kissed me and we went into her bedsit. She came from north Wales and told me to stop moaning and get on with it. After she had made me bacon and eggs on Sunday morning, I drove home. Nanny lifted an eyebrow and said, "We expected you on Friday evening." I said, "I got delayed." The eyebrow remained hoisted but nothing more was said. I got on with answering the condolence letters and took the children up to London and to the Zoo, and eventually the gloom slowly evaporated.

My business and local government affairs now meant that I had to spend much of the week in London. So I got a flat in Marsham Court, Victoria and bicycled around town and started to make the most of Sixties London.

Chapter 18

RUNNING WATER

Although I had lost my seat in Coleshill on the District Council in 1958 and was then out of local government until I was elected to the County Council to represent Water Orton in 1964, in the autumn of 1961 Warwickshire County Council had to find a representative for the Trent River Board. Historically it had always sent the northern-most member, who was then a Labour N.U.R. man and the station master at Wilnecote. On promotion to Tamworth station he found he couldn't cope, and the County Council asked me to be their representative. So began my 38 years in the water industry.

When I got to Trent River headquarters in Nottingham I found it was run by a very dour magistrate from Newark, a Mr. W. A. Muddell, who was interested only in the land drainage side, full stop. He knew the Trent River Board's days were numbered, and a new Trent River Authority was to be created after Parliament passed James Ramsden's Water Pollution Bill. However, he and Marshall Nixon, the engineer, had masterminded the Trent flood alleviation scheme after the disaster of 1947, when thousands of acres were inundated and scores drowned. A very able man in his sphere, Marshall (a lefty Royal Engineer colonel from the war) had already done wonders with the Ouse and Nene in the Fens when a similar disaster had occurred. The clerk was Ian Drummond who had come from West Ham Borough Council. He had six solicitors working for him and the legal work bored him. The Board was dominated by six representatives from Birmingham City Council – all Labour bar one Tory. They were led by Alderman Chaffey who was the Cadbury directors' lavatory attendant at Bournville and a keen T.G.W.U man. Muddell knew what he wanted but, as the money largely came from Birmingham, the Board members from there did everything they could to slow the work. The government was Tory and, as a result, all the cities and some of the counties were Labour controlled. The remainder of the East Midland cities and the Potteries all loathed the way Birmingham ruled the roost.

I enjoyed the work and was a bit surprised when Muddell called me into his office and asked whether, as the new River Authority needed a new hand at the tiller with different skills, he could groom me to succeed him. I thought it could be fun to do and instantly agreed. He said he was going to do one more year and then go. So, when the new authority was set up, I continued to represent Warwickshire and was elected chair of the River Pollution Committee. No sooner had I set up the committee when a busy foreman at the Tame & Rea sewerage works kicked away the penstocks when doing maintenance work, and let about a week's untreated Birmingham sewage into the Tame. As a result every fish between Birmingham and Burton-upon-Trent was poisoned and died.

There was a tremendous outcry from the anglers and I persuaded the committee that they had to prosecute the Tame & Rea, the Birmingham sewerage enterprise. Although the committee had executive powers, Chaffey requisitioned a special meeting of the whole authority. In the end the decision to prosecute was upheld by one vote and didn't need a casting vote. The case was heard by the Birmingham Stipendiary Magistrate and fines amounting to £600 were awarded, but the costs were many times greater. This was a major first in the battle against big cities economising on sewage purification at the expense of their neighbours. A glance at the map reveals Birmingham at the head of the Tame, the Potteries at the head of the Trent, Leicester at the head of the Soar, Derby on the Derwent and Nottingham on middle Trent after all the major tributaries have joined it. Birmingham and Tame & Rea were furious but took immediate steps to improve matters, and I was elected chairman of the National River Pollution Prevention Committee of the Association of River Authorities in London, which was entry to the main arena.

Trent River Authority needed a new head chemist/administrator for my committee, and I had a great slice of luck when Fred Lester from Essex River Authority got the job. He was the son of a miner in Nuneaton, had joined the borough engineer's department as a sewage works labourer at fifteen, and had progressed upwards from there. Seven years of night school had got him a fellowship of the Royal Society of Chemistry. A strong Methodist, he and I hit it off at once and the national team welcomed him as a very live wire. The national scheme for clarifying the pollution risks from road tankers was entirely his idea and was forced through a very reluctant Home Office and Ministry of Transport. It is now, 30 years later, regarded as indispensable.

In spite of efforts by the Birmingham contingent to prevent it, I was duly elected chairman of the Trent River Authority the following year and set about trying to deal with the rivers, water supply and river purification. The East Midlands badly needed a new reservoir and our preliminary investigation showed that the cheapest and most efficient site was Hassop, a stone's throw from Chatsworth. The dam needed only to be 300 yards long. The snag was the Roman lead mines which, if they had penetrated the strata, would mean that the site would never hold water. I, accordingly, wrote a polite letter to Andrew Devonshire, with whom I had been brigaded in Italy, explaining the situation. I got a furious response, which perhaps was not unexpected. But I was surprised to get a letter from Roy Jenkins who was, I think, the Minister of Civil Aviation, warning me off and saying the Devonshires were powerful people whom one should never tangle with. In the event it was discovered that the lead mines went through the strata and so the site would never be suitable.

The next site we looked at was the Manifold Valley, where the River Manifold disappears underground for about four miles before re-appearing in time to join the Derwent. Most of the land belonged to the Harpur-Crewes but there was a fascinating block of small farms of up to 180 acres, which seemed to be owned by a long line of unmarried mothers going back to the 15th Century. They were very reluctant to give up their ancestral holdings. We were pondering the next move when we received a flat refusal from the National Water Resources

Board saying that, as it was just inside the Peak District National Park, we should look elsewhere, suggesting a pumped storage site at Carsington in the Derwent Valley. The Carsington reservoir was a chapter of disasters, ending in a major slip in the newly constructed dam. The slip bankrupted Hills, the consulting Civil Engineers, and the contractors only escaped bankruptcy through their third party insurance. By then I had just retired and I got a message from Don Reeve, the Chief Executive, to say he thought a flight over Carsington would be interesting. We met at Coventry Airport and flew up to see that the whole of the top end of the dam, which was of clay construction, had slipped outwards and downwards. Don Reeve said it was well known that if you continued to bund (pile it up on top of itself) wet clay without giving it time to dry it would slip.

But to return to the water pollution business, which was where my great interest lay. The Association of River Authorities had as its secretary David Kinnersley, who had come from the Coal Board where he had been head of Lord Ezra's private office. As a result, he had a great many friends and allies on the Labour benches which proved to be invaluable after 1964, when the Wilson government took over. We had a succession of ministers running Environment: Tony Crosland, Roy Jenkins, John Silkin, Peter Walker, Peter Shore, Denis Howell and Jeff Rooker. I got on well with all of them except John Silkin, whom I found very unfriendly and suspicious. The first two were only too anxious to move on to Economic Affairs and the Treasury, but, as I had known them both at Oxford, they were very ready to listen to what I had to say. Peter Shore I rated the best at the job, as he took much more trouble to listen to the pros and cons and always wanted a steer from me on anything I asked him about.

Denis Howell I had known in Birmingham politics. A football referee and a bass in St. Paul's Church choir, he was a man of many parts. When he was Minister of Sport the Jockey Club invited him down to Newmarket and I was then put in charge of taking him round and going to watch the early morning gallops, etc. On the second day of his three-day visit at the second October meeting, we got back to the Jockey Club Rooms for breakfast and there, sitting alone at the head of the table was Lord Sefton, the Senior Steward, reading the *Sporting Life*:

D.H. "Good morning, my Lord, I have had a marvellous trip watching Noel Murless's and Captain Boyd-Rochfort's strings."

Lord S. "I am so glad, have some breakfast," and the Sporting Life resumed its position in front of the Sefton visage.

D.H. "Isn't it extraordinary what politics can do for you? Here I am a kid out of the Birmingham slums and sleeping in Edward VII's bed and rolling all over Newmarket with the Jockey Club."

Lord S. The paper lowered. "If you believe that, you'll believe anything." And the paper shuttered back up there.

I ushered Denis up to the sales where he continued to enjoy himself and did not seem upset by the perfunctory Lord Sefton.

Denis was to do me a good turn shortly afterwards. I was rung up by the *Daily Telegraph* at four in the morning to say my integrity had been strongly attacked in a debate on the adjournment by Jeff Rooker, the M.P. for Erdington and an ex-A.E.U. official. The T.R.A. had decided that in order to clean up the River Cole it needed to dig a new channel along the railway at Blyth. Seeing the problem of conflicting interests I had told the Authority to negotiate direct with Winterton's, my chosen valuers, and I would accept whatever they came up with. Jeff Rooker had clearly had a tip off from a Birmingham member of the Authority, but luckily it was all in writing. Denis defended me strongly in the House and called for a report which, when completed, allowed him to rebut the accusation. Peter Liddell, the North West Chairman, was less lucky. A car number plate buff, he had bought number plates for himself and David Kinnersley, NWA1 and NWA2. This got into all the papers and Denis made an example of him in the House, so he was not re-appointed as Chairman.

Marshall Nixon was still worried about a further possible flood disaster so we commissioned a study that replicated the Norfolk storm of 1913, when 14.5 inches of rain fell in five hours, as if centred on Nottingham. We invited all the Clerks, Chief Executives, Chief Constables and the Head Fire Officers of the Midlands – in all about 90 – to the Hydraulic Research Station at Wallingford on a Sunday. We all sat round the model of Trent, Derwent, Soar and Tame and watched as the inches of rain fell in an area 50 miles around Nottingham. The assembled brass refused to believe it as Trent Bridge Cricket Ground and The Meadows disappeared under 22? feet of water. The fall-out as far as Leicester, Derby and Newark was enormous, and the flash flood did billions of pounds of damage. Whether any planning ever took place as a result I doubt, but I was pleased to get a letter from Mr. Vine, the Town Clerk of Nottingham, to say how his eyes had been opened to what could happen in a summer mega-thunderstorm.

Fred Lester and I featured in an article in the *Telegraph* about the river pollution problem. Hitherto, all England had continued to put its effluent through overloaded and outdated sewage works. The English water supply was as good as anywhere in the world, but our rivers were disgusting and some of them were so polluted that they were no more than open sewers. The effluent from Imperial Metal Industries at Witton was, at our request, put straight into the Tame as it was so much cleaner that what emerged from the various Birmingham sewage works. However, aided by the Council for the Preservation of Rural England, agitation was now under way about the next round of reservoirs, which were being planned for the West Country, the North East and the East Midlands. The Government thought that cleaning the rivers would allow water to be taken out from them for consumption several times over.

Jack Beddoe, the Deputy Secretary at the Environment Ministry, started to bring the message to the industry. I took an immediate liking to Jack, the son of an East Anglian carpenter, who had had a brilliant career as a historian at Peterhouse, Cambridge before becoming a civil servant. Politically he was well on the left, but was always well liked and admired by us on the right. I got him later as Chief Executive of Severn Trent Water, when Marshall Nixon died, and he did us proud for four years. Peter Liddell, David Kinnersley and I used every form of persuasion to get him to see that uniting all forms of water management – supply, purification, land drains, river management, fisheries and reservoirs – under one body was the answer. On the subject of boundaries we argued, and he accepted that the determining factor should be where the water was used. This meant that Severn Trent should also comprise the Wye, and that we would lose Lake Vyrnwy to the North West.

Mr. Wilson called a general election in 1970 and the Heath government was elected. Jack had prepared two schemes for a white paper: one nationalising all the private water companies like East Surrey and Bristol if Labour were to be returned, the other leaving them private if the Tories won. So the latter was unveiled as the white paper and Peter Walker, my conqueror at Worcester, was put in charge of it. However, the Tory Secretary of State for Wales (the M.P. for Hendon!) immediately objected to the size of the Welsh area and insisted on the Wye being in Wales. This drove a wagon through the proposals as it would mean that Birmingham would have no control over the Elan Valley reservoirs, whence came about 85 per cent of its water. I had two interviews with Beddoe and one with Walker, both of whom agreed, but said the Tory position on Wales was so weak they were sure that we would lose and so we did, defeated by water nationalism.

The Act setting out the water re-organisation was passed in 1973 and was designed to give single authorities responsibility for the complete water cycle from sky to sea. So the Water Authorities were set up, and I went to Whitehall to be invited to be chairman of Severn Trent. This was my first paid job in water. Severn Trent was charged with the responsibility for potable water supplies, pollution control, waste water disposal, land drainage and fisheries for the area stretching from the Humber to the Bristol Channel. I accepted and began to make plans for the new authority. I set up temporary headquarters in the Billiard Room at Merevale. The Trent River Authority provided me with two solicitors, Fred Lester, and several assistants. I asked Don Reeve, the Chief Engineer of the Tame and Rea, to come over and work for me on the engineering side. He arrived, breathing deep suspicion and reservation remembering our run-in over the pollution incident. It took about a year of almost daily interaction to overcome, but thereafter we became close allies and friends.

My plan was quite simple: the new system had to work from the outset; once it was working, new comprehensive operating divisions would be formed; once they were operating the system would be pared down to a lean, tight operation. The first block was Marshall Nixon who, being a river man, wanted to exclude the rivers operation and just have two river divisions, water supply and purification. This opposition magnified when Marshall was appointed as the Chief Executive. The favourite was Ian Drummond but he badly mishandled his interview, which he mistakenly thought was a coronation and not a selection. So Marshall was installed; and as Peter Walker had promised Birmingham that the new Severn Trent headquarters would be in Birmingham, we had to find premises there.

Our members from local government were mostly Labour and they formed most of the interviewing panels. I used Bill Jarvis, an up-and-coming Birmingham councillor, to chair many of the panels, only reserving for myself the Finance, Legal and Pollution chairs. I asked Jarvis and Len Lees from Mansfield to head up the others. All officials in the public sector tend to be Labour rather than Tory, so I urged them to be ruthless in looking for talent. The Labour Party, influenced by the relevant union, made various attempts to get good party men, rather than outstanding talent, appointed, but my two Labour warhorses mostly saw them off. However, the Labour caucus thought my private office needed a political commissar and they appointed Kitty Mackenzie to head it up. She was the N.A.L.G.O. queen at Tame and Rea. She came to see me and we hit it off from the outset. Loyal, hardworking and well informed, whenever there were industrial problems she invariably knew to whom it would be wise to talk.

One day we were interviewing for the Finance Director and I was accompanied by Councillor McLatchie of Coventry, who was from Rutherglen and knew the score. "One further question Mr. –. I understand ye come from Glasgow. Are you a Rangers or Celtic supporter?" "Oh, I'm Queen of The South." After he went out, McLatchie said, "I thought he was probably a Papist and you don't want one of them." Anyway we somehow collected a very good and effective team. We made a few mistakes but they were usually because of incompatibility rather than incompetence. As we had a team of twelve at Merevale, and all the other authorities had a Chairman and only one or two assistants, we were a long way ahead of the rest on vesting day.

Marshall and I set out to secure an H.Q. in Birmingham. As he had moved to Sheepy Magna, on the Warwickshire/Leicestershire border, and I lived at Coleshill, we thought the east side of Birmingham was preferable and we were able to secure Abelson House on the Birmingham-Coventry road. It had been built as a speculation by Mr. Abelson, my old friend and the owner of National Spirit (champion hurdler of the late 1940s), and was standing empty. We first got a lease and then purchased the freehold, and it remains to the present time as Severn Trent headquarters.

Sadly Marshall got viral pneumonia at a weekend and his wife, a literary *New Statesman* sort of person, sent him to bed with a bottle of whisky. On the Sunday he went into a coma from which he never emerged. He was greatly loved by all of us and, besides being a personal blow, he left us leaderless just as the sparks were beginning to fly. The Chief Officers and I had a series of meetings after the funeral and it was decided that Don Reeve and I would act as Chief Executive and begin the search for Marshall's successor immediately.

The political situation was very interesting. The whole concept was an initiative of the 1966-70 Wilson government. The Heath government enacted a slightly revised version and set up the new authorities, but they lost the election of 1974, and then the Wilson/Callaghan government found themselves administering a scheme they had first thought of. Roy Jenkins was bored by water, Tony Crosland was interested in macro-economics; and it was not until the arrival of Peter Shore and Denis Howell that we got a consistent administrative approach from the top.

The method of charging council tenants for water was changed. Previously council tenants had paid a combined rent, rates and water rate but now the water element was to be removed and charged separately. It was thought that tenants would get a reduction in their council charges as a result but this did not happen because it soon became clear that councils considered this money to be how they got extra funds for whatever project they wanted to do. So the early years of the new system were taken up with mitigating costs for tenants, and resulted in the water authorities being unable to threaten disconnection in the event of the non-payment of their bill.

The Welsh water situation was one to which I had to give a lot of thought. As a result of the Wye being removed from our catchment, and us having to pay a due to the Welsh water authority, we were unable to be master in our own house for the next stage of the Elan Valley water reservoir development. We needed to raise the output of the three reservoirs and use the Elan Valley aqueduct more intensively to solve Birmingham's and the Black Country's mounting problems. I pinched two of the greatest water resource experts from the Water Resource Board when it was wound up: Barry Rydz, a wild and imaginative Pole, and Graham Sharpe, who was staid and less far-seeing but very adept on the technical and political sides. They provided us with the intellectual expertise to take on all comers. The Welsh soon ran into a financial problem and we were able to do a deal which re-established our rights to decide what to do, but it cost us many millions, which we should not have needed to shell out. Similarly at Lake Vyrnwy, North West Water, who used it for Merseyside, was able to negotiate rather more easily.

Chapter 19

SEVERN TRENT

The arrival of a Labour administration at Westminster in 1974 caused local government to go into reverse, and the consequent Tory local take-over saw many of my trusty Labour old guard no longer available. I fought a battle or two with the new Tory group, led by a Loughborough University lecturer, Brian Scarlett, who was the greatest living expert on the theory of extraction of oil from sand. When the first flush of victory had diminished, he established a good but intensely wary relationship with the old guard.

I had early thought that, if my three point plan went through to stage three, we would need to have a very trusting relationship with the workforce. So, when Lord Nugent of Guildford, the first chairman of the National Water Council, called for volunteers to negotiate terms and conditions with the unions, I put up my hand. The three big unions in the workforce were G.M.B., N.U.P.E. and the T.G.W.U. in descending order. Negotiation was a charade which flowed in stately fashion from Ministry of Labour, through Public Sector Committee of the T.U.C., National Conference of the Union, Regional Secretary, Industry Official and down to branch level. Dicky Nugent was an urbane, articulate old Etonian, who had had minor office in several Tory administrations when M.P. for Guildford. He had a very good knack for saying the right thing to the right people and we had little strife. However, as an ex-Tory M.P., he was anathema to the back bench government M.Ps and he had to go. He was replaced by Sir Robert Marshall who was the Second Permanent Secretary of the Department of the Environment. I think Denis Howell thought he was of the true faith, but he emerged at a by-election as the local Liberal Party Chairman. Anyway, Marshall quickly established an inner negotiating elite consisting of himself, Eddie Newall of the G.M.B., and Mick Martin of the T.G.W.U., thereby infuriating those excluded.

The inner elite left, after any meeting, to go upstairs to the National Water Council chairman's office and the remainder of us sat and gossiped in the general office below. We usually did *The Times* crossword puzzle collectively and were pretty good at it (we had lots of practice). One evening while we were thus employed (actually at about three in the morning) the phone rang and, as nobody moved, I walked over and picked it up. The voice said, "Is that the water negotiations? It is Albert Booth here." I knew this to be the Secretary of State for Labour and the M.P. for Barrow. "I just want you to know the Cabinet has just agreed that you can have another 2.5%, so go ahead and ask for it." "Sir", I said. This is Grenadier-speak for whatever your context implies. I did not pass the message on as I was asked, and we eventually settled at where we were at.

The negotiations opened my eyes to many matters about the Trades Union movement. The tricky ones were always the moderates, who are always nervous of a left-wing dagger between the shoulder blades. The left wing, on the other hand, always have a target and, once achieved or unable to be achieved, lose interest and walk away until the next time.

Our chief negotiator was James Dickens who had been, until unseated, a Labour M.P. for a south of the Thames constituency. In spite of each being very nervous of the other to begin with, we struck up a good friendship. A left winger, born and bred in Glasgow, he had an even more fiery wife. They came to Blyth for the weekend and at Saturday breakfast in the Old Kitchen overlooking the lawns, beyond which a herd of cows were grazing, they asked:

J.D. "To whom do the cows belong? Are they the local peasants'?"

W.D. "No, they're mine. The tenants' land starts over the road."

J.D. "What is a tenant, on what terms do they operate?"

W.D. "Oh, we have a legal agreement and they pay rent twice a year at Lady Day and Michaelmas."

Mrs. J.D. "But you can eject them when you want?"

W.D. "Oh no, they're there for life."

J.D. "I never realised they had any security."

Anyway, Jimmy got along fine with Sir Robert and made many improvements to terms and conditions, which much needed doing.

At Severn Trent I thought that no local branch A.G.M. should go unattended if I was invited, and I went all over the region and Wales. My spiel was quite simple – we were all on trial to deliver a new economic and technically up-to-date service. They would be kept fully informed of our thinking as it evolved, and consulted if either we or they thought it necessary. We invariably got on to pay. It was during the mammoth pay increases when we had global inflation, and, while attempting to be fair, we had to think about the bill-payer too. The one thing that did come over was that they were delighted to have the boss there, who listened in silence, and who didn't argue till they had finished. In this way, I got to know all the local officials of all the unions and this was to pay off in spades later on.

When Jack Beddoe was appointed as our new Chief Executive he started immediately on phase two of the plan. The two rivers were to be divided territorially with, initially, eight divisions and with the possibility of reducing to four later. All functions would be handled from each divisional headquarters. Land drainage and rivers would go with the rest (Marshall no doubt turning in his grave). Jack did an immense job of getting all this through and running. But he was much less certain than I supposed on handling the administration of the consultation and, when his four-year contract was up, we thought he was not the man for stage three and that Don Reeve would do this part of the plan better. He was very upset at his departure and hardly ever spoke to me again.

At the time of the start-up, the received wisdom was that all the brainpower of the industry resided in water supply. They were pashas in a vast municipal sultanate. However, I very quickly came to the conclusion that this was not the case and the real brainpower and dynamism resided in water purification. In fact our two star managers were both chemists from the back offices of large sewage works. Fred

Lester, always the chemist, wanted to take all his staff off to Coventry sewage works, and I had a real struggle to get him to move into the top floor of Abelson House. Happily, he took to administration instead of analysis and proved a great success and the perfect ally in some of my struggles.

Our first Director of Finance came from the African operation of a large conglomerate. A nice man and technically proficient, he struggled somewhat in the arcane systems of public accounting and finance. When Don Reeve took over as Chief Executive, the Director of Finance tried to organise a putsch with some members of the Finance Committee. This was seen off and he had to go, but negotiating his pay-off with me and Don took quite a long time. On the basis of poacher turned gamekeeper we appointed John Pawley, who had previously been the union man for N.A.L.G.O. and was now the clerk at Tame, as our personnel man. He was also the long time lover of my Kitty Mackenzie, who was delighted to see him installed on the floor below, and between them I received many vital bits of authority gossip, which wouldn't otherwise have come my way.

I was anxious to continue the dynamics of radical change to our operating systems so I introduced a group, which became known as My Angry Young Men. The membership was floating, according to what I wanted to discuss, but Vic Cocker, who later became Chief Executive, and Graham Sharpe, and Ian Sinclair, the solicitor, were more or less regular members. People from about the third tier down seemed to welcome being invited in to my office for tea and later a gin and tonic to discuss problems, both actual and future.

Mrs. Thatcher had led the Conservatives to power in May 1979 following a winter when the country had been beset by strikes. Another election was due in 1983/4 and by this time the Thatcher government was not very popular nationally. The Trades Unions and Labour party thought that recreating what had become known as the "Winter of Discontent" might help them in the battle to oust Mrs. Thatcher. Word reached me from a civil servant in April 1982 that the T.U.C. Public Service Committee had discussed the prospect of a strike – and the strike generally thought to be the most important was water. Don

Reeve was also, at that time, the President of the Institute of Civil Engineers and he received information that a water strike was to be discussed at the national conference of the G.M.B.T. at Whitsun. I got him to write down the things that would cause the water service to collapse. We thought that Wales, Merseyside, the northeast and London would be the worst hit.

I had become friendly with the Holland brothers, who were the N.U.P.E. leaders for northeast London and East Anglia. During a London transport strike I had walked from Queen Anne's Gate to Kings Cross carrying one side of a Holland holdall and, as a result, communist and Tory were on good terms. "What do you think is the likelihood of a water strike over pay this winter?" I asked the younger Holland brother during the summer. He looked rather startled and said, "I suppose it all depends on how the employers handle things." When I told Don Reeve of this, he said he was actively pursuing things with the Chief Executives and that all were reviewing their problem areas. He added that all the old Metropolitan Water Board pumping stations were coal-fired, and he was trying to get them to introduce electricity as back-up.

As the senior chairman on both manual and staff panels, I had the pick of which I would chair. Len Hill, the Chairman of South West Water, was the next senior. However, Sir Robert Marshall rang me to say that as he was worried about my abrasive personality, he proposed to veto me at manual, and would I chair the staff panel instead? I protested, but couldn't make him change his mind, so there it was. The staff was usually a doddle as you offered what had been agreed. The manuals were the key to whether there would be a strike or not. Len Hill was a great friend, ex-Labour leader of Devonshire County Council and Plymouth. He had started as a fire-lighter in the engine shed at Plymouth and progressed to driving the Paddington express. There was little he didn't know about the unions and he had had his problems with them, particularly in Plymouth. I told him what had happened and said I was disappointed, but he said he would be glad to have me around.

Then the government announced the privatisation of the water industry and the abolition in due time of the National Water Council. Sir Robert was out of a job and my colleagues suggested that I should be the new Chairman of the N.W.C. until it was abolished. I was to take over in December. But the news on the Labour front was not good; various local Trades Union secretaries got in touch after their national conference, and confided that it looked like a strike was planned even before we started negotiations. Don Reeve reported that all the water authorities were doing what they could to prepare, and all we could do was to await the start of the negotiations.

Eddie Newall of the General and Municipal Workers' Union opened the negotiations with a very tough set of demands, which was punctuated by occasional hear hears from his side. Jimmy Dickens replied, and then Len Hill added that the water industry had been strike-free since the General Strike in 1926 and he hoped this would continue. This friendly intervention was met with a long and hostile silence.

Tom King, the Minister of State at the Department of the Environment, then asked us to go and see him. Sir Robert was in command but, as he was in his last month, most of the talking was done by Len, Jimmy and me. We learnt that the government intelligence was that, whatever we offered, there would be a strike for political, rather than industrial, reasons. Tom was of the mind to let us make a normal offer and, if there was a strike, it would have to be resolved in the usual way and would take time. He asked me what I thought of our ability to withstand a long strike. He didn't think stand-pipes would be tolerated for long. I pointed out the problem of the Thames pumping stations and he said, "Don't forget Parliament and the political party headquarters are all in London."

The strike started and all the supposed hot Labour areas did much better than we dared hope. The new Chairman of the North West Water Authority was George Mann, an ex-stoker in the Navy. He was also Chairman of the Manchester Fire Brigade Committee which had had some very large labour problems in the "winter of discontent". He knew what to do and did wonders with Manchester and Merseyside. The northeast coped well, as did Wales to my surprise, but there were problems in South Yorkshire.

Jimmy Dickens got Sir Robert Worcester to organise a Mori poll on the issue. It was fun trying to devise questions that looked innocent, but were really loaded. A quick poll showed that most people thought our offer was reasonable and therefore there should be no need for a strike. So we landed an early defensive blow and the papers were predictably mostly on our side, but with the *Guardian* and *Daily Mirror* moderately hostile. Television was aggressive but not hostile. Len went on television and gave a fairly straight bat to some awkward questions. I was asked to go on the Brian Walden Sunday lunchtime programme. I was worried that Brian, (an ex-Labour M.P.), was likely to leave a very aggressive and hostile question till last, and that this would lead into him saying whatever he had in mind to say. The interview progressed easily until five minutes from the end when the question came. "If the government asked you to give more and call off the strike would you do so?" I said the government was the government and that we would have to consider seriously whether to comply with their request. He was on me like a flash saying that clearly it was a government engineered and controlled strike and I was just a puppet. I hit back as best I could but he wanted his headlines and he got them.

I was running the Severn Trent end of the strike as well as the national one in London. My day was Severn Trent until tea time, then driven up to London in the Authority car by Ron Hopkins, my driver, to be at the National Water Council from 6-10.30 p.m. At 10.30 p.m., we went round to either the House of Commons or Tom King's flat in Hamilton Gardens, opposite Marsham Court. I then had to be back at the National Water Council by 6.45 a.m. as the calls came in: from Number 10 Downing Street – Mrs. Thatcher would be on the phone about once a week, otherwise a private secretary would telephone – and from Len Murray, the T.U.C. Secretary, personally on the phone at about 7.15 a.m. Soon after that, Gerald Kaufman, the Labour industrial Shadow Minister, would come round. He was consistently and confusingly hostile and I learnt to have a completely empty desk for his visit as he could read upside down. When I had seen the overnight reports at about 8.30 a.m., Ron then drove me back to Abelson House where I arrived soon after 10 a.m. This was a seven-day-a-week schedule.

After about fourteen days Pat Lowry, the head of the Government Conciliation Board, decided to play a part. At our first meeting he outraged Len and Jimmy by his apparent partiality towards the union side, but after several meetings it became clear that anything else would have caused the union to walk out. After 29 days Mrs. Thatcher decided that enough was enough, though on the whole the authorities were coping very well. But Thames and Yorkshire were beginning to run into difficulties. Thames, needless to say, had not bothered, or been able, to electrify the pumping stations so on three nights, led by Hugh Fish, the Chief Executive of Thames Water, we went down to Hampton and Twickenham and humped sacks of coal and coke up a gang-plank from a barge into the pump houses. Fun to do occasionally but not regularly. The hottest union areas decided that a great show of indignation once a day allowed more routine operations to go on in an underhand disguised manner. The unions were now terrified of what the nation would think if they stopped peoples' supplies and they wanted "out" too.

Every night at A.C.A.S. we were greeted by rent-a-crowd of East End water workers led by the Holland brothers. Their anger was usually directed at their own reps rather than us. But we got a good boo as we arrived at the front desk in St. James's Square. On the Sunday evening, presumably because the union had thought it was settlement night, the crowd was about three times bigger and the T.V. cameras were much in evidence. Negotiations were re-started at about 10.30 p.m. and Eddie Newall said he wanted to talk to Jimmy alone so they disappeared into a side room, and Pat Lowry, after giving the rest of us stiff whisky and sodas, popped in after them. Len and I sat on a sofa with Ron Keating of the N.U.P.E. and Mick Martin of the T.G.W.U., and talked about previous strikes they had handled. All through the strike the relations between both sides remained very friendly because we all knew what a charade it was. At about midnight both sides, with a fresh whisky, withdrew into their separate rooms. Jimmy then outlined in detail the proposed settlement. It amounted roughly to £175 per annum for the average manual worker. As the strike had lasted 35 days and the average worker had lost about £1,600, it would take about nine years to win back that money, but of course there would have been annual wage increases along the line. At about 2.15 a.m. the union announced they were ready to meet us in a "Plenary Session". More whisky for all and then Len read out "our final offer", which Eddie then accepted on their behalf.

Mick said to us, "You remain behind and have a final whisky while we tell the boys about the great victory we have won for them!!" We had about two more whiskies and Len had a right go at Pat Lowry for his partiality. Which Pat laughed off while refilling the drinks. At 3.30 a.m. we went down into the hall and saw the union headmen having a rotten time of it, with spittle dripping from all their faces. "Rent-a-crowd", who could do elementary maths as well as the next man, had vented their ire. It had been 35 very anxious days but both sides had learnt a great deal – particularly us – about which processes must be automated and computer-controlled, and which were the crux points for continued operation. The unions had learnt once more that strikes for politics, and not for money, don't carry the Indian signals for success.

One of the more amusing events during the water strike was my dinner for the Trade Unions at Scott's Restaurant in Mount Street. I was the head of the Training Committee of the National Water Council and when the government launched a programme to encourage training I was keen to participate, as I wanted to get rid of the distinction between manual and white-collar workers. I had written to all the Unions in July to say I would host a dinner with all the Unions' top brass, in an attempt to get manual workers to upgrade into management. Accordingly, I set a date in December and hired the private room at Scott's for a dinner. The room held about 18 at a pinch, and Len Hill and I and Jimmy Dickens would host the dinner. I picked the menu: Crab Claws, Chateaubriand steaks and Soufflé Grande Marnier with adequate supplies of liquor. As the strike was starting I received a call from Mick Martin to say he knew we had a dinner planned and that he couldn't see why it should be cancelled, as life would go on when the strike was over. So I notified Scott's that we were proceeding.

The guests all came in taxis and, with faces concealed by mufflers, scuttled into the restaurant. I had laid on Sidecar cocktails before dinner and they were consumed at a rate only equalled by my 80th birthday party nearly twenty years later. Dinner was a lively affair and second helpings were demanded of the Chateaubriand and the soufflé. The New Zealander, Ross, who was head of the agricultural section of the T.G.W.U., which represented rivers and land drainage operations, was particularly keen on the soufflé. As a result, after schooners of cognac, we did not end till 2.30 a.m. when agreement was easily reached on the points in Jimmy Dickens's spiel and training the manual workers for management. But, before the guests would leave, Len and I were despatched into Mount Street to make sure that the paparazzi were not there to photograph their departure.

With the strikes behind us, I got down to running the National Water Council. All of the employees would be redundant with the winding up of the Council on privatisation, but there would need to be a London body to back up and lobby for successor organisations. Most of them knew what they wanted to do. Peter Stott, the head man, got relocated as the Professor of Civil Engineering at Kings College, London; and I was very keen to land David Walker, the second man, for Severn Trent. He had several offers so I was pleased when he opted to come and subsequently he had a distinguished career as a Manager for Severn Trent both at Shrewsbury and at Tame House in Birmingham. The National Water Council office very soon became a very dreary place except when there were meetings with the Trade Unions. I had told the Department of the Environment that, after eleven years, I did not want to continue as Chairman of Severn Trent. They took a very long time to find my successor, but eventually a new batch of members at Severn Trent included John Bellak, the Managing Director of Doulton, the porcelain firm from Stoke-on-Trent, and at the next meeting I noticed him taking notes assiduously. Don Reeve caught my eye as we both saw it at the same time, so it was no surprise when he was appointed as the next Chairman. I was given a farewell lunch by the Authority and I sailed off into the sunset.

Chapter 20

WARWICKSHIRE COUNCIL

I must now backtrack a little, to the Swinging Sixties. I was spending quite a lot of time in London, footloose and fancy free, and returning to Blyth at the weekends. I took the children to see the Beatles twice (their passion, not mine) and in 1964 I threw a party at Annabel's. Belinda's family were wonderful with the children and kept an eye on me as well. But it was Nanny who looked after the children and the house, day-to-day.

I had begun to see a lot more of sister-in-law Harriot's flatmate, Cylla Mount. I thought that she would be a marvellous successor to Belinda, were I lucky enough to land her. My children seemed to like her and, in 1967, when I asked her to marry me in the kitchen at Blyth, she was so surprised she sat on the hotplate – which had the opposite effect to inflaming her ardour. But she said yes and it was the start of our happy 40 and more years together.

After my election to Warwickshire County Council in 1964, we Conservatives struggled to run it with lots of Independents and a very strong and well-organised Labour group. As a result, in the 1968 election, we decided to run a Conservative candidate late in every seat. We gained a large majority and were clearly going to control the council. I was elected as chairman of the group and asked to organise the takeover. So Neville Spencer, Deputy Chairman of the conservative group, and I went along to see Sir Edgar Stephens, the clerk, to tell him that we wanted to change the whole way the Council operated. Previously the clerk had formed the committees but now we intended to present a list of members of all the committees and their chairmen. We proposed to vote this through at the annual meeting. Sir Edgar accepted it as a sign of the times but, as he said goodbye to us, he said, "I fear your dear father will be turning in his grave."

I put myself in charge of the overall Policy Committee and Neville in charge of the Finance Committee. I had a study weekend with all the chief officers and told them that I wanted the budget to be all-embracing, and that I would keep control of expenditure. I would only depart from this policy to help out if there were new and unpredicted expenditures. I emphasised that I would expect, in general, the budget to be accepted as final. The only chief officer who didn't want to work with us was Mr. Chenevix-Trench, the Director of Education, and brother of the headmaster of Eton. The leader of the Labour group was Bill Wilson, the M.P. for Coventry South West, whom I found to be sensible and pragmatic. I was sad to lose the two existing Labour chairmen of committees, but it was inevitable.

My first problem was getting all my team of forty odd Tories to vote together. Some of the old independent-minded Tory ladies were not used to being told how to vote and they thought, as females, they had all the answers in education and social services. In addition, the housewives all wanted to leave by 4 p.m., in order to get home and cook the evening meal for their menfolk. As a result we tended to lose votes if the meeting continued after that. The Labour group cottoned on to this and realised that the Education Committee, with the help of the teachers' representatives, could be swung their way.

I had agreed with the Director of Education that the education budget be contained, and not to make any dummy cuts only to reinstate them as soon as the budget meeting was over. Imagine my fury at finding that, after 5 p.m., he had instigated the passing of amendments in the Committee to nullify the overall control of education expenditure. Next day I went down to Shire Hall and asked him to come and see me. I asked him why he had gone back on our agreement. He had the cheek to say that he hadn't really agreed with what I wanted, and saw an opportunity of "putting things right." I lost my temper and gave him the sort of dressing down I used to give recalcitrant subalterns in the War. I told him I would not trust him again, that I would ensure the amendments were nullified at the next Council meeting, and that all Education Committee meetings would end if the controlling party lost its majority. The next day I heard he had had a fatal heart attack while mowing his lawn. I hoped it was not my rocket that caused it, but a more financially aware director was an urgent necessity. I then had a very difficult meeting with the ladies to persuade them they must stay until the business was put to bed.

The arrival, in 1964, of Dick Crossman as Environment Minister provided us all with plenty to discuss and to do. He had singled out Warwickshire for solving Birmingham's slum clearance problems. After a typically aggressive speech from the Minister, who berated us for objecting to Birmingham's plan, we decided that we must co-operate as far as we were able. So Alderman Harry Watton, the Birmingham Labour leader, was invited to lunch and a meeting afterwards. He was a true old-Labour patriarch who combined extreme toughness with a good dollop of class. After a jolly good lunch in the Judge's Lodgings, we all adjourned upstairs to one of the many grand rooms. Harry Watton took a chair at the middle of the table facing me. All the army of Birmingham officials sat in a half circle behind him, briefcases on their laps. I said, "Oh, Alderman Watton I hope there's room at the table for your officials," to which the Alderman replied, "Young man, I have come to talk to thee. They (with a wave of the hand) have come to advise me."

In spite of this daunting opening, we got on very well with what had to be done. I pointed out that the menfolk from the new town of Chelmsley Wood (which was set to contain 64,000 people) would presumably have to seek employment back in Birmingham. I questioned whether the Birmingham people had considered the pressure on the existing roads into Birmingham. Harry Watton said to me, "What do you suggest?" Without asking for support from my side, I said that at least a new dual carriageway, out of Chelmsley Wood and into the Birmingham hinterland, was essential. So the Collector Road was born. As constructed it was not ideal, but once Birmingham saw how badly it was needed, they attempted to put this right with an extension into central Birmingham past the old Jaguar factory. The new town was built on 1750 acres of land, mostly owned by Simon Wingfield Digby.

It had two shopping centres and no identity at all. The houses could only be let to people on income support as the economic rents were so high. But as the people were all, in theory, from the outdated estates of Ladywood and Saltley, their economic capacity was low, so there was some sort of logic to this. However, Chelmsley Wood was incorporated into Solihull in the boundary changes of 1974 and it seems to be surviving as a suburb rather better than its neighbours at Castle Vale, who remained with Birmingham.

I next tried to persuade the Labour party that, in the north of the county, the comprehensive system was not working for the able children. The choice at sixth form was very limited and I felt something else was needed to encourage able children to do more varied subjects. So I took Bill Wilson, the Labour group leader, out to lunch and we had a very friendly and informative discussion. Bill was a solicitor who had worked his way up the hard way, starting as an office boy. I outlined my worries and Bill said, "I quite agree but what you want to do is completely impractical, as it flies in the face of accepted Labour dogma." By 11-plus the figures were already illuminating: 9 per cent passes in the north of the county compared with 54 per cent in Solihull and 47 per cent in Sutton Coldfield. But he did point out that, "With your majority you'll get it through in spite of our 'furious opposition'." So the Sixth Form College in Nuneaton was born and later, when Labour controlled the Council, I was taken round by a Labour friend who claimed all the credit for it!

Bill and I used to sit on the sofa outside the Council Chamber and bargain our way through the agenda. He had a political nose and knew exactly how to process the business. He wanted a row at every Council meeting for the benefit of the local newspaper and, once that had been satisfactorily concluded, after anything up to three hours, we usually got through the rest of the agenda quite neatly. The Liberals were never predictable – any deal would be immediately scrubbed if they saw the possibility of party advantage. Luckily, the numbers meant that they could be contained. But, after 1972, they held the balance of power and the difficulties of dealing with the business became much more pronounced.

The next major problem for the Conservatives was the proposed boundary changes. They had been designed by Baroness Sharpe, the formidable Permanent Secretary of the Department of the Environment, for the Labour government. And now Peter Walker, the new Department of the Environment supremo for the Tories, was unwise enough to accept them as they stood. This meant that the Birmingham boundaries were moved a long way towards Coleshill. We lost Castle Bromwich to Solihull, which was a strong pro-Tory village. Warwickshire lost Solihull as a County Borough, and Sutton Coldfield entered into Birmingham. I went to Tory West Midlands' H.Q. to see the chief agent and received no support from him. He harboured the belief that, with Sutton Coldfield, Birmingham would invariably be Tory. This has been proved since to have been disastrously wrong. I also got myself an interview with Peter Walker but did not succeed in persuading him either. And I found myself in Pseuds Corner in *Private Eye*, to the great amusement of my children, stating that "Warwickshire without Sutton Coldfield is like an apple without cheese (or like a kiss without a squeeze)."

The next problem was Coventry, which had gone Tory just before the national election in 1970. Under the Act Coventry could only keep the educational authority if it opted to join West Midlands rather than remain with Warwickshire, and so we lost Coventry. Hence the extraordinary new shape of Warwickshire, and the shrinking of our population from over a million down to just under half a million. From being the eleventh largest county in terms of population, Warwickshire now became the fourth smallest. The Tory Bill became law and Warwickshire had to get its act together. Being such a small county meant that all our officials were either old men, who had not made it elsewhere, or young thrusters, who came to make a name for themselves and then move rapidly on to a larger authority. Warwickshire's team thinned rapidly, mostly because of enticements, and it was not long before we had a new Chief Executive and new Directors of Finance and Education. The new boundaries meant that the balance of power had changed and it was not long before the Conservatives, although the largest party, were outnumbered by a Lib-Lab alliance. Bill Wilson, the

Labour leader, gave up but soldiered on as an M.P. but there was a succession of Lib-Lab leaders. My duties at Severn Trent were becoming more demanding so I planned my departure. Michael Hammond, my successor, was, I think, pleased to be stepping up and my resignation took most people by surprise.

My time in local government was always interesting, and demanding when in the chair of a committee. As the leader of the majority party I was Prime Minister, Chancellor of the Exchequer, Leader of the House and Chief Whip all rolled into one, which suited a power-mad leader like me! Involving one's colleagues at an early date in one's ideas and plans got them on board from the start. Once the officials realised that the Tories were set on changing the whole system they co-operated whole-heartedly, with the possible exception of the Education Department. The Labour government, as usual, tried to rig the grant system in favour of their own locally-controlled authorities, but our new system of financial control was usually able to cope. Social Services was the exception but, at that time, the ageing population trends had not begun to have a significant impact on the old folks' home system.

Chapter 21

AIR RACES

Ilove driving and I love driving fast. I sped up and down to London in my 6.8 litre Jensen beating my own record many times just as the motorways were being built when, to begin with, there were no speed limits. But in 1964 I became worried that my motoring might be curtailed by the system of points and totting-up introduced by Barbara Castle (Labour Minister of Transport in Harold Wilson's government). I thought, entirely incorrectly, that learning to fly ought to be a useful hedge. So, after asking around for helpful advice, I set out for the Warwickshire Aero Club at Elmdon, the Birmingham Municipal Airport. It was shut. I was led to the Midland Air Taxis on the service road where I was introduced to the chief pilot of their Piper Aztec operation, Mike Holloway, an ex-R.A.F. Squadron Leader instructor. I had my first lesson there and then, in a Cessna 150, and was duly hooked, so I signed up with them. I went solo after 13 hours and then my qualifying cross-country flight was from Birmingham to Gloucester and on to Bristol. As both the airports were a mile or two off the Bristol Channel this was not a very difficult feat of navigation. I duly got my Private Pilot's Licence after 32 hours, and was set on my piloting career.

With the arrogance of the novice, one day I set off with my daughter Charlotte, aged 11, to fly anti-clockwise around the Birmingham conurbation. When we got to Wolverhampton, the clouds came in from Wales and I was faced with some instrument flying. Luckily the clouds became thinner and I was able to regain "straight and level" every five minutes or so. But, by now, Charlotte's nerve had gone. She collapsed sobbing in her seat and got her legs entangled with the co-pilot's rudder, which only made matters worse. It cleared when we got to Coventry, and our return to Elmdon was largely trouble-free, but it made me realise that basic instrument flying was a must, and I enrolled for a further course on a simulator. Confidence in this art only came after much trial and many errors, when I had had my instrument rating for about 50 hours.

The more I flew, the more I wanted to fly. Even so, it was not until I had married Cylla that I took the next step and bought my own plane. We had hired a plane to go to Newmarket and, on the return trip, I had great trouble in controlling it. On landing we asked the hirer to have a look, and he found that the elevation control cable had slipped off the pulley, and I had therefore been pulling with no leverage. Cylla said she would never fly with me again in a hired aircraft. She also said that either she learnt to fly or that I had to give it up. So she enrolled with Mike Holloway and it wasn't long before she went solo, appearing in the *Birmingham Mail* taking off "to beat those traffic jams."

I answered an advert in *Private Pilot* and the sales manager came to see me, offering me first refusal on a Cessna 182, which was on its way from America. I put myself in the hands of Mike Holloway who ordered a complete set of Narco avionics for it and a transponder for giving your position to air traffic radar. It would be a state of the art small single-engine aeroplane, with four seats and a range of about 800 miles. The plane arrived 10-12 days late, by which time we had gone fishing on the Spey and the sales manager, who was building hours like everyone else in General Aviation, immediately volunteered to fly it up to Lossiemouth and collect us from there. The sales manager, a friendly Indian, had prepared the return route using radio beacons all the way. We had to deviate as far as Talar but, after that, all the way under the airways. The Indian's beguiling manner with Prestwick had us in contact all the way south, and we arrived home in Birmingham at about 7.30 p.m. in the twilight.

The next morning I rang Mike Holloway and asked for a training flight. After some discussion we opted for St. Malo. He said it would give me four hours of precision flying, and off we went. It was interesting sitting in the pilot's seat watching Mike working us down over

Reading, Southampton and Jersey, with interludes with French air traffic control at Cherbourg. He was in his most didactic R.A.F. instructor mode. He kept saying, "If you are not going to kill yourself, you must attain a much more precise method of flying, dealing with drift, and being quicker and more clued-up on the radio." At St. Malo we had a very good lunch in a bistro outside the airport, and then filed our flight plan for home. We each had had a Calvados after lunch but, at Flight Level 100 (10,000 feet) I felt so ill that I never broke the eight hour bottle-to-throttle rule again. I signed up for some instrument flying training under a hood and set out to polish my performance.

All was going swimmingly when suddenly the Indian rang to say he had a Twin-engine Beechcraft for sale and would take the Cessna in part exchange. Cylla was ecstatic – she always imagined the worst whenever we crossed the coast – and thought two engines just the ticket. I contacted Mike who said, "Go ahead but it will cost you a lot more!" Neither of us had a twin rating so I rang up the Oxford Air Training School and asked for details. They offered me a trial lesson with Wing Commander Duff-Mitchell A.F.C. He had got this medal when flying a Beaufighter, which lost an engine over the North Sea. He succeeded (almost the only pilot so to do) in landing it back at base after a turning circle with a radius of about 100 miles to get back on reverse track. The Wing Commander kindly came up to Birmingham and, in four days' solid flying, I mastered single engine and engine out procedures and theory. Lo and behold I had the twin rating. I could now fly it to Oxford and continue training.

I had become a director of The Phoenix Assurance Company in 1969. The junior directors sat at the bottom ends of the long elliptical boardroom table and there I found myself next to Hugh Astor, whom I had known slightly at Eton. He was a pilot of both aeroplanes and helicopters and one day he produced some papers about a potential air race from London to Sydney to celebrate 200 years of the Commonwealth of Australia. Having probably had a gin and tonic before lunch, I immediately accepted to go with him. He had already done some research into the handicapping and had decided to ask Desmond Norman, of Britten-Norman, to supply a plane. He not only supplied a brand-new Twin Islander but also put us in touch with someone who would buy it in Australia, when we got there. The only worry was that neither Hugh nor I had the necessary instrument rating (involving so many hours under instruments and so many hours under the hood with an instructor on a simulator) and having that, or an R.A.F. green card, was an essential requirement to compete. So immediately we got in touch, via the Oxford Air Training School, with Flight Lieutenant Jankowicz, who had just left the R.A.F. and had both – his last job had been testing repaired R.A.F. planes at St. Athans in Wales. We put him on the payroll to become the third member of the team for the race and, with the help of Pip Hicks, the Britton-Norman sales manager for Islanders, started to convert the plane (which was designed for short heavily-laden cross-water flying to island aerodromes) to be able to do 1000+ mile hops. The seats came out and tanks for extra fuel went in. Whoever was not either pilot or co-pilot would have a rubber mattress and a sleeping bag on top of the tanks.

There was no hope of either Hugh or me getting the necessary instrument ratings in time, but we both started to train frantically at Oxford on the instruments and in the air. This was to prove crucial in the race, as events turned out. The aeroplane was delivered to Biggin Hill for the fuel alterations. I insisted that we did a fuel test in the air to evaluate its capabilities so, with Pip Hicks in the pilot's seat, we took off from Biggin Hill and went northwards up the east coast, around the Shetlands, and returned back up the Channel. Hugh showed us a page in the aircraft manual which stated that, by turning the plane on its side and having maximum rudder trim, we could literally run each tank on one side dry and then repeat the process on the other side. This was to save our lives in the race. We tried it out in order to know what to do and found that we could do about 1500 nautical miles at a filling. At 128 knots that was quite a lengthy flight. Back at Biggin Hill the final preparations were made. We bought some women's silk underwear – vests and tights – to keep us warm on the trip and Cylla went shopping at Fortnum's for some delicacies to eat en route. Unfortunately, they rolled off the platform behind a fuel tank and we only got our hands on them at Adelaide.

The race was due to start from Gatwick. Each plane was given a start time but, as might be expected, the weather was vile and the start was postponed for 24 hours. Janky had done the flight planning on his own and we had a seminar (such was the rush) during the postponement to discuss the route we would take. In the end we chose Gatwick to Athens (going over Mont Blanc to Italy and then round Corinth); Athens to Abadan (as already the Iraqis were being difficult over Basra); Abadan to Karachi. Then, by special dispensation, we were to go direct from Karachi to Calcutta; Calcutta to Singapore; Singapore to Bali; Bali to Darwin; Darwin to Alice Springs; Alice Springs to Adelaide and finally, Adelaide to Sydney. The first leg would be flown by Janky, with Hugh as co-pilot. The second leg by me, with Janky as co-pilot, and then the Basra-to-Karachi leg by Hugh, with me as co-pilot.

I got into the sleeping bag before take off but, when the engine spooled up for take-off, I rolled off the Li-lo and it slipped between the tanks and the wall of the plane so I had a very uncomfy flight. Nevertheless, I went to sleep and woke up, between Zurich and Mont Blanc, to see the main wheels covered in a ball of ice and ice everywhere. I decided there was nothing I could do and went to sleep again. The flight over Mont Blanc, designed to be twenty minutes at 18,000 feet had, in fact, lasted fifty because of the head winds. We came down from 18,000 feet at Florence and flew the rest of the leg at 9,000 feet. For Hugh and Janky, who were both heavy smokers, it was half an hour too long at high altitude. I, as the non-smoker, survived the flight much better. It is interesting to note that the flight behind us iced up completely, went down killing its crew, and was only discovered in the spring when the snow melted.

We forced Janky to do the flight planning for the next leg. Hugh and I checked the oil, topped it up and rubbed the windscreen clear of the remaining ice. However, Janky was in such a bad way he had to be put to bed and was hors de combat until half way to Calcutta. Hugh was not much better, but bravely slumped in the co-pilot's seat and tuned the radio. We took off in the late evening and flew on to Rhodes, Cyprus and Beirut. As the dawn broke we were flying over a remarkably frosty desert near Damascus, and on to Baghdad. We had a good steer from a B.O.A.C. flight and we tuned into the Baghdad beacon until it suddenly went off. We woke Janky – he said stick to the flight plan timings and then fly east for Basra after passing my estimated time of arrival over Baghdad. So, at watch time, we turned S.S.E. I had a look at the fuel, which was getting very low. I did some calculations and we decided to use both engines on the port tanks, empty them, and then switch over to starboard. We staggered along at a bank of about 15 degrees, and the tanks emptied. The engines stuttered and I switched over to the other side. After what seemed an age they started again. When we got to Basra, we turned for Abadan and the plane ran out of fuel as we taxied to Abadan's B.O.A.C. office. The B.O.A.C. manager, having heard of the postponement, had taken his girlfriend for a picnic on the beach. The second-in-command, a girl, finally went out to find him. Getting him back, and getting fuelled up took 4 hours 40 minutes instead of the 45 minutes which had been planned. The delay didn't cost us the race, but it prevented us being the overall second.

Janky was still hors de combat so we did the weather and filed the flight plan, and had to keep putting the departure time back. We finally took off with me at the controls and Hugh as co-pilot, with Janky still on the platform on top of the tanks. We had a marvellous day-time flight down the Gulf, and a night-time flight along the shores of Waziristan to Karachi. It was my first night-time landing in the Islander but I managed it all right. We made up some time and were off for Calcutta very quickly. India and Pakistan had closed their frontiers, so we awakened Janky and he replaced Hugh to watch the radio and deal with the very excited Pakistani and Indian air-traffic controllers. Dawn broke as we approached central India and we could see the flames from a series of blast furnaces. When we made Calcutta in the heat Hugh, who had developed the squitters, shot past two men looking like Bengal Lancers at the door of the Air Traffic Control. He re-appeared to take the controls with Janky, with me back on the platform. I was so tired that I slept all the way to Singapore and awoke to see Janky getting out the Jepperson navigation manuals for our landing. Changi Airport was using both runways in alternate directions depending on whether you arrived as an odd or an even number at the arrival beacon

(V.O.R.) We put on speed to ensure that we were an odd number, landed and refuelled. Hugh and Janky went off to do the paper-work. Suddenly I was violently attacked from behind. My assailant was the well-known lady aviator, Sheila Scott. She was flying alone in a Piper Comanche, and was being looked after by the Royal Navy as she had been a Wren during the War. She had a very good auto-pilot, but had been forced as an even number to re-think her approach procedure to the reverse runway. The Captain R.N. and the Wren commander, who were the welcoming party, dragged her off me and put her to bed to recover. Next stop, Bali. We went the wrong way round the island and lost another 45 minutes, but we made a quick get away and flew off for Darwin.

After an hour we flew through the worst thunderstorm I have ever been in. I was frankly terrified but luckily Janky, with his great experience, was back in the pilot's seat. At one point he said to me, "Kindly remove your hands from the controls and leave it to me." The storm was still continuing as we approached Darwin but Janky made an immaculate landing in severe downdraughts – rather him than me. We were through the Darwin immigration and customs and away for Alice Springs as dawn seemingly ended the thunderstorm, about 300 miles on our way across the Northern Territory. When we got to Alice we were met by the Phoenix manager there, which was not what we wanted as we were tired and in a hurry. Out of Alice I had an altercation with Air Traffic Control. He was very rude and demanded our immediate return to face an instant fine. However, Hugh, from the rear platform, turned on all the charm and mollified him somewhat.

Next step was Adelaide where the whole race was halted in order to have a mass arrival and descent into Sydney. But, as it turned out, the weather was so bad that we were halted at Griffiths on the frontiers of New South Wales and Victoria for four days. Charlie Shelburne, Hugh's nephew and also in the race flying a single-engine Bonanza, organised a night out with the Griffiths High School old girls' graduation class of 1967. They were a bunch of extremely pretty and gung ho girls who took us all skinny dipping in an immense irrigation canal at dawn. I still have my sorority pin to prove my honorary membership.

When Charlie and his Uncle Hugh and I were running on champagne mid-morning with other race-entrants on the grass, we were summoned to a press conference held because of weather conditions. There would be a mass departure at 2.30 p.m. to ensure our arrival en masse in Sydney. It was a racing flight – all 81 competitors took off at one-minute intervals and we were in and out of scudding clouds all the way. I saw two large reservoirs in the Blue Ridge Mountains but then it was back into cloud. We landed at Sydney and were besieged by a crowd of teenagers for autographs – they departed in disgust when my trousers, relieved of pressure by several days of foodless flight, descended in a swish to my ankles.

In 1971 another air race loomed up: from London to Vancouver for the Vancouver bi-centenary celebrations. This time Hugh acquired a Britten-Norman Trislander from Desmond Norman to fly. It had three engines, the third being on the rudder a long way above the ground. We acquired, as a co-pilot, a Hurricane veteran from the desert. He was a real old curmudgeon but as good a pilot as I have flown with. As always, getting the aeroplane ready for the race was a rush. We did the logistics and left the race-planning to him. The take-off point was the R.A.F. base at Abingdon and, in order to accommodate the single-engine planes, several stops had to be made before Quebec, our first scheduled stop in Canada. We opted for Reykjavik to Narssarssuaq in Greenland, then Goose Bay in Labrador with one extra stop in Nova Scotia. Cylla and Emi-Lou Astor were to fly out to Vancouver to join us there. The stops after Quebec were all scheduled and were concluded with an overnight stay. This had the effect of reducing the race to a mere rally and the Canadian Ministry of Transport, terrified of an accident, grounded the whole race at the least sign of bad weather.

The weather on the flight was awful. The visibility at Keflavik in Iceland was down to about 300 yards with a cloud base of about 150 feet. I was glad it was the Hurricane Jock who had to make the landing. Nevertheless I considered it just my luck that I was perched on a ladder 18 feet up, adding oil to a new engine that was losing plenty, and trying to balance in a 40 mph wind. We were off again after about 25 minutes and it was a problem at various levels to 7000 feet trying to avoid icing up. Once again the Hurricane Jock came up trumps. I was flying the aeroplane with my new instrument rating and he was dozing beside me. Every time I changed course as the magnetic variation altered he woke up and, obviously not trusting me, checked my calculations and then dozed off again. But, as we approached the three-fjord entrance to Narsaq, he woke up and, as I made the choice, he said, "If you've got it wrong, you'll only get out with a loop and a roll," so I spent a very uneasy 10 minutes until we picked up the aerodrome beacons. The runway was sharp up hill, away from the water, and our landing roll only about 150 yards. The Hurricane Jock said, "I'll order breakfast and you check the engine oil, fill up and come and join me." Hugh went to get the weather and, once more, I climbed up the ladder and filled the three engines with lots of oil – incidentally the last for the rest of the trip, as they had apparently bedded in the pistons, etc. by then.

Anyway, I went into the hotel, which was a haunt of Danish fishermen over for the Atlantic char. We had an enormous Danish breakfast of scrambled eggs, ham and cheese. Hugh informed us that the weather was continuing cloudy all the way to Quebec. Then we were back on board and charging down the incline towards the icy water. We lifted off right at the end of the runway and down the fjord towards the Atlantic. As we got out of the mountains we heard a Mayday call. A single-engine plane was running out of fuel and announced that it was ditching in the Atlantic, about 100 nautical miles to the south. The Hurricane Jock said firmly, "I hate that there is nothing we can do – the survival time will be about five minutes." In the event the plane, which was of wood construction, floated long enough for a Danish search and rescue helicopter to haul them off the wing. The helicopter subsequently went back and hauled the entire plane out of the water and carried it to Narsaq, where I think it remains to this day, as it was too expensive to return it to the U.K.

We flew, with the magnetic variation altering about every ten minutes, to Goose Bay, Labrador when, in a blinding snow storm, I climbed my ladder once more and nearly got blown away. The rest of the flight was busy with continued grounding, due to thunderstorms. The only noteworthy thing was a herd of deer on the prairie near

Regina being able to run faster than our three-engine plane because of a strong headwind. On the final leg we passed Mount Baker in a thunderstorm, and landed at Vancouver. Cylla and Emi-Lou joined us and we went on some garden visits on Vancouver Island – a famous horticultural site because of its climate.

Hugh had sold the Trislander to an island hopper taxi company in Fort Lauderdale in Florida so, after a few days, we headed south for San Francisco. Hugh had an invitation to Astoria, an ex-whaling station north of San Francisco, founded by the first Astor plutocrat. They were celebrating its centenary so it was left to the Hurricane Jock and me to fly on from San Francisco to Fort Lauderdale, with one stop at Denver. When I was on the radio to a St. Louis air traffic controller he said, "Just say it again, I simply love your old world accent". After handing over the plane, we flew back via Miami.

I had got my top instrument rating the year before after two failures, which enabled me to fly on instruments in controlled airspace at major airports. The first examiner was an ex-R.A.F. Group Captain with a D.S.O. After we got into the plane I ventured a joke and he said, "Mr. Dugdale, I am here to assess your capability as a pilot, not as a comedian." The temperature in the cockpit dropped about 15 degrees and he abandoned the test as I was well off course on the approach to Birmingham. I failed the second time with Wing Commander Silk who was a different character and very pleasant. The third test was again with the Wing Commander and was a complete success – I didn't put a foot wrong. He asked if he could fly Papa Delta back to Oxford "as I get so little left-seat experience these days". It was fun to watch a master pilot doing everything so smoothly, with a particularly exemplary landing in cloud at the end. A good professional pilot is a joy to watch – everything falls into place and nothing has to be rushed to move the plane towards its landing wire.

Chapter 22

CHURCH FINANCE

I had become a Churchwarden in 1954 and, after a few years, was invited to help with the Diocesan finances by Bishop Wilson of Birmingham. I did not like him and got fed up with the way the Diocesan Board of Finance operated and its impotence in controlling expenditure. So I was surprised to be asked by the new Bishop, Hugh Montefiore, to be the Chairman of the D.B.F. in 1969. I thought of refusing but Cylla encouraged me to do it, so I accepted by letter.

After I was appointed I went to see the Diocesan Secretary who was a retired colonial service man from West Africa. He was horrified to find that the Diocese was, in fact, bankrupt. Overspent by £150,000 during Monte's first year and very overparsoned, the Diocese had a large overdraft. The Secretary was taking a "little boy's finger in the dam" approach to get by. The trouble was caused by the young parsons who, enthused by Hugh's reputation as a "thoroughly modern" Bishop, flocked to fill vacant livings. As a result the Diocese was at a pre-war strength of over 250 incumbents. With a full house there was only one way for the overdraft to go – and that was not downwards. So I went with the Diocesan Secretary to see the local director of the Midland Bank and persuaded him to give us more time. However, the Diocesan Secretary was over 65 and thought it was time to retire.

I was dreading the Diocesan Synod, which would approve the accounts. When I arrived at the Birmingham Council Chamber, where the meeting was to take place, Monte was sitting in the Lord Mayor's chair, with the chairman of the House of Laity, a retired Edgbaston doctor, sitting beside him. I said, "Good evening my Lord, where should I sit?" (Thinking my place was on the podium.) Monte replied, "Anywhere as far away as you can get from me. We must be clear that God and Mammon don't mix." So I sat right at the back – as high up and as far away as the seats would allow.

I drafted an advert for the *Church Times* for a new Diocesan Secretary which Hugh didn't like and re-drafted it to suit his objectives. I wanted good financial skills and Hugh wanted evangelism, so it was not certain we would get such a combination. Each candidate was interviewed at Bishop's Croft by Hugh, and then the candidate walked over to the Diocesan Office to meet me. This was very effective and meant that Hugh and I did not get together till after we had seen all ten on the shortlist. There was, in my book, just one sound candidate – a rather fat American clergyman, with a beard that was both scanty and long at the same time. I went round to see Hugh who said, "Well, what do you think?" I replied that there was only one I thought would do. "The Beard," said Hugh and, without more ado, we agreed to get him back the next week to see if he continued to shine at a second interview. He did and, at the end, Hugh said, "Just one thing," looking at his black suit and tight clerical collar, "are you an Anglo-Catholic?" "No," said the beard, "I adapt to where I am." Not to be outdone I said, "Could you possibly stand closer to your razor?" "No can do, receding chin," said the beard. So Hugh engaged him and the Reverend Jim Pendorf became the new Diocesan Secretary.

The more one got to know him, the better he appeared. He was always available to anybody in the Diocese, and he was immensely helpful to incumbents whenever they asked for help. We began to plan an assault on the overdraft and annual deficit. We decided on a two-pronged attack: on the parishes, to get them to contribute sums more nearly attuned to their assessments; and on the Bishop, to get the parsonical establishment down and adjusted annually to Diocesan circumstances.

To tackle the first I thought I would have an overnight study seminar at the Diocesan Retreat House at Wast Hills for all Rural Deans and Churchwardens. After discussing it with the Archdeacon I luckily decided to pay for dinner and the necessary red wine myself. The programme was designed to get the Rural Deans and Parsons to back the new regime, and the Churchwardens and Treasurers to be encouraged to actively raise their duly appointed imposts. It seemed to go very well until after dinner when the Area Dean of Aston, who was a chartered accountant before he became a parson, got up and gave me a tremendous dressing down for attempting to suborn the parishes, and for using Diocesan funds to entertain them. There was a long and embarrassed silence until I got up and said I had personally paid for the supper and drink. I added that I thought, as they had all come to discuss the Diocesan finance problem, a little social party might help things along. Undeterred, he returned to the attack saying that if I thought alcohol would bring people round to my way of thinking, I was in for a big surprise. Nevertheless, it all ended peaceably with early Communion the next morning and I got several thank-you letters from priests who had enjoyed it.

The Diocese was in an uneasy mood and it was reputed that the Bishop and two Archdeacons did not see eye to eye. However, the Archdeacon of Aston became the Bishop of Middleton in the Manchester Diocese, and Gerry Hollis, the Archdeacon of Birmingham, retired; when John Cooper and John Duncan succeeded them as the two Archdeacons, life became much easier and friendlier.

One day Bishop Hugh asked me to go round and see him. "I want to do something for ethnic girls, to bring them into mainstream British life," he said. I attempted to cross-question him on what he wanted but he just said, "Go and work something out." As I went out of his study I saw the Senior Industrial Chaplain, Reverend Dennis Claringbull, and said to him that it seemed a wide remit. We talked and he suggested that there was redundant space in St. Paul's Church in the Jewellery Quarter which might do as premises for a start. I placed an advert for a man to run the Diocesan Lay Employee Agency, as we called it, and got several good applicants. The winning one was a former actor who had been made redundant by Blue Arrow, the employment agency firm. He proved a very good choice and got some excellent people to help him, the most noteworthy being an ex-accountant from Geest Industries, the banana people. Between them they got the show up and running in no time at all.

The Afro-Caribbean element was keen to join, but less keen to put in the effort required. The Muslims were extraordinarily keen. They turned up every morning at 8.55 a.m. wearing the chador, with only their black eyes showing above the veil. They disappeared into the ladies and reappeared on the dot of nine in the shortest of skirts, fish-net stockings and six-inch stiletto heels. At 4.55 p.m. they disappeared again, to reappear in the chador once more. However, they worked like beavers, were excellent mathematicians, and took to book-keeping and computers as to the manner born. We soon had Birmingham employment agencies clamouring to sign them up on completion of the course. We started charging the agencies a signing-on fee, which they were very willing to pay. Birmingham Corporation was very helpful and, as our numbers grew, they offered us a disused school which, after repair, we opened as a training place for plumbers and painters as well. The first year accounts showed we had made a profit of about £60,000 and our profits climbed sharply for the three years I ran it. After the second-year accounts were processed and passed on to the Diocesan Office, I got a message from Bishop Hugh to go and see him. When I arrived at Bishop's Croft (his home), he was in a tetchy mood.

Bishop H. "What is all this profit you are making out of the Training Academy? It seems out of all proportion to me."

W.D. "We charge everyone a signing-on fee when they recruit our girls and we are getting a long waiting list of firms wanting our people."

Bishop H. "It seems terrible to me, exploiting all the ethnic girls. We should be doing no more than break even."

W.D. "I don't think that would work, as there are so many unbudgetable expenses. After all, the profit goes straight into the Diocesan funds."

Bishop H. "It makes me very uneasy. I don't know what my colleagues would say if it gets into the papers."

Still, shortly afterwards, the Bishop of Manchester (Booth-Clibborn), having been told what we were up to by Hugh, came down with the Bishop of Middleton to see how it worked. I explained how the budgeting was done, and emphasised that the thing only ran with very tight financial controls and needed a very efficient in-house accountant. They set up a similar arrangement with three clerics running it and, after incurring very heavy losses for nine months, they had to close it down. Meanwhile our profits grew and grew, much to the delight of Jim Pendorf, the Diocesan Secretary, but it did not please everyone. I was summoned once more to see Hugh who said that the large and growing profits were anathema, and he wanted out. I was to sell it. The out-of-work actor had long since been re-recruited by another agency, so it was the accountant who now controlled our activities. I discussed it with him and he said it ought to fetch about a quarter of a million, but he would like to consider a management buy-out. I thought that in many ways that would be the most satisfactory outcome. The deal was done and the sale price was £278,000, to be paid in four installments. Hugh never mentioned it again, but the enterprise had, one way or another, contributed almost £500,000 to Diocesan funds. As it happened the Government passed a new education act and the operation of the facility became much more difficult – perhaps luckily, our timing had been spot on.

I have always been a great believer in the power of commercial property to generate funds and, as the overdraft was paid off by the Diocese, I began to look for commercial opportunities in Birmingham. I was much encouraged by the partners of James & Lister Lea, the Diocesan surveyors, to undertake this venture. Their judgement was nearly always very sound and, aided by the Banks, we embarked on a series of shop and office purchases. This did not evoke universal approbation from the hierarchy and the properties were all sold fairly quickly after my departure as Diocesan Board of Finance Chairman. However, profits were to be measured in millions rather than thousands and the subsequent investment of all monies in gilts turned the clock back, with the Diocese having an investment increase but little capital gain. In addition, the D.B.F. was cut down to size by Bishop Santer, who transferred most of its funds to a committee composed of clerics, where the chairman of the D.B.F. had a seat but no power.

All the Church of England's 43 D.B.F. chairmen were on a rather odd body that agreed the stipends of clergymen. On the one hand, the commuter dioceses (Southwark, Chelmsford, Bristol, Newcastle) often wanted large increases; on the other hand, the rural and deprived dioceses (Lincoln, York, Durham, Carlisle), which had large rural parishes with small congregations, wanted the minimum. The loudest voice was Southwark whose chairman was John Smallwood, a banker from the Bank of England. I wanted Birmingham to pay top wages even if it meant a few fewer parsons and, at the end of my stint as chairman, Birmingham was one of the three or four dioceses that paid the top of the scale. But I lost out on pensions. While parsons were earning £2,000-£5,000 a year, paying their pension contributions was sensible but, once their stipends equalled police inspectors and head teachers of primary schools, I couldn't see why their pensions should remain non-contributory. I never got near to overturning this, however hard I tried.

Hugh's wife, Eliza, sadly got Alzheimer's and he found that looking after her was made much more difficult by his regular House of Lords' weeks. So he resigned and the Bishop of Kensington, Mark Santer, was appointed to succeed him. The new regime started with problems. Hugh had entrusted to the Bishop of Aston the organisation of an anti-apartheid weekend, starring Archbishop Tutu. The Bishop came to me and asked for a budget. I said I thought the Diocese could afford £30,000 and, if pushed, I might be able to find a little more. He got on with organising it and the highlight was to be hiring Villa Park on a Sunday for a service and gala. The Bishop did not consult me again. On the eve of the weekend Jim Pendorf rang to say that the BBC, who were covering the events, would not come until their fee of £22,000 was paid in advance. After arguing that this would only be the tip of the iceberg, we paid the money. The gala at Villa Park had acres of empty stands and barren areas and we knew the worst. Jim and I sat up all night working out that the total shortfall was £160,000. Luckily, a female worshipper gave us a substantial donation and we ended up losing only about £60,000, which was a let off. The *Birmingham Post* had a picture of Tutu and Santer dancing to the African drums just showing their feet.

I hated the Diocesan Synod where the young turks among the clergy tried to make their names as protagonists of a radical agenda.

Once I was being given a hard time by a young incumbent dressed in a multi-coloured rugger shirt. I wondered what to say to rebuff his views and, as I didn't know his name, I referred to him as "that chap dressed in the Duke of Westminster's racing colours." To my surprise the whole Synod erupted into roars and roars of laughter and it was never forgotten. I had a much easier time from the clerics after that.

By bullying the Bishop about the number of parsons which he could actually have, as against the annual establishment, we reduced our stipend outlays. The overdrafts were paid off and a healthy surplus began to give the Bishop some financial leeway. In addition, the property investments, made before the recession had ended, rapidly increased in value. The new plan of financial control in the Diocese greatly reduced my ability to influence affairs. Jim Pendorf said that after 11 years it was time to go and I agreed; I said as much to Bishop Mark Santer and he agreed. He found an eminent Birmingham accountant to succeed me, and I bowed out with a portable computer as a leaving present.

Chapter 23

ASTON VILLA

All my life I have supported Aston Villa from the first match I went to in September 1932, when I saw the great Billy Walker help defeat Leicester City 4-2. In 1972 Pat Matthews buttonholed me after a Phoenix Board meeting and asked if I would put some money up to re-constitute Aston Villa, as it had gone bust in 1969. He was trying to get it back to play once more. Pat had already got funds from eminent Birmingham citizens and proposed the re-founded club should be led by H.D. Ellis, who was a Birmingham City director. The re-build had not gone smoothly and Ellis had got rid of two of the directors. Joe Mercer, my old P.T. instructor from Sandhurst in 1941, was the manager but he was removed as the club slid down the second division table. He was replaced by Tommy Docherty, a very extrovert Glaswegian.

But the new board received a major blow in 1970 when the club was relegated to the third division for the first time in its career. Tommy Docherty was sacked after 13 months and was succeeded by Vic Crowe, the ex-Aston Villa Welsh international. In the first year of Vic's reign the club failed to get promoted, but they did get to Wembley in the League Cup, where they lost to Tottenham 2-0. The following year they got promoted by winning the third division title.

I went to a couple of Villa games in the Director's Box and met the remaining survivors of the board that had attempted the revival. Harry Kartz and Alan Smith were two very different people. Harry had made his money with one of the numerous companies that made parts for the motor manufacturers. Alan was Secretary of the Warwickshire County Cricket Club. He was Birmingham born and bred, and educated at King Edwards. Clever and good at everything he did, he had taken up soccer while at Brasenose College, Oxford and had been an outside left of the all-conquering Pegasus Club. They had won the Amateur Football cup several times in the fifties. The remaining member of the board was Eric Houghton, who had been my boyhood hero. He had played on the wing for the Villa and, as a result of the excellent service he received from Billy Walker, he had played a few times for England until superseded by Cliff Bastin. He had managed the Villa when they won the Cup in 1957 and was claret and blue to the tips of his fingers.

I had my first taste of the resurgent Aston Villa in 1972 when, as High Sheriff of Warwickshire, I had taken Sir John Ashcroft, the West Midlands Presiding Judge, to Villa Park for the semi-final leg of the League Cup against Manchester United. Ashcroft was engaged in trying Father Fell, the Roman Catholic priest, who was subsequently convicted for being a commander of an I.R.A. active service unit in the Midlands and therefore had a high degree of police protection. We sat in the first row of the directors' box, flanked by two armed special branch officers. A third special branch officer looked backwards and upwards, in case of an assassin at the top of the stand. When Andy Lockhead scored the winning goal I jumped to my feet and knocked my glasses off my nose. They fell into the standing enclosure below. One of the special branch officers leaned over, gun in hand, and said, "give me back those spectacles." The spectacles came flying back like lightning and I was able to see the end of the match.

I continued to watch the Villa on a regular basis and was not too surprised by Pat Matthews' invitation to join the board in the spring of 1973, subject to putting up £25,000. The other new arrival was Harry Cressman who was the dynamic head of Bristol Street Motors, the Ford dealership in Birmingham. Villa had just been promoted from the third division to the second. Doug Ellis had just had a row with the two directors, Messrs. Hartley and Parkes, whom he had got rid of. (They had not liked being dispatched and, when I left some five years later, I was amazed to receive a very smart silk claret-and-blue tie with the initials S.B.E. on the front – with a card from Jim Hartley saying it stood for "Sacked by Ellis".) The board now consisted of Ellis, Harry Kartz, Alan Smith, Harry Cressman, Eric Houghton and me.

My first surprise was the role of the board. Instead of discussing cash flow and plans, we spent an hour or more each meeting discussing the team's performance in the games since the last meeting. No doubt of great interest but, with a club teetering on the verge of bankruptcy, there were other worries to confront. Vic Crowe, the manager, was a very nice man and, for perhaps that reason, never really attracted the enthusiasm of the board. He was in the process of collecting a very useful team of old warhorses and young men just out of youth sides, who had been discarded by grander clubs. My first impressions on meeting the players and staff were rather like those joining a battalion, when all the hardened veterans wondered what horrors they were in for under the newly arrived officers. The Rioch brothers were there and, as I had known their father, the redoubtable Drill Sergeant and later R.S.M. of the Scots Guards, there was an immediate way-in for ice-breaking.

The training ground at Bodymoor Heath had been established and built but the work of the original builder was so shoddy that I was put in charge of getting it right and improving the facilities. I talked to the chairman, whose firm had been used, about this and he said that they were so short of cash that they had had to skimp in order to make the money eke out. Anyway, I put my estate building staff in and they did an amazing job of replacing inadequate roof timbers, and the beams that held up the hot water tanks etc. Whilst we were sorting out the training ground, the squad were brought to train at Merevale several times, running up and down to the ridge from the front drive. They compared it to the 1965 film "The Hill" and were not enthusiastic about coming regularly. As I went down to the training ground almost daily, it was a good introduction to the club and its workings. The chairman, coming to the Villa from Birmingham City, was very anxious to be more Villa than anyone and he turned up with a claret-and-blue Rolls Royce with an AV registration number.

We often went to away matches on the team coach. I used to sit on the back seat and gossip with Harry Cressman and Alan Smith. The tables in the coach were all used for the various card schools for the gambling players. The manager sat at the front of the coach on a single seat, but would move to the double seat opposite if he wanted a discussion with anyone. The coach usually started up very early because, with the kick off at 3 p.m., there had to be three hours between the players' midday meal and the start. To save money we usually had lunch and then went on to the ground. As the club became more affluent we were able to put the players to bed for a couple of hours after lunch.

The second division was a different cup of tea from the third. Although there were moments when we thought we would go straight on up to the first division, we were thwarted towards the end of the season, finishing fourth and having to stay for another season. The board was very disappointed and decided to sack Vic Crowe as the majority thought he was unlikely to take the club up to the first division. Vic felt very let down – it was quite unusual for the manager to be dispensed with for finishing fourth in a division of twenty-two clubs. He remained a Villa supporter and had a season ticket just in front of me throughout the 80s and 90s.

The next task was to select a new manager. The board advertised and had several possible applications. However, the first meetings took place at Doug's house in Sutton Coldfield, leaving only two applicants still standing. One was clearly impossible; and the only choice that remained was Ron Saunders, who had been the manager of Norwich City for several years, and then had gone to Manchester City but had only lasted a few months there. Doug was very anti-Saunders and tried to veto his appointment but Harry Cressman said, "Who else is there?" and moved that we appoint him. After much argument and discussion regarding re-advertising, we left Doug to discuss terms with Ron. Whatever happened there we shall never know, but Ron and Doug were not on the same wavelength from Day One.

Ron Saunders had never hit the jackpot as a player with Everton and, after a season in the reserves, and occasional appearances he had moved onwards and steadily downwards. However, he had shown signs of management ability at Norwich and had done pretty well with a small budget. Yet, he had not hit it off at Manchester City and Peter Swales, the chairman, had got rid of him after several months. But that was probably par for the course. Ron had abundant self-confidence and the ability to get the most out of a situation. He could beat any of the players at table tennis and usually beat his assistant, Roy McLaren, a 4 handicap, at golf even though Ron's official handicap was 14. His meteoric style was far removed from Vic Crowe and the close season saw him begin the changes that were to lead to our promotion to Division One in his first season.

Our financial worries had begun to ease with our appearance at Wembley in the League Cup final in 1971. But there were still no pretences of flashing an open chequebook like the top elite. However, Ron gathered a team of backroom staff that were to take us to the top. He engaged Tony Barton as his chief scout and talent spotter – a man who was later to be the manager when the club won the European Cup. He produced the players for Ron to organise. Ron had a strong Roman Catholic bias with an Everton background and a Roman Catholic wife and, while Aston Villa was not the Midlands hub of the Catholic faith, we no longer became a no-go area for Irishmen.

I thought out carefully what I should do and not do for the club. I became friendly with the club's auditor, Edmund King of Deloittes, and the commercial manager, Eric Woodward. The money side of the club was not being given the crucial attention it needed; if the money was right, everything would follow in due course. After a great deal of discussion we got a computer program which would enable the club secretary, Alan Bennett, to put a monthly figure on the Manager's desk of the money available, should the Manager wish to enter the transfer market. The board liked to be able to approve transfer opportunities in advance but that did not appear to be a practical possibility as any move into the transfer market needed to be secretive and rapid. As a result, and again after a long discussion by the board, I was allowed to negotiate at board level with Ron Saunders, under my overall control, free to negotiate with other managers. This worked quite well and, while at a water industry conference at Bournemouth, I was rung up by Ron who said we could have a young centre forward from Dundee if we moved fast. I negotiated all night with the Dundee chairman and in the early hours bought Andy Gray for £120,000. The cheque was returned, as it had to be made out to the Scottish chairman personally! When I came to pay my hotel bill I found the cost of my telephone calls had reached £465, so I paid the bill myself rather than have questions asked by Severn Trent.

Andy was a most brilliant athlete and I still remember with pleasure a thrilling individual effort to raise our half-time score to 5-0 against Liverpool one night at Villa Park. Andy being a native of Drumchapel, a housing estate in Glasgow, had no reason to be a Villa enthusiast and Ron always had trouble with him over wage negotiation. The offices at Villa Park were the old living quarters of the Giraffe House of the Menagerie in the Villa Lower Grounds Pleasure Park whose bankruptcy at the end of the nineteenth century enabled the Villa to build its famous ground. The boardroom was up high with windows on all sides looking over the tarmac concourse towards the Trinity Road Stand. One day I was asked to finalise the deadlock in wage negotiations with Andy Gray which had been reached by Ron and Alan. When I came into the room I saw that Andy had got a small card table with two chairs eyeball-to-eyeball in the middle of the room. We argued with each other and every so often Andy got up and walked across the room and looked out of the open window. I could not make out what was happening until I got up and followed him to the next window along where I saw he was making tic-tac signals with raised fingers to his agent who was standing below. The next time Andy got up I went to the other window and leant out which brought the signalling to an end. As a result we reached agreement soon after.

The next transfer I dealt with was Denis Mortimer, from Coventry, which came up on a Sunday afternoon. The board was inclined to grumble at each transfer but came to accept that they could not be involved in the whole transaction ab initio. Messrs. Mortimer and Gray had a tremendous influence on the team that eventually won the European Cup.

I was rung up one evening by the *Birmingham Evening Mail* and asked for my comments on Ron Saunders' move to Saudi Arabia. As nothing had been said by Ron when we last met, which was admittedly several days before, I played dumb and asked for details. I was told that Ron was going as the manager of the Saudi international team at a salary of £1,000,000 plus bonus. I said that, much as I loved Ron, there was no way a resurgent Aston Villa could even approach a salary of that size, and we must sadly stand and cheer Ron on his way. I rang Ron and asked him to come and see me – if true, this was a blow of the first order because he had clearly begun to pull the club up the rankings. However, when Ron appeared his new post seemed a lot less certain than the *Evening Mail* had implied. He asked for a rise in salary and I said the board were always ready to examine whether his remuneration had fallen behind but that, in general, we were in favour of sticking to his contract. Ron said he would bear in mind what I had said. I asked him when he was proposing to go as the club couldn't match a million a year. There was the usual five days' press bonanza and then everything went quiet, so I imagined that all was well and that it had been a bit of kite flying.

We had won the League Cup in 1975 at Wembley in my first year as Chairman – I had been elected after yet another boardroom scuffle. We beat Norwich City with a penalty goal in the last five minutes. The penalty had been taken by Ray Graydon. The Norwich goalkeeper made an excellent save but Graydon kept his wits and side-footed the rebound in past him. As Graydon ran up to take the penalty, I had tapped the front of the League President's box with my toe. "Keep your foot still; he is taking the penalty, not you," said the cup presenter with brutal accuracy. And the goal, although scrambled, still counted! We got one million pounds at that final and, two years later, we did the same thing again and won the League Cup by beating Everton at the third attempt. Each of the replays got us an additional million and our financial troubles were greatly eased. But the relaxation of financial stringency meant some loosening of the common ties that united the board in its endeavours to resuscitate Aston Villa.

The new stand, the building of which I oversaw, was our talisman of the club's regeneration. I was surprised to be challenged at a board meeting about its name. I hadn't thought about it and when Harry

Kartz asked, I could only come up with either the Witton or North Stand. I realised afterwards that they did not want it called the Dugdale Stand, something I had no intention of requesting. We got the stand finished on time and on budget, although the raising of the large beam to hold up a pillarless roof had caused everybody to have qualms about the design. The contractors from the north-west, who were building the stand, cannot have made much money out of it. The financing had gone well and all the boxes on the two tiers below the seating had been let for several years in advance.

Winning the League Cup meant an entry to European football. We travelled to Turkey, Poland, Spain, Portugal and elsewhere and made many friends across the Continent. Aston Villa officials were very well liked for doing more than was necessary to help continental sides when they came to England. It is the custom for the visitors to be entertained to dinner the night before the game by the home board, and we had many happy evenings as we did the rounds of Birmingham hotels. I was very touched when Bilbao wanted to entice Bobby Robson from Ipswich, and then made a special visit to Birmingham to consult me on the best way to go about it. Ipswich naturally demanded a "transfer fee" and Johnny Cobbold, their chairman, asked for £250,000 which Bilbao was reluctant to pay.

When we had a Scottish Villa player selected for a Scotland home international, to be played at Tynecastle, the Heart of Midlothian ground in Edinburgh, Ron and I were offered tickets and I said I would fly him up and back from Birmingham in Papa Delta, my Beech Baron. Ron was initially keen on the idea but when I got to the hangar at Birmingham he was nowhere to be seen. He finally turned up holding a clutch of mini whiskies. We had a trouble-free flight up in glorious weather to Turnhouse and could see the Forth Bridge as we made our descent. After an early supper we made our way to the ground and I was given a chair at the top of a staircase in the old Tynecastle stand. Needless to say, I toppled over; I and the chair fell about 25 feet down the stairs to ground level. My riding experience came in handy – I tucked my head in my chest and really wasn't hurt at all, though rather shaken. We enjoyed the party afterwards and had a good night's sleep at the airport hotel.

The next morning was again brilliant sunshine so I was surprised to learn that Birmingham Airport was closed due to fog. The forecast said it would "burn off" by the time we got to Birmingham, so off we set. We flew in sunshine but, after crossing the Solway Firth, we could no longer see the land as it was blanketed. When I switched to Birmingham approach I was surprised to find the airport still closed. I got my clearance to make the Instrument Landing System approach, but a British Airways pilot ahead was over-shooting and he said to me, "You'll be lucky if you get in; it's at minimum." Anyway, we sailed down on instruments but, at decision height, I still couldn't see the ground so we overshot. Meanwhile Ron's store of miniatures was disappearing at a rate of knots. We made one more attempt and I then had to consider my options, as Dublin and Manchester were the only two airports open. I opted for Manchester and, back in sunshine, we sailed up to the beacon and Congleston. Manchester said they were just about above the minimum level of cloud base required for a legal landing so I could try. Ron's store had by then completely disappeared and we made a trouble-free, but visually hampered, landing on the long runway. We were now told Birmingham was open and we could go back. Ron was by now almost incoherent and refused to go any further with me, so he hired a taxi to take him back. I completed the return to Birmingham which by now had no restriction on flying. Ron refused ever to fly with me again: if you fly in an airliner you can only look out of the window – in a small plane you have 180 degree visibility to the front.

I enjoyed seeing Ron evaluate the players, young and old, and promote the best and transfer the rest. He was greatly aided by Tony Barton, his chief scout, whose unerring view of who would flourish in the first team almost invariably proved to be correct. I made it a point of honour to go to all the youth team matches and any reserve fixtures that I was able to, since the Villa agreement that a director would always go with the reserve team was honoured more in the breach than in the observance. Because of the attempts by one director to collect a "private army" of the players to try to undermine Ron's all-embracing direction, Ron was very suspicious of directors travelling on the coach.

Ron usually came to see me about once a week for a whisky and a chat. One evening he asked whether I had noticed how many of the young players were the children of shopkeepers. I said no, I had never enquired. Ron said he was going to make investigations. Sure enough he came back about a month later to say he was sacking the youth coach, who was having his car boot filled with groceries, etc. Ron advertised in the N.U.T. magazine for a graduate teacher who had been a pro footballer. We got a surprising number of replies and he eventually recruited a man from the north east, who had been on Middlesbrough's books but had gone into non-league football. He was, amongst other things, the holder of a postgraduate degree and a very nice person. Ron thought we needed a schoolmaster who talked the language of the comprehensive in order to try and collect talented schoolboys to join the club as they left school – to train up local young talent gives any club an enormous financial advantage should they make it professionally. The Roman Catholic Church has always had a hotline to the Catholic community in recruiting talent for the traditionally catholic clubs (in the Midlands, Wolverhampton Wanderers) and we needed an antidote at school level.

Shortly after my arrival in the chair, Ron Bendall arrived on the board, and divisions soon became apparent. Doug Ellis ceased to play any meaningful part in our discussions and Ron Bendall was looking to control the club, which had a certain inevitability to it since he was the biggest shareholder and was buying more shares all the time. He was an accountant specialising in liquidations in the Midlands with an enormous practice, selling up bankrupt small businesses. Ron wanted to remove Alan Smith from the board and insert his son in Alan's place. Having been alerted to this, I went to Ron Bendall and suggested that removing Alan was not in the best interests of Aston Villa. He said he saw no reason to enlarge the board beyond the size it was already and that his son would be a very good addition, bringing youth to the forefront. The board meetings were soon a fortnightly horror to be endured rather than enjoyed. Alan Smith and Harry Cressman remained their usual cheerful and practical selves. Harry Kartz, who thought he ought to be have been made chairman instead of me, alternated between his usual chirpy self volunteering incisive football analysis and sarcasm on the side lines. Doug sat and sulked and, when asked his opinion, usually hedged. He was obviously making notes for his auto-biography, which duly appeared some years later.

I made a last effort to persuade Bendall to alter the Articles and increase the board numbers to allow Alan to continue. But I failed and Harry Cressman suggested the three of us should chair a meeting to discuss what to do. This we held and we decided that we would all resign en bloc and have a press conference to announce our departure, since it was plain that if Alan went, Harry and I would follow soon after. I was very sad to do this as I enjoyed running Aston Villa. My work with Ron Saunders resulted in a stable financial position for the club, and a team which won the First Division the following season and the European Cup the year after. Harry Kartz became chairman after me but soon gave way to Ron, as chairmanship was not Harry Kartz's style.

As a footnote to the whole miserable story, Bendall was found to have had his palatial Worcestershire home redecorated at the expense of Aston Villa and, no doubt urged on by the West Midlands Police, he resigned. Doug went to see him at his eyrie on the Isle of Man and persuaded him to sell all his shares to him, so founding the empire that lasted until Doug, in his turn, sold out to Randolph Lerner, the American entrepreneur, in 2006. And now in 2010, Aston Villa is once again putting the top teams of the Premiership under constant pressure, coming sixth in the 2009/10 season.

Chapter 24

GÉNÉRALE DES EAUX

In 1987, after I had left Severn Trent, I received a call from David Kinnersley, Secretary of the Water Companies Association, to say that the French firm Compagnie Générale des Eaux were looking for a chairman to drive their venture into the English water service. I was feeling rather under-employed and jumped at the chance to do something active again when invited to France to meet the President, Monsieur Guy Dejouany. I went over for three days to first meet the directors and see the installations in the Paris area. The water industry in France was divided between three main groups; Générale des Eaux (the biggest), Lyonnaise and Bouyges. Paris was divided; right bank was Générale des Eaux and left bank Lyonnaise. Générale des Eaux had contracts with about 1500 French municipalities of varying sizes. It had a department of 200 people in Paris whose main duty was to help all the contracts to run smoothly and prevent defections. The company was at least apolitical, as it was in good standing with every French political party. They sensed an opportunity in England with water privatisation and had already acquired North Surrey and Folkestone and Dover companies before I arrived.

I was quartered at the Royal Monceau and, after three days, I lunched with the President and he offered me the job. The English managing director was a "pied noir", Jean Claude Banon from Algeria, who had had a brilliant career at the École des Mines (where all the best post-graduates in engineering and sciences went). He had built holdings in several of the larger private water companies and our immediate concern was to convert these holdings into outright ownership. Jean Claude was no financier and was very conservative in his approach to the purchase of the remainder. He failed to make a final offer when he was dealing with the purchase of South Staffs and Mid Kent. We did, however, buy Tendring Hundred and Three Valleys water companies. But we stopped short of the dominating position we had hoped for. Nevertheless, we were in the privatised water industry with a largish stake. Jean Claude's immediate boss was Jean Pierre Tardieu whom I liked enormously and we got on very well. Alas, he fell foul of the French commercial code with a deal in the island of Réunion and was made the fall guy. He was sentenced, most unfairly, to two years which was immediately suspended, but it was a blot that stymied his otherwise successful career.

To begin with I used to visit Paris once a week but that was gradually reduced over my eleven years at the helm to nil. I caught the 6.35 a.m. plane out of Birmingham and landed at Charles de Gaulle so I was in the office at Rue d'Anjou by 9 a.m. before many of the top guns had got there. We worked from 9.45 a.m. to 12.30 p.m. and then adjourned to one of the restaurants around the Madeleine: Goumard or Alexandre were the most popular. We had a large and alcoholic lunch and then went back to the office at about 3.30 p.m., where the work continued often as late as 10.30 p.m. The secretaries also were used to working late, but came in to ask permission to catch the last train back to their homes in the Banlieue.

I usually missed the last plane back to Birmingham at 7.45 p.m. and then had a choice of catching the 9.20 p.m. to Manchester, or having another night in Paris. I swapped the Royal Monceau for the Bristol, as it was nearer to Rue d'Anjou. Rue d'Anjou to Charles de Gaulle was relatively simple but, when we moved to La Défense – an enormous office development sponsored by Générale des Eaux which was slow in letting – the problem became much more difficult. One day in April I was told that the French Air Traffic controllers had gone on strike and that if I wanted to get back to England I must leave immediately by train. A nightmare taxi ride to the Gare du Nord was followed by a fast train to Calais where I found that it was too rough for the hovercraft to go across the Channel. I caught a P&O ferry at 9.30 p.m., arrived in Dover at 11 p.m. and caught the slowest train from Dover to Charing

Cross. I got into the forecourt at Charing Cross at 2.15 a.m. and hailed a cab at the stand. "Where to Gov?" "Stratford-upon-Avon." "Wait a moment while I phone the wife." The fare was £170 which I paid in cash and, at 5 a.m., got into bed beside my wife in the Shakespeare Hotel. I was President of the Shakespeare Birthday celebrations that year and had to be on parade at 8.45 a.m. When I got to the hotel I felt as if I had been done over by the Gestapo with a rubber truncheon.

I had been alternating with Charlie Smith-Ryland (and, after his death, with the Bishop of Coventry) as the President of the Shakespeare Birthday Celebrations on April 23rd, or the nearest Saturday thereto, for many years. This continued until, in 2004, I said I would be too old to continue when my turn came round again. I and the Lord Lieutenants stuck firmly to our briefs and scripts, but it was always too much of a chance for the Bishops (Barrington-Ward, Bishop Gibbs and Bishop Bennetts) to indulge in a bit of frothy man of the people stuff. The first time I did it the actors of the Royal Shakespeare Company and Equity were demonstrating against the presence of the South African High Commissioner. They pelted me with rubbish outside the Church as I was standing in front of him. I was livid and demanded an apology but did not get it.

Générale des Eaux', or rather General Utilities' as the English investments vehicle was called, original British H.Q. was in a Mews close to Belgrave Square where we were very happy. But we expanded so fast under the insatiable urge of the French to snap up what they could of the former nationalised utilities which were being put on the market, one by one, by the Thatcher government, that we needed more space, so we found new H.Q. at the back of Queen Anne's Gate. Générale des Eaux applied for, and got, the Charing Cross to Dover line and South West suburban train commuter network for Waterloo. I fought long and hard against this proposal on the basis that those lines, even under the inspired direction of my father-in-law, Willy Radnor, had made huge losses for many years before nationalisation, which had then given an inevitable upwards surge to the losses. Nobody took a blind bit of notice of my stance and the lines were acquired, only to be removed after 1997 by the Labour government, who supported the anti-French and anti-modernisation stance of the A.S.L.E.F.

Under nationalisation the drivers attended Union Branch H.Q. at the nearest station on a Friday and, after handing in their hours due, were given, in return, the roster of duties for the following week. The French management, being a rational and logical bunch, decided to post a computer print-out of everyone's duties on Thursday evening for the following week. All hell broke loose; the union were denied a simple way of collecting the subscription, and the workers were denied several hours of overtime at premium rates. Strike after strike ensued. It was never resolved before the lines were expropriated in such a way as to lose the poor French many millions of pounds. If they had been given a free hand, and some support from the Ministry of Transport, there is little doubt that the French regime would have resulted in two much more efficient railway lines, saving a great deal of money and commuter fare rises.

Générale des Eaux remained the largest shareholder in Bristol, South Staffs and Mid Kent water companies but, because of Jean Claude Banon's reluctance to pay the necessary bit over the odds to clinch the deals, the holding was still below the 30 per cent needed to trigger an automatic bid in these companies. It is, of course, a fine judgement as to how much over the odds one is prepared to pay to claim a sale but, if it is decided to stick to bare values, one's chances of obtaining a result narrow perceptibly. I attempted to encourage Jean Claude but he was reluctant to have to go back to Guy Dejouany and ask for approval for more. Judging by the rise in share prices for these companies in later years, we could have paid a lot more and still have made a handsome profit. In the case of Bristol, my old water colleague John Wills was the Chairman. Being a Wills he was reluctant to sell off Bristol's water heritage. However, later on, all three companies fell to another bidder.

We were warmly welcomed by the Bristol and South Staffs; but not by Mid Kent where, after a long enquiry by the Monopolies Commission, we were forced to give undertakings on several aspects which made a complete take-over more unlikely. I was a veteran of the Monopolies Commission enquiries, having done it before at Severn Trent. They were run from offices in Carey Street, appropriate perhaps, as the former site of the bankruptcy court. We hired a large room in a pub opposite. Our solicitors were Simmonds & Simmonds and they handled the proceedings with quiet efficiency. We all adjourned there at 4 p.m. after the Commission rose, and stayed until we had been through the day's business and discussed the likelihood of what would transpire on the morrow. At around 9 p.m. a bit of work was handed to the army of admitted girls who were doing the donkey work for the partners. They had to be ready with the answers when we re-convened at 8 a.m. the following morning so that we could finalise our approach for the ensuing day.

I got on the list of attendees for the July 14th junket at the French Embassy in Kensington Palace Gardens. It was fun wandering around the mammoth attendance to see which of one's friends and acquaintances had been invited as well. But Générale des Eaux was clearly about to undergo wholesale changes. It had been criticised by a French Government commission for supporting all three major political parties. The President had stomach cancer and clearly, at his age, was heading toward retirement. The search for a new Chief Executive continued for some time when suddenly a political whiz kid was announced as the next head. M. Messier was under 40, had a political appointment, and was involved in just about everything that was going places in France.

When Dejouany handed over the job, he said that as there had only been three heads of Générale des Eaux in almost a century he hoped M. Messier would last as long. Guy Dejouany had presided over a long, slow and inexorable expansion of the company throughout the world. Aided by a favourable tax system and a majestic and positive cash flow, the company had bought into America, South East Asia, Australia and South America. It was the largest and most adeptly managed water business. It had a large research establishment at Maisons-Laffitte (next to the racecourse!). It handled problems neatly and, if necessary, expensively. When the North Banlieue was short of a treatment plant and a site for a supply reservoir, it bought the Château of Méry-sur-Oise from the Ségur family. A dynasty so old it pre-dated the Salic law, the head of the family was the eldest daughter. The negotiations involved the head of the house aged 99, her daughter aged 73, her daughter aged 49 and the youngest, aged 23. All around the walls were portraits of the stallions (all notable figures in their own right) who had sired the female owner. However, the Château, built around 1480, had many acres of roof and, on the transfer, the French Ministry of Heritage seized a golden opportunity to get the Château put back in order. Générale des Eaux was using it as a cultural centre and I went to a couple of events there which were pretty impressive, accompanied, as all Générale des Eaux events were, by a pretty impressive vintage Moët vin d'honneur.

Messier was keen to make his mark. The media was where the next great push forward was to be. The company's name was changed to Vivendi, and the water companies were downgraded and their name changed to Veolia. Jack Page, President of the Water Companies Association, had kindly suggested to Jean Claude Banon that any replacement for me ought to be a colourful character who had, for instance, been in the French Foreign Legion and then the taipan of a large company in Hong Kong! I was awaiting the date of my retirement when Jean Claude Banon and Messier staged a party at the Victoria and Albert Museum to introduce Messier to England. I arrived and stood in the receiving line and Jean Claude introduced me to Messier as "Our English Chairman". The handshake was limp and the greeting:

"M. Dugdale, you are 76."

"That is correct, M. Le President."

"But I am 38."

The next sentence should have been "Goodbye" but I was already on my way towards the champagne. M. Messier in his drive to turn the company into a media behemoth made large and loss-making acquisitions in TV, radio and related industry in America. He acquired a large company flat on 5th Avenue, New York at the top of the market and generally lived the life of a media tycoon before the organisation was properly established and was still making immense losses. The whole episode ended in disaster with Vivendi in debt to the tune of 35 billion Euros in 2002 and the Paris establishment had to institute a rescue programme to stave off imminent insolvency.

But perhaps the best epitaph is in the history of my Générale des

Eaux shares. I acquired the holding in 1987 when I joined and subsequently added to it, reaching a six figure valuation, which was reduced to £6700 after the inevitable crash and the necessary sort out at French pistol point.

I had enjoyed my time at Générale des Eaux; perhaps more so in the early years than at the end, when my authority weakened and passed into the hands of Jean Claude Banon. They had got the initial timing right, but subsequent *crises des nerfs* had perhaps blunted the impact of a great company intent on dominating world water. Two men called Jack made life much more fun during the last three years. At the end of 1991, Jean Claude wanted to shake up the management of several companies and wished to remove the then Chairman of Tendring Hundred. He asked me to be Chairman and I immediately agreed, although I thought it was a long way from Blyth. Jack Page was to remain as Chairman of Three Valleys, and Jack Jeffery of North Surrey would carry on until Three Valleys and North Surrey could be merged. Jack Jeffery would then succeed me at Tendring Hundred while remaining as Jean Claude's hatchet man. Jack Jeffery was a remarkable character, the son of a Durham miner, who succeeded brilliantly in all he attempted. He was the personification of my theory that chemists, for whatever reason, make much better managers than engineers. He was the chosen blue-eyed-boy of Sir Leonard Millis, Secretary of the British Water Authority, who had picked him out as the chemist who would succeed him in management and had groomed him accordingly. Eminently likeable (as the son of a miner should be), he was strongly Labour, played both the piano and excellent cricket, and was one of the founding fathers of Durham County Cricket Club's new ground at Lumley Castle, as well as a lifelong Sunderland supporter. He was an outstanding example of how talent can succeed in Britain. We all got on like a house on fire and, after he succeeded me at Tendring Hundred, I was delighted to be asked to remain on the board. We used to meet the night before board meetings at the Pier Hotel in Harwich to put the world to rights on a excellent dinner of fish and good white wine. Jack Page had been the M.P. for Harrow for many years and was a strong supporter of Maggie Thatcher. A master of the art of the doggerel he wrote witty rhymes on every significant occasion in the career of General Utilities.

On another business front, I had been in America in the late summer of 1982 and had dined with an old friend of Belinda's, who was a leading corporate lawyer in New York City. In conversation he mentioned that Continental Insurance, who owned 30 per cent of the Phoenix, was in deep liquidity trouble. He added that it was common gossip on Wall Street that its only really feasible way out was to realise its stake in the Phoenix. At the next Phoenix board meeting, when directors were asked if they had anything to bring up, I reported this conversation. I was astounded at the reaction I got. The chairman, Jocelyn Hambro, and the chief executive both flew at me, saying it was quite untrue and that it was wrong to scaremonger in this way. I knew that, with the departure of Bill Sidney and Bill Harris, the previous chairman and chief executive, I did not have the same relationship with the two newcomers. But I was still astonished at the way they took my remarks.

Three weeks later we were summoned to an emergency meeting on a non-board Wednesday. Jocelyn told us that the Continental chairman had flown over and said that Jocelyn had to dispose of the Phoenix holding in days rather than weeks. Jocelyn went on to say that he had gone round to the Sun Alliance that morning and had sold the Phoenix to Toby Aldington. Sir Arnold Hall, the chairman of Hawker Siddeley, said, "Don't you need a board meeting to do that, Jocelyn?" to which Jocelyn replied, "That is why you are all here." The price Jocelyn got was just about OK, but not what we would have got with a slower sale. Arnold asked, "Don't you think you would have got more with more time?" Jocelyn replied, "The last thing I wanted was to set up an auction by hawking it around the city." That ended the meeting but there was no resolution. Hugh Astor, the senior non-executive, and Arnold set up a meeting in a side room and we left it to them to see Jocelyn on our behalf and find out if anything could be done. But the news, needless to say, had already leaked and Arnold, who had immensely more experience than the rest of us, decided that the agreement had to stand. Accordingly, a fortnight later Toby Aldington came round and gave us the bum's rush – Jocelyn and the chief executive, alone, had seats on the Sun Alliance board after the purchase.

Chapter 25

CYLLA AND CHILDREN

My father and mother both died in 1965 and I decided to carry on living at Blyth and, although we used it for summer holidays when we didn't notice the cold, Merevale remained empty until Matthew and his family moved in in 1995.

I have been lucky enough to have been married to two women who, in their very different ways, have brought happy family life to Blyth. Belinda was an ex-Wren and London career girl who also loved horses, country life and travel; Cylla is a painter and collector. Her love of the country came from being brought up at Wasing in Berkshire, her family home which she was later to inherit.

When Cylla married me she also took on four young children and a well-established Nanny. There was inevitably a tricky adjustment for everyone. Nanny had been with us since the birth of Laura and, after Belinda's death, had had seven years of running the house and the children. She retired shortly after I married Cylla and there was a great deal of sadness when she left but she soon settled into life in Earlsdon, Coventry, in a house I bought her near to her sister. The children visited her regularly and she often came to Blyth. (At Christmas and on her birthday I had, over the years, given her small parcels of about £200 worth of blue chip shares. She had put them in the bank and forgotten about them. I was the administrator of her affairs and when, at the age of 92, she had to be looked after, they amounted to over £99,000. As a result, she was forced to pay for her own care home.)

Nanny's departure unified the family and Cylla, who had been having a rough ride with the three girls, soon got back on to happy working terms, although it was not until the girls got married that she succeeded in turning us all into the united gang we are now. Cylla gave birth to Adelaide in 1970 and Joshua in 1974, born 21 years to the day after Laura. My family was now complete.

I was working and playing hard, but Britain's economy was sinking and inflation was a huge problem. I re-thought my horse-racing activities. Belinda had really worked hard at the Stud and we were beginning to breed competitors in some of the major races. Cylla's interests lay more in the artistic world. As well as this, the performance of my Lloyd's syndicates gave increasing signs of the disaster that subsequently overtook them. So I started gradually to reduce the number of horses in training. Atty Corbett's death – he was run down by a lorry on the Bury Road – caused me to move to William Hastings-Bass. He started off at the Hamilton Stud and then became trainer to the Queen and moved to West Ilsley. I failed to replace Rufus in the north until I found Steve Norton at High Hoyland. I also sent horses to George Bridgland in France. We had great fun flying ourselves to France to see the horses race, and always included a trip to the Arc. Our best horse probably was Peace and Concorde (fourth in the Oaks) – I received a lot of stick from friends who thought that she could have done better with a jockey who knew the Epsom course, instead of the stable jockey of the French trainer. Reluctantly I decided to end my stud enterprise as I no longer had the time to devote to it that was needed.

As far as schooling my children rather than horses was concerned, I made the decision to separate the twins. Charlotte was to join a pony-oriented establishment in Northampton, Tilly was to join Laura at Hanford School in Dorset. All would probably have gone well if the Northamptonshire school had not gone bust in the middle of Charlotte's career. Nanny and I visited umpteen schools and we finally settled on Stonar, a school in Wiltshire, because Nanny liked the headmistress and thought she ran a happy ship. So she did, but there were too many children for the capacity of the school buildings and, though Charlotte was happy enough there, she did not make much academic progress. But she had acquired some O levels when she left and went on to the Castello di Vicchiomaggio in Greve in Chianti to learn Italian, and drawing with Signora Simi.

Laura and Tilly continued at Hanford and then passed into Cranborne Chase, a large girls' school in Wiltshire at Wardour Castle. It had a first-class headmistress and good staff. But the headmistress retired and the governors appointed a man as the head. In Laura's last summer she was caught having a crafty cigarette on the roof and I was summoned to the school to be told that Laura was no good and wouldn't get any A levels, let alone pass the entrance exam to Oxford, as was her plan. In the event, she left with very good A level results and booked herself into Westminster Tutors for the Oxford entrance. The next term she won an exhibition to Somerville College to read PPE. At the following school speech day the headmaster referred to Laura in glowing terms, ending by saying, "We all knew she had it in her," much to my and Tilly's disgust.

Laura spent 3 months learning French near Tours, and then went up to Somerville where she had three happy years and got a good degree. I went to spend a weekend with her in Oxford. I arrived on the Friday night and she had arranged for two friends to entertain me while she had a tutorial. As we went out to dinner, I noticed pairs of winter boots outside nearly every room. Thinking Somerville must have a grade one valeting system, I made some comment only to be told the boots meant that a man was being entertained within. After her first year in college she moved out to Jericho, where she lived in a very restricted condition with a crowd of friends, both male and female. How she found time to do any work I shall never know. On leaving Oxford she got various temporary jobs before she turned up in a business suit, having got herself a traineeship at Viznews, a TV news agency.

Tilly was determined not to be seen to follow in Laura's footsteps and, after three very good A levels, ended up at Sussex, which she did not enjoy and dropped out after a year to go and work in London. So I had two daughters working in London; Tilly in advertising making TV commercials, and Laura now a graduate trainee at ITN after leaving Viznews. London not being big enough for both twins, Charlotte had gone off to New York where she got a job with John Chancellor, selling antiquarian books and then with Marco Grassi, picture dealer and restorer. While she was there she got a taste for real estate and, with a large loan from an indulgent bank, purchased a wing of a federal penitentiary in the West Village. I went to visit her in her apartment when I was over and, while drinking my second dry Martini, was amused to see that I was eyeball to eyeball with the captain and helmsman of a Soviet cruise vessel, docking at the pier across the road. The pay-off came several months later when I opened an official looking US letter to Charlotte to find that it was a demand from the Internal Revenue Service for several hundred thousand dollars.

Charlotte returned to London in due course to share a flat with several other girls in Chelsea and she blossomed in several marketing posts, where she soon developed the skills to sell ice to Eskimos. Then she turned up at Blyth, after a long absence, to announce her engagement to Gerard Noel. The wedding took place at Merevale in May 1985 and Hugh Montefiore, the Bishop of Birmingham, refused to read the homily on marriage in the 1662 Prayer Book. However, Gerard's Ampleforth housemaster, Father Walter Maxwell-Stuart, volunteered and read it perched, as monks do, on the top of the altar. Hugh, showing signs of great disapproval, averted his eyes.

Charlotte was followed to the altar shortly afterwards, first by Laura and Arthur Hazlerigg, and then by Tilly and Marcus May the artist. It was interesting to note the champagne statistics: Charlotte's guests in May consumed 1.25 bottles of Moet per head; Tilly's guests in April got through 1.075 bottles per head; and Laura's in February were down to .48 per head (although, as it was a particularly cold day, the consumption of spirits and mulled wine made up for a good deal of the difference). It was fun doing the organisation for the weddings and, if anyone is interested, get your daughter to choose a day in the depths of winter – it is a real economy.

Matthew was in Philadelphia when he got engaged to Paige Perkins and he rang to say that he was getting married in Bryn Mawr on February 24 1990, which was about 10 days on. I thought we must be there and, as I was in the middle of some important water business, there was no alternative to a return ticket on Concorde for Cylla and me.

That set the trend so I booked a room at the Pierre for the two nights. Tony Samuel, a very good friend, was also in New York staying at the Algonquin, arranged a stretch limo to take us all to Philadelphia from New York.

We arrived at the church about half an hour before the event and were greeted by two rather haughty ushers who said, "Bride or Groom" and hearing "Groom" put us all in the last pew on the bridegroom's side. About ten minutes later the bride's mother appeared, looking stunning in a pale blue and pink Gainsborough hat. She eyed us sitting at the back and advanced saying, "You aren't the British parents are you?" to Tony Samuel. He pointed to us and so we met our new in-law for the first time and were moved up to the front pew. After the wedding I congratulated Matthew, to whom I hadn't spoken earlier, and he asked, "Have you got your American Express card with you?" He then told me that the bridegroom's father pays for the pre-wedding party, which had been held the night before at the Four Seasons Hotel in Philadelphia. He took the card and phoned the hotel to give them the number to pay the bill. So I found, sadly, that the rule of the bride's father paying for everything did not apply in the USA. The reception at the family home was going great guns when, at about 10 p.m., our driver came in to say the blizzard was getting much worse and, if we didn't go at once, he couldn't guarantee the road would not be closed. So we made our excuses and left. He was quite right and the road was closed during the night, but we got through just in time. The next morning, rather bleary, we caught the 9 a.m. Concorde and, with a strong westerly tail wind, we broke the record for the fastest crossing of about two hours or so.

Grandchildren followed in droves, starting with Charlotte's Belinda. Matthew's marriage was blessed with the arrival, at regular intervals, of four grandchildren – Clementine, William, Fernanda and Nathaniel. I suggested to Matthew that he should move to Blyth but he preferred to go to Merevale direct, which was possibly the correct decision.

When I was forced to re-roof Merevale in 1986 I was luckily able to sell a piece of land for development to defray most of the cost. As a result I bullied the architect, Michael Reardon, to design a lift that reached from the basement to the top floor. It entailed hacking away at the oolite on which Merevale is founded, but meant that Merevale became much more manageable with the small staff that modern economics demands. When he moved in, Matthew rejigged the kitchen and entrance to make it the modern and comfortable family home it has become. Paige first turned her attention to furnishing the house in a modern way with Christophe Gollut, her Swiss interior designer, and then turned her attention to the garden, where she made a great many changes to the terrace and rose garden. She found an enthusiastic assistant in David Kirkland, the new head gardener, and Merevale garden once again became the provider of all the household plants, flowers, fruit and vegetables.

The changes forced on Matthew by the Common Market Agricultural Policy and the loss of relief for milk meant that my cherished Friesian herd, which was just beginning to provide around 8000 litres a cow, had to be sold. Milk at 12.7p a litre meant that only a family farm, where no labour was employed, could survive. But Matthew produced plans to enable the family farm to continue, albeit in the hands of contractors. Matthew and I swapped offices and we continued to share Judith Hutchinson, whose knowledge and reliability made things much easier for Matthew, as he took over the complete running of the Merevale and Blyth estates. I was left with Blyth and the garden, with income from the sand and gravel deposits surrounding Blyth, but I felt that, after about 40 years, it was time for the generation to change and a new regime to take control. I remained on top of things to begin with but soon realised that I had to keep my mouth shut if family harmony was to be maintained. I still occasionally get consulted about things, but any questions of finance remain firmly in the hands of the new regime.

The world has not been kind to the traditional agricultural estate since the second world war. That we have survived at Merevale is due largely to the determination of its employees to change their chosen methods to suit the constant changes in agricultural and leisure regulations and legislation. Harry Stangoe, who arrived as head keeper in 1954 and now retired, is still with us at 87, Les Huxley has been with us very many years and is still in charge as head of repairs and maintenance. Jason Douglas is now the head keeper and leader of the commercial game enterprise. Mike Holder, the head forester for many years, has improved not only our woods but also our relations with English Nature and the Countryside Commission

I had worked with four agents during my watch. I had got on very well with Robert Pardoe but he was obviously destined for higher things and it was no surprise when he left us for the Raby Castle estate in County Durham. He did a great deal to revitalise the estate as we re-positioned to take account for the loss of the colliery. We failed to buy the Whitacre estate when Mr. Swynnerton-Weston died, which I have always regretted as it would have fitted in well, and could have been acquired at a price which would have greatly increased over the years.

Robert Pardoe was succeeded by David Compton who came to us from the Crown Estate, when he heard that he would not be succeeding Sir Eric Saville as the Crown Commissioner at Windsor. An old Harrovian, who had been badly wounded in north west Europe when serving with the Irish Guards, he was a good administrator and a keen gun dog man. He, in turn, was succeeded by Hilary Bladon who came from Overbury. I then, to my lasting regret, took on a firm on the recommendation of the estate auditors. This soon proved to be a great mistake: the commission on selling things is larger than fees from administration.

I had been asked by Cylla's father, Bill Mount, to take over the farming at Wasing but when it came down to practicalities, he didn't like it, so I withdrew. However, some three years later my mother-in-law, Nance, and the agent at Wasing, Hanslip Long, came and said I really had to take it over as Bill couldn't cope, so I took control from 1988 to 2002. Once I had got a new keen young manager in Neil McLean it wasn't long before the farming was once more contributing to the estate budget. I got on very well with Cylla's parents apart from one jolly day at Goodwood when I made a joke about Cylla, who had just given birth to Adelaide, and got pursued across the paddock by Nance and her handbag, much to the amazement of Tilly and Charlotte who were with me.

My two youngest children, Adelaide and Joshua, achieved well at school and then attended the universities of their choice. Adelaide is a great linguist speaking both French and Spanish fluently, and is making her mark as a journalist. Joshua, too, is a great communicator and has produced and directed some very highly acclaimed films, as well as turning Wasing into the modern, profitable estate that it is now. Adelaide's wedding did not take place until July 2006 and, as the bridegroom was Spanish, the delicious dry sherry he brought with him, when iced, reduced what would have been a colossal consumption of Bollinger to much more modest proportions.

I have been lucky all my life – lucky in my home – lucky in my parents and siblings – lucky to return from the war when so many of my friends did not – lucky in my two marriages to two kind and responsible women who melded with my life and led me into theirs – lucky in my choice of career and happy all my life at what I happened to be doing. I have drifted into job after job, possibly because I find it difficult to say "no", and lucky again that my drifting led seamlessly from one career to another. I have been lucky in that my chosen amusements – hunting, skiing and steeple chasing, flying, fishing and travel – did not end in disastrous accidents; lucky in that my six children have all reached adulthood without any of the sorry tales of wasted youth, though not because I was a father involved in childhood and teenage activity, as now seems to be the norm. Now my children and grandchildren come and go secure in the knowledge that Blyth is always available to them if they should need it.

ACKNOWLEDGEMENTS

I would like to thank everyone who has helped in producing this book, from encouraging me to write it to the finished article. In particular I want to thank Judith Hutchinson, Enid Savatard, and Geri Reaves for deciphering my handwriting; Jane Ridley, Roger Hudson, Charles Merullo and his marvellous staff at Endeavour London for editing, advice and criticism; my family for their support and patience but particularly my daughter Tilly for her hours of work pulling it all together. I am also grateful to The Memoir Club, particularly their editress Mrs. Meg Ross who gave me much help in the first draft. My thanks also to Hugo Swire for suggesting the title.

I have relied on Arthur Old for checking my chapters on the water industry and Canon Jim Pendorf for the chapter on the church so many thanks to them. I have referred constantly to Nigel Nicolson's definitive history of the Grenadiers in World War II and other Grenadier publications, for which I am most grateful.

I must also thank Aston Villa Football Club and Lt. Col. Conway Seymour at Regimental H.Q. of the Grenadiers for their permission to reproduce photographs and maps and Viscount De L'Isle for allowing me to use photographs from his own archives.

If I have omitted anyone from this list, please accept my apologies and know that I am very grateful for their contribution. Finally, any mistakes or inaccuracies should be laid at my door.

INDEX

PICTURE CREDITS

All illustrations and photographs in this book are from the writer's own collection with the exception of the following for which permission is kindly acknowledged:

Aston Villa Football Club 189 middle & bottom; Daily Graphic 179 bottom; Getty Images 37, 178-179 top; Gillman & Soame 38; Grenadier Guards Regimental HQ /Crown Copyright 40, 42, 44, 75, 84, 103, 107, 120, 129, 133 ; Race Finish Recording Co.Ltd. 185 middle; Solo Syndication 186 bottom; Sports Argus 189 top left; Viscount de L'Isle 43 top.